STORIES FROM THE ROYAL HONG KONG POLICE

Fifty accounts from officers of Hong Kong's colonial-era police force

Founded in 1938, the Royal Hong Kong Police Association brings together former serving police officers. In this book, fifty members of the association share real-life accounts of policing the streets, housing estates and harbours of colonial Hong Kong from the 1930s to 1997.

STORIES FROM THE ROYAL HONG KONG POLICE

Fifty accounts from officers of Hong Kong's colonial-era police force

The Royal Hong Kong Police Association

BLACKSMITH BOOKS

STORIES FROM THE ROYAL HONG KONG POLICE:
Fifty accounts from officers of Hong Kong's colonial-era police force

ISBN 978-988-79638-8-2 (paperback)
Text and photographs © 2020 the contributors as noted

Published by Blacksmith Books
Unit 26, 19/F, Block B, Wah Lok Industrial Centre,
31–35 Shan Mei St, Fo Tan, Hong Kong
www.blacksmithbooks.com

Typeset in Adobe Garamond by Alan Sargent
Printed in Hong Kong

First printing 2020

Contents

Preface 9
    Keith H. Lomas

Historical Background 11
    Keith H. Lomas

Organisational Structure of the RHKP 19
    Keith H. Lomas

Glossary 24

Policing in the 1930s 27
    Norman Gunning

1956: Crashes and Riots 37
    Charlie McGugan

Ping Chau First Aid 44
    Peter Leeds

A Dutchman in the the Auxiliary Marine Police 46
    Frank Goldberg

A Day In the Western Police Station Charge Room . . . 49
    Charlie McGugan

Central Police Station: 1956 54
    John Turner

The Establishment of the Police Training Contingent . 59
    Ivan Scott

Black Sleeves and Panda Faces – Traffic Days 61
    Ian Stenton

Tokyo Olympics 66
    Mike Watson

Snippets of Empire 74
    Jim Prisk

Monsoon Shipwreck 78
    Charles H. Fisher

A Harbourside Duel 83
    Graham Harper

A Thai Catch 86
    Graham Harper

The 1967 Riots and the Dockyards 89
    Duncan L. Macrae

A Lo Wu Incident – 1967 94
    Chris Fraser

Serve the People 98
    R.A. (Bob) Steele

The Cultural Revolution at Sea 112
    Frank Goldberg

Thirty Years of Policing Hong Kong 115
    Richard Tudor

Hello Sailor 124
    Keith Braithwaite

'Luck Be a Lady Tonight' 128
    Ian Lacy-Smith

Midwife Duty 135
    William C. Trotter

Bizarre Justice 138
    Roland Dibbs

The Agency of Last Resort 139
    Peter Halliday

Riding Out Typhoon Rose 143
    Iain Ward

Grass-Roots Diplomacy 151
    C.R. Emmett

A Salty Solution 154
    Roland Dibbs

The '633' Squad 156
    John Murray

Incidents in Traffic Division .163
    John Murray

The Po Sang Bank Siege 170
    John H.T. Griffiths

Marksman Unit 1973–1978 .174
    Bill Duncanson

Vietnamese Refugees Arrive .188
    Ian Lacy-Smith

The *Huey Fong* and *Skyluck* Refugees 195
    John Turner

The Police Negotiation Cadre 201
    Tom Delbridge

Leading Her Majesty Astray 207
    Barry Griffin

Building an International Drug Case 210
    Paul Dalton

A Junior Inspector in Sha Tin and Tai Po 214
    Simon Roberts

A Detective Inspector in Tsim Sha Tsui, 1981–3 222
    Gordon Elsden

Light-Hearted Leadership 229
    Peter Webb

Special Duties Unit – Water Team 233
    Sandy Macalister

The Phantom Wire Cutter 235
    John Macdonald

Snakes and Lawyers 238
    Rose Johnston

The 1984 Taxi Riots 246
    Jim Prisk

Gun Battle In Causeway Bay 254
    R.A. (Bob) Steele

Special Duties Unit Selection 258
    Gordon Elsden

A New Territories Kidnapping 262
    Peter Halliday

A Tragic Career Development 267
    Peter Halliday

A Murder in the Vietnamese Refugee Camp 270
    Simon Roberts

Baguio Villas Landslide, 1992 276
    Keith Braithwaite

The Approach to 1997 280
    Simon Monaghan

A Postscript: The RHKP Memorial 287
    Keith H. Lomas

References and Further Reading 290

Preface

Keith H. Lomas

Whenever former members of the Royal Hong Kong Police meet on a social occasion, talk inevitably turns to yesteryear, and stories of interesting incidents or characters are bandied about. This is true of any military or police organisation, or indeed of any organisation where the nature of their work of necessity relies on trust and comradeship.

These stories in their way are a historical record of life in Hong Kong, and of events which were not necessarily printed in official records. The accounts of incidents are often one man's view of what happened, and do not give an overall picture, or indeed may be at variance with the official view or the public perception.

The 'Royal' Hong Kong Police ceased to exist in 1997 following the return of sovereignty of the territory to China from British control. However, under the terms of the Sino-British Joint Declaration, expatriates in the Hong Kong government administration, including police officers, could continue their career until retirement. As the years pass, officers with knowledge of the Hong Kong scene and incidents pre-1997 get fewer. There is no doubt that now, some twenty-odd years after the Handover to China, many good stories have been lost forever.

This book is an attempt to ameliorate this situation and it may be that interest will be stimulated to encourage a second edition.

As indicated above, these accounts are individuals' perceptions of Hong Kong life, and are the personal responsibility of the authors. The editorial sub-committee made it clear to contributors that their articles should not be used to criticise any individual or the Royal Hong Kong Police Force.

This is not to deny that mistakes were made, nor that the Force did not have dark periods. Notably there were serious problems with corruption, as was present to a greater or lesser degree throughout the Hong Kong administration, and in the private sector, up to the 1970s. The corruption issue was tackled by Sir Murray MacLehose, the governor of Hong Kong from November 1971 to May 1982. Legislation and the creation of the Independent Commission Against Corruption in 1974 resulted in the territory probably having the most corruption-free administration anywhere in the world. From that dark period, the Royal Hong Kong Police emerged to be a fine force of which its members were, and are, justifiably proud.

But this book is not a history, and the corruption issue is well documented elsewhere.

The articles have been collected and reviewed by a sub-committee of the Royal Hong Kong Police Association (*www.rhkpa.org*), consisting of Keith H. Lomas, Keith Braithwaite and Simon Roberts. With many different writers, inevitably the quality and styles are uneven, but we hope that readers will find it a light read and may obtain some idea of police activity, and of Hong Kong life in general, in the pre-1997 era.

Historical Background

Keith H. Lomas

The following is a description of major events or incidents which affected Hong Kong from the end of the Second World War to the Handover of sovereignty of the territory from the United Kingdom to China in 1997.

Hong Kong, an island of some thirty-two square miles, was ceded to Great Britain by China in 1841 following the First Opium War, and was intended to facilitate trade with China, albeit the main export to China was opium in exchange for silk, tea, chinaware and other goods. Hong Kong Island, at the mouth of the Pearl River was chosen for its ideal natural harbour. At that time the population was a few thousand, mainly farmers and fishermen, which then rapidly increased. A year later the population was estimated to be around 20,000. Crime was rampant, piracy was common, and so a police force was formed.

Subsequently, following two further wars with China over the opium trade, the territory of Hong Kong expanded, first in 1861 to include Kowloon on the mainland of China and then, in 1898, by another three hundred and sixty square miles, including some 235 islands ranging in size from Lantau Island (twice as large as Hong Kong Island) to others which are barely more than rocks. Whilst Hong Kong Island and Kowloon were ceded in perpetuity, the 1898 treaty only provided for the additional land, referred to as the New Territories, to be leased to the United Kingdom for ninety-nine years. This arrangement meant that this land would revert to Chinese sovereignty in 1997.

The terrain is mountainous and urban development initially was focused on the north side of Hong Kong Island and on the

Kowloon Peninsula, although since the early 1980s it has perforce expanded greatly into what were more rural areas north of Kowloon.

In its early years, although trade with China continued, Hong Kong was something of a backwater. At the outbreak of World War II, the population consisted of about 1.6 million inhabitants. Following the invasion and occupation of Hong Kong by Japanese military forces in 1941 and the British surrender, the population declined due to the Japanese policy of encouraging inhabitants to return to China and shortages of food and medicines. It is estimated that at the end of the war in 1945, there were only about 600,000 Hong Kong residents.

Following World War II, the police force had to be rebuilt and this became the main task of Commissioner Duncan Macintosh. He was an energetic, professional officer who having inherited a force of less than 2,000 officers, worked hard to make it an effective organisation, demanding better pay and conditions of service for his officers. Personnel were a mixture of European, Pakistani, and Chinese officers, with senior ranks almost entirely European.

At the end of 1946, only some twelve months after the cessation of hostilities, the population had returned to about the same level as had existed pre-war and in the ensuing years, the population increased even further due to refugees fleeing the civil war in China, which culminated in the communist victory in 1949. By the end of 1950, it is estimated the population had reached over two million.

This dramatic increase caused severe problems for the Hong Kong administration, including for the police. Housing was scarce and existing flats with two or three bedrooms became the home of several families, each occupying a room, with the toilets and kitchen shared. Homes made of wood and sheets of metal were established in stairways and scavenging lanes, on roof tops and in crude insanitary shanty towns built precariously on hillsides. There were obvious pressures on education, medical facilities and public transport.

A serious fire in a shanty town in Shek Kip Mei in 1953, resulting in over 50,000 people being made homeless, forced government into improving housing, and it commenced building cheap resettlement blocks where families resided in one-room flats, with communal toilets and washrooms. Whilst far from ideal, it was the start of a massive low-cost public housing programme and, over time, considerable improvements in housing, education and health facilities came about.

The main problems for police immediately following the end of the war, apart from its own reconstruction, were illegal immigration and drugs, principally opium. Commissioner Macintosh built small hilltop posts, or forts, to overlook the Sino-British border – but it remained a porous border. Refugees continued to enter Hong Kong for the next decade or so. With regard to opium, this trade with China had ceased early in the twentieth century although consumption of the drug within Hong Kong was not illegal until after the war.

The victory of the communists in China naturally caused some tension and fear of attack in Hong Kong, particularly when People's Liberation Army troops arrived on the border. However, the PLA were careful not to infringe the border and British troops were also not deployed in that area. The border remained a policing responsibility. Tensions eased. The outbreak of the Korean War in 1950, when China allied with North Korea, whilst the UK participated with United Nations forces in defending South Korea, caused tensions again to rise. All British subjects resident in the territory were required to serve as a volunteer in an armed forces unit, in the Auxiliary Police, or in the Auxiliary Defence Services, unless exempt by employment in an essential occupation. This remained the situation until 1961, although the Police Auxiliaries continued after that date on a voluntary basis, and continue to this day.

The Korean War caused a depression in Hong Kong as trade with China was embargoed by the United Nations. But the large influx of Chinese refugees, some of whom brought business experience, skills and capital with them, proved to be of value and Hong Kong started to develop what would become a flourishing industrial base.

In 1956, serious riots broke out in Hong Kong. 'Double Tenth', the tenth of October, is the National Day of the Republic of China, defeated by the communists in the Mainland, only surviving in

Taiwan, the island to which the Kuomintang (KMT) had retreated in 1949. Many of the residents of Hong Kong who had fled from communism took part in the celebration. Dinners were arranged, and banners and flags flown. On the morning of the tenth, posters supporting the KMT were displayed in the Lei Cheng Uk Resettlement Estate. This was against the letter of the law and an overzealous government resettlement officer began to remove them. This resulted in protests by residents of the estate which escalated into fights with communist supporters, and was used by triad and rogue elements as cover for looting and extortion. Rioting spread through the colony, vehicles and buildings were set alight. Before the disturbances were brought under control by the police, supported by the British Army, fifty-nine people had been killed including the wife of the Swiss vice-consul, and hundreds were injured. Over six thousand people were arrested although most were released after questioning, the remainder being brought before the courts.

As a result of this serious incident, the police reviewed their tactics and established the Police Training Contingent, later renamed Police Tactical Unit, which aimed to give every member of the Force appropriate security training.

In 1958, there was a further large influx of refugees from China, following the 'Great Leap Forward' campaign instigated by Chairman Mao Tse-tung. His purpose was to move the basically agrarian economy to a socialist society through collectives and rapid industrialisation. Land could not be privately owned but was made the property of the collectives, large groups of villagers, whilst at the same time farmers were encouraged to leave the land and produce steel. The policy was a disaster, resulting in a severe lack of food and tens of millions of people died in the famine – some estimates are around 30 million people. The police in Hong Kong were under considerable pressure in trying to prevent another flood of refugees, and in returning those arrested back to China.

In 1966, there were riots when it was proposed that the cost of a journey on the Star Ferry, which conveyed passengers between Hong Kong Island and Kowloon, should be raised from 20 cents to 25 cents. This was opposed by a prominent urban councillor who was supported initially by one individual, So Sau Chung, who appeared at the ferry concourse and declared a hunger strike. From this small beginning there developed full-scale rioting in Kowloon, involving looting and burning of shops. The rioting only lasted a few days, being brought under control by the police supported by the British Army. It was estimated that the cost of the arson was over HK$20 million whilst the entertainment industry centred in Kowloon lost considerably more than that in profits.

The following year brought more trouble. China was in chaos as the Cultural Revolution gained impetus. Mao alleged that bourgeois elements had infiltrated the government and society, aiming to restore capitalism. His real objective was to eliminate his rivals within the party by re-imposing 'Mao Tse-tung Thought' as the ideology of the Chinese Communist Party, and by instigating class struggle.

This caused considerable civil unrest as individuals were denounced as counter-revolutionaries. There was ideological ferment as factional groups formed in the military, civil population and within the Communist Party itself. Bands of 'Red Guards' roamed the country seeking out the revolution's enemies. Millions of people were persecuted, suffering public humiliation, torture, imprisonment, hard labour and even execution. The Hong Kong Marine Police were picking up corpses which had floated down the Pearl River, the individual often having been tied up before being executed.

This turmoil spilled over into Hong Kong and a labour dispute at a plastics factory escalated into very serious disturbances. Leftwing supporters organised large demonstrations and waved the famous 'Little Red Book' of Chairman Mao's thoughts. This developed into rioting with the burning of vehicles and attacking buildings. There was a shooting incident on the Sino-British border which resulted in the deaths of five police officers, and a bomb campaign. The disturbances lasted for several months and resulted in many civilian and police deaths. There was real concern that China was preparing to take control of Hong Kong. Eventually the security forces stabilised the situation and in recognition of the steadfastness of the Force during this difficult period, it was honoured by Her Majesty the Queen with the title 'Royal'. Her

Royal Highness Princess Alexandra was appointed as the Force's Honorary Commandant General.

In the 1960s and early 1970s, the United States was involved in the Vietnam War, and Hong Kong, along with Japan, became a major rest and recreation centre for the thousands of American servicemen. The red-light areas in Wan Chai and Tsim Sha Tsui boomed. However, given the circumstances, and the strain which many of the troops had endured in the war zone, they were comparatively well-behaved – not least because of their healthy respect for the US Navy Shore Patrol.

The end of the Vietnam War in 1975, with the surrender of the South Vietnamese forces and exodus of United States military personnel, was followed by a very large influx of Vietnamese refugees into Hong Kong. They made their perilous journeys from Vietnam often in ramshackle boats, suffered attacks by pirates and occasionally bad weather, to reach Hong Kong. Some more seaworthy boats endeavoured to travel further to Indonesia or the Philippines. No one knows the loss of life at sea during this period but it must have been significant. In Hong Kong, the refugees who over time numbered around 200,000, were placed in camps, until they were accepted for immigration by other countries. Unfortunately, many years later, some were obliged to be returned to Vietnam as no country would accept them.

In the 1980s there were many armed robberies carried out by Mainland China criminal gangs. They came well armed, including with AK-47 rifles, and attacked banks and goldsmith shops. They were not averse to using the weapons and posed a serious problem, particularly because, at that time, liaison between the law enforcement bodies of China and Hong Kong did not exist.

In January 1984, some seventeen years after the last outbreak of serious rioting, disturbances again erupted in Kowloon. The government had proposed steep rises in taxi fares and licences, and the drivers held a two-day strike to protest. This provided a spark for thousands of mainly young people to start rioting, with looting, attacks on vehicles including buses, and arson. Again, police were called into action and the situation was quickly stabilised.

In this same year, the Joint Declaration on the future of Hong Kong was signed between the United Kingdom and China setting out the terms under which sovereignty of Hong Kong would revert to China in 1997, following the ending of the lease of the New Territories. It was agreed that the existing economic, legal, administration and social systems, including freedoms, would continue in Hong Kong for a further fifty years from 1997, while the territory would be run by local Hong Kong Chinese under China's sovereignty. Recruitment of expatriate officers on pensionable terms ceased, with subsequent appointments on a contract basis only. Training of Chinese officers for the top posts in the administration and in the police was stepped up.

In 1989, serious unrest in China caused considerable concern to the people of Hong Kong. Following the reforms in China in the early 1980s which encouraged rapid economic development and an embryonic market economy, there were anxieties among the political class and also in the general population of China. The developments had positively affected some of the population but others felt left behind, and questions were being raised about the one-party system. Students were at the forefront in seeking democracy, greater accountability and freedom of the press and speech. The Chinese government was initially somewhat ambivalent about these protests and demonstrations, but on fourth June 1989, after several hundred thousand students had occupied Tiananmen Square at the centre of Beijing, troops were sent in to clear the area. They used firearms and estimates of students who died vary from a few hundred to several thousand. There was international condemnation and in various cities worldwide there were demonstrations in support of the students, including in Hong Kong.

This action by the Chinese government not surprisingly raised concerns about how Hong Kong residents would be treated following the 1997 handover of sovereignty. In 1997, the territory was hugely successful, having developed into a major commercial, financial and tourist centre. Its population numbered around six and a half million people, and law and order was being well maintained by the 28,000 uniformed officers, supported by some six thousand auxiliary police personnel with an equivalent number of civilian staff. By this time, the Force was almost entirely Chinese, including the commissioner and his two deputies, with only a few hundred expatriate officers, the last recruitment exercise for the latter having taken place in 1994.

However, currently (2019–20), there has been a very strong reaction from the community to a Hong Kong government proposal to introduce an extradition treaty which would allow accused people in Hong Kong to be extradited to the Mainland. The justice system in China is widely distrusted and there have been large-scale protests which have since morphed into general pressure for more democracy in Hong Kong. These demands were strongly resisted by China and, on 30 June 2020, resulted in the National Security Law which contains strong penalties for secession, subversion, terrorism or collusion with a foreign country. How the present unrest in Hong Kong develops remains to be seen.

Organisational Structure of the RHKP

Keith H. Lomas

It may be helpful in reading the articles in this book to understand how the rank structure and organisation of the Royal Hong Kong Police has evolved.

The articles basically cover the period from the end of World War II, when the population of Hong Kong, depleted by the Japanese occupation, exploded from about 600,000 to around 6.4 million in 1997. Over the next five decades, as the territory grew from a backwater to an international city, and technology, training, and tactics all advanced, there were necessarily organisational changes within the police. There were other minor changes over this same timescale but in the cause of simplicity, only the main ones are mentioned.

Rank Structure

Before the war, by far the largest proportion of the Force was Chinese, with a large contingent of Indians. Caucasian officers recruited largely from the United Kingdom, and also from the Commonwealth countries, joined the Force in the rank of *constable* and moved up the ranks from there. The officers, *inspector* and above, were mainly Caucasian but there were a few Chinese. Selected individuals from the United Kingdom could join the Force at *assistant superintendent* level and be promoted in due course to the senior levels of the Force. For the majority of the Caucasians who joined at constable level, the highest rank they could hope to achieve was *chief inspector*, although a few did move into the *superintendent* grade.

After the War, the Force recruited a small number of Pakistani officers. Caucasians from the United Kingdom or the Commonwealth joined as *probationary sub-inspectors* and together with selected young Chinese, formed the basis of the officer grade.

Constables/sergeants/station sergeants with good records could be promoted into the inspectorate grade or indeed further, and this became more common as Hong Kong's education system improved. It is possible that a very few individuals were recruited directly into the assistant superintendent grade, as had been done pre-war, but the practice ceased in the early 1950s.

It should be mentioned that the term 'Chinese' covered a wide range of people who spoke different languages and enjoyed different customs. The very large majority of the Hong Kong population were Cantonese, but following the civil war in China in the 1940s, there were communities of Shanghainese, Chiu Chau, Shan Tung, etc., coming into the territory from other parts of China who, at least initially, did not speak the local language of Cantonese. The police perforce recruited from all the communities but ensured that they were able to speak Cantonese. But as can be understood, there were some communication difficulties when dealing with non-Cantonese inhabitants.

In the 1950s, the rank structure was as follows:
Commissioner
Deputy Commissioner
Assistant Commissioner
Senior Superintendent
Superintendent
Assistant Superintendent
Chief Inspector
Inspector
Sub-Inspector (recruitment rank)
Staff Sergeant Class I
Staff Sergeant Class II
Sergeant
Corporal
Constable (recruitment rank)

In 1960, the rank of *senior inspector* was introduced, and the *sub-inspector* rank abolished.

In the mid 1960s, the additional ranks of *senior assistant commissioner* and *chief superintendent* were introduced.

In 1971, the rank of assistant superintendent was abolished and in the early 1970s, the ranks of *staff sergeant* I and II were combined and renamed as *station sergeant*.

In the mid 1970s, the rank of *corporal* was abolished.

Thus, from the 1970s on, the rank structure became as follows:
Commissioner
Deputy Commissioner
Senior Assistant Commissioner
Assistant Commissioner
Chief Superintendent
Senior Superintendent
Superintendent
Chief Inspector
Senior Inspector
Inspector (recruitment rank)
Station Sergeant
Sergeant
Constable (recruitment rank)

Force Organisation

In broad terms, post-World War II, the Force was organised into a headquarters for the administration of policy, finance, personnel and training; and operational support with forensics, communications and transport. It also included territory-wide operational units such as Special Branch, Major Crime, and the Narcotics and Triad Bureaus. The territory was divided into two districts, each commanded by an *assistant commissioner*, namely Hong Kong Island District (ACP/HKI), and because they were sparsely inhabited, Kowloon, New Territories and Marine District (the waters and islands of the territory – ACP/K, NT & M).

Subsequently, with population increasing, in April 1957 Kowloon became a separate district from the New Territories and Marine, again commanded by an assistant commissioner (ACP/K). Later still, in the early 1960s, the New Territories and Marine District separated into two districts, each commanded by an assistant commissioner (ACP/NT and ACP/M).

Each assistant commissioner had his headquarters staff for administration as well as operational teams for serious crime investigations and vice, and with a Traffic Division (T), and an Emergency Unit (EU) for 999 response.

The districts were divided into divisions, commanded by a superintendent (DS), and each division comprised one or more police stations commanded by an inspector, entitled *sub-divisional inspector* (SDI). The SDI would have other inspectors in his command who would head uniform patrol sub-units, and special squads dealing with vice and drugs. The inspector in charge of the report room inside the station which received all initial reports, was termed the *inspector-on-duty* (IOD).

Each division would also have a crime investigation component consisting of teams of detectives each headed by an inspector, the whole of this unit being commanded by a *divisional detective inspector* (DDI). If there was more than one police station in the division, then a number of teams would be assigned to the other station(s) with an inspector in charge, the *officer commanding, Criminal Investigation Department* (OC/CID), a misnomer really as this crime investigation unit was only part of the Force Criminal Investigation Department.

There were some minor changes in the 1970s, primarily in Kowloon, and the overall picture changed more substantially in the early 1980s when, as a result of the rapidly increasing population, districts were renamed 'regions' although still commanded by an assistant commissioner (RC); divisions were renamed 'districts' and the commanding officer upgraded to a *chief superintendent* (DC); whilst sub-divisions became 'divisions' commanded by a superintendent (DS).

The detective component of the regions, districts and divisions continued as before but the rank of the commanding officers was similarly upgraded with the former divisional detective inspector position being upgraded to superintendent and renamed *assistant district commander, crime* (ADC/C). Divisional detective teams continued but again the officer commanding was renamed from officer commanding, Criminal Investigation Department to *assistant divisional commander, crime* (ADVC/C) and was usually a chief inspector.

The increasing population necessitated a further reorganisation in the late 1980s when both Kowloon and New Territories Regions were divided into two: Kowloon East (RC/KE) and Kowloon West (RC/KW), and New Territories North (RC/NTN) and New Territories South (RC/NTS). All regions continued to be commanded by an assistant commissioner, while the organisational structure of the regions was otherwise unchanged.

The Marine Region basically followed the same organisation with regard to the police stations on the islands, although the command of Island District was graded at senior superintendent level. The harbour and territorial waters of Hong Kong, around 1,850 square kilometres, were patrolled by some 150 launches, varying in size up to 32 metres. Depending on the size of the launch, it could be commanded by a chief inspector/inspector/station sergeant/sergeant. The sea area was divided into two districts, each commanded by a senior superintendent, and was further divided into five divisions, including Harbour Division, each commanded by a superintendent. The divisions were allocated a complement of launches to control their area. The detective units were based either on island stations or at Marine Headquarters.

Glossary

Hong Kong words, mostly Cantonese

bom baan	police inspector
chai-yan	police
che tau	unit vehicle fleet manager
dim sum	small breakfast dishes
fei din	radio operator
foki	traffic police, co-worker
godown	warehouse
gweilo	Caucasian, literally 'ghost man'
jik haak	quickly
laan jai	bad character
lathi	long wooden staff
mahjong	popular gambling game
nai cha	milk tea
paak pei zhu	white-skinned pigs
sampan	small rowing boat
siu yeh	late-night snack
tai chi	martial art and exercise
triad	criminal gang
wong pei gau	yellow-skinned dogs or running dogs
yum cha	snack

Acronyms

ACP	Assistant Commissioner
ADC/C	Assistant District Commander, Crime
ADVC/C	Assistant Divisional Commander, Crime
BMH	British Military Hospital
C&E	Customs and Excise Department
C/F	Chinese female
C/M	Chinese male
CID	Criminal Investigation Department
DC	District Commander (usually a chief superintendent)

DD	dangerous drug
DDI	Divisional Detective Inspector
DO	District Office(r)
DPC	Detective Police Constable
DS	Divisional Superintendent
EU	Emergency Unit
HKTC	Hong Kong Telephone Company
HMOCS	Her Majesty's Overseas Civil Service
HSBC	Hongkong and Shanghai Banking Corporation
IED	Improvised Explosive Device
IOD	Inspector On Duty (report room inspector)
KCR	Kowloon–Canton Railway
KMT	Kuomintang, the Chinese Nationalist Party
MU	Marksman Unit
NT	New Territories
OC	Officer Commanding
OSCB	Organised and Serious Crime Bureau
PC	Police Constable
PHQ	Police Headquarters
PL	Police Launch
PLA	People's Liberation Army
PLB	Public Light Bus, 14-seater minibus
POLMIL	Police/Military Combined Command and Control Centre
QMH	Queen Mary Hospital
PSI	Probationary Sub-Inspector
PTS	Police Training School
PTU	Police Tactical Unit, formerly Police Tactical Contingent
PWD	Public Works Department
QA	Queen Alexandra's Royal Army Nursing Corps
RAMC	Royal Army Medical Corps
RC	Regional Commander
RHKP	Royal Hong Kong Police
SB	Special Branch
SDI	Sub-Divisional Inspector (station commander)
SDU	Special Duties Unit
SDS	Special Duty Squad (vice squad)
SFCP	Senior Force Clinical Psychologist
S/Sgt	Staff Sergeant, later renamed Station Sergeant
SSP	Senior Superintendent
UB	Uniform Branch
UNHCR	United Nations High Commissioner for Refugees
WPC	Woman Police Constable

Policing in the 1930s

Norman Gunning

Norman Gunning arrived in Hong Kong in December 1936 to begin his police training. The following are edited extracts from his 2005 book Passage to Hong Kong *and describe life as an ordinary police officer in pre-war Hong Kong.*

'Albert is so amused that I have got the island of Hong Kong,' wrote Queen Victoria to King Leopold of Belgium in 1841. But while her husband could see the funny side of it, considerably less amused was Lord Palmerston, the foreign secretary! He regarded the acquisition as a massive error by Captain Charles Elliot, Britain's superintendent of trade in China, who had negotiated the deal with British commercial interests at heart. 'A useless and barren island with hardly a house on it,' Palmerston raged in a letter to Elliot, but the captain, being a naval man, had seen Hong Kong as a safe anchorage for ships of all kinds in one of the finest natural harbours in the world.

We sailed into this harbour in December 1936, on the SS *Ranpura* and eventually berthed alongside at Kowloon Wharf where, for many years, P&O liners had tied up beside each other every two weeks, one homeward bound and the other on its way to Yokohama. When we disembarked, things moved fast and we were welcomed by Sergeant Bill Gowan, an ex-Scots Guard instructor whose bark was worse than his bite.

First it was to Central Police Station to meet the Inspector General of Police and then before a magistrate to be sworn in as a police officer. Next, a medical at the Government Civil Hospital, my one and only visit there because within a few weeks the hospital was closed and the new Queen Mary Hospital at Pok Fu Lam opened. Kitting out was a big job – rough blue serge with high collar; three white uniforms of the same design; three khaki shirts and shorts; overcoat, raincoat, etc. There was interesting head gear with seven different styles: white helmet with pugaree and spike, white topee, khaki sun hat, blue peaked hat with white, khaki and waterproof covers.

At the Police Training School (PTS), which was then in Kowloon on the corner of Nathan Road and Prince Edward Road, now used by Traffic Division, Kowloon, in the Mong Kok Police Station complex, we were four to a room. Each had a small wardrobe and there was a dressing table, open fireplace and overhead fans. The veranda looked out on a large parade ground which was also used for football and hockey. At night, lying beneath a mosquito net, our peace was disturbed by the croaks of bullfrogs across the road in a smallholding, and also by the double thumps of flying cockroaches, the first as they hit the wall and the second when they dropped to the floor, before taking off again.

The approximate number of personnel at the PTS was as follows: 1 European commandant, 1 European instructor/lecturer, 2 European drill/musketry instructors, 10 Indian instructors, 5 Chinese instructors, 12 European recruits, 80 Indian recruits and 60 Chinese recruits.

The main contingents within the police were European, Indian, Chinese and Russian, but there was yet another group from Wei Hai Wei (in China) who were much taller than the Cantonese and were used mostly on traffic duty.

Training lasted twelve months, about nine months at the school then three at a large divisional station. In our case, however, the course was a little reduced because of a fear of anti-Japanese riots (the Japanese had invaded China) and we were needed on the front line. Life was rigorous at the school with morning parades at seven o'clock. On the first morning the senior drill instructor looked at us with a jaundiced eye and told us to start running round the parade ground until he told us to stop. Five weeks on a P&O liner with large meals and Bass Export had left us in poor condition!

At the PTS, European recruits had to learn the art of drilling a squad. On one occasion a squad of Chinese and Indian recruits were approaching the end of the parade ground and were waiting for the order 'About Turn'. Unfortunately, the hapless recruit 'drill instructor' became tongue-tied and couldn't get the right words out. The assistant musketry instructor Sergeant Penfold, ex-South Wales Borderers, yelled out, 'For God's sake say something, even if it's only goodbye!'

Square-bashing was followed by breakfast and school started at 9 am. The first hour was devoted to the study of Cantonese in small groups and then it was to the classroom for the morning session on policework. The Police Code and Police Regulations were our 'Bibles'. The afternoons were reserved for practical work and were always full of interest. The use of arms played an important part and during the course we handled the following: .38 Police Positive Webley Scott revolver; .303 Lee Enfield rifle and bayonet; Lewis gun; Thompson sub-machine gun; Vickers machine-gun (used mainly on large Marine Police launches); Very light pistol and Greener shotgun.

The .38 Smith & Wesson revolver was light and more suitable for plain-clothes duty. Police truncheons were part of uniform dress and were made of Lignum Vitae. *Lathis* (long wooden staffs) were kept in store but rarely used; I have seen Indian police using them and they are a dangerous weapon. There was also the newly formed emergency unit, a large armour-plated van with a hatch in the roof for the commander.

On our course, there was also the second batch of Chinese sub-inspectors, an idea that did not work. The previous class had all been dismissed for one reason or another. Later on, the most efficient Chinese police officers were those promoted from the ranks.

There was further drill later in the afternoon, followed by compulsory sport, and we all got fit with this very busy training programme. One Saturday afternoon I was watching the football at Chatham Road ground, very much minding my own business, when I was asked to play in goal for the police team against the Royal Welch Fusiliers, because our goalie was indisposed. A penalty was awarded, which I saved, but in doing so I dislocated a finger and ended up in hospital.

At about this time I joined the Victoria Recreation Club on the waterfront close to the naval dockyard. There was a swimming pool and gymnasium but by present-day standards the facilities were primitive. Every year there was a swimming competition between the police and the prison department in which I took part. There was also a regatta and a cross-harbour swim. The Cantonese meaning of Hong Kong is 'Fragrant Harbour' – a lovely expression but sadly inaccurate! I gave the cross-harbour swim a miss.

The afternoons were very well organised with something different every day. There were visits to other government departments including hospitals, prisons, Customs and Excise, Harbour Department and, of course, the mortuary. Having been quite bilious as a child, I must admit I was a little apprehensive about watching post-mortems immediately after lunch. Strangely enough, though, I survived better than some of the others. Visits within the Force were an essential part of our training and these included regular courses on the revolver and at the rifle range and armoury. The police had bullet-proof vests – heavy and uncomfortable but rarely used – and our instructor had recently been in Shanghai on a course. From fairly close range he was shot in the chest by a .38 revolver. He certainly felt it and was left with a large bruise.

Every section of Police Headquarters was visited during the training, and towards the end of the course, we accompanied officers on patrol at the larger stations. Our instructor, Inspector Len Tyler, was a 'local knowledge' fanatic and the rambles he organised for us were a work of art. We were taken to a starting point and then we walked uphill and down dale taking notes along the way. There were remote islands and isolated villages, and *en route* we always visited the local police station where the hospitality was good and instructive. Then it was back to the PTS by a different route and invariably we were tired out after a strenuous day. The training inspector really was an expert at this kind of planning and timing, and a few days later there was the inevitable examination on what we had seen on the days out.

A day trip to Macau, forty miles away, was included in the training. The description 'Monte Carlo of the East' was a bit of an exaggeration and the only game I saw was fan-tan which was not very exciting. It is interesting to note that the Portuguese had been in Macau 283 years before Hong Kong became a British crown colony.

Passing out was a big day for all the contingents of recruits and I managed a credit pass. I was posted to Number 7 Police Station, 'West Point', on Hong Kong Island. I was issued with a .38 revolver and ammunition with instructions to wear the gun at all times, both on and off duty. Occasionally we were told to carry the small circular six-bullet holder now called a speed-loader. On looking back, I can hardly believe that, for years, I carried this quite heavy weapon and also managed to disguise it.

On arrival at West Point, an old mission house, I got into trouble on my first day out. The patrol was 4 pm to 1 am with one hour for dinner. I wore a clean white uniform and helmet and, in Queen's Road, quite close to the station, a body had landed in the middle of the road having fallen from the third floor of a tenement building. It emerged that the man had enjoyed a meal without the money to pay for it and had left in a hurry. Did he fall or was he pushed? I cannot remember the outcome of the enquiry but it was a real mess in the road with the usual large gathering of sightseers. I made the mistake of calling for an ambulance instead of the 'dead box' and got a slap on the wrist.

The routine was mostly evening and night patrols throughout the district, signing books at places like Kennedy Town slaughter house, Pok Fu Lam sub-station and the Leprosarium. I called at various cinemas, which were very popular with the Chinese. They loved chatting and sometimes quarrelling during the performance, standing up, walking about and shouting to each other across the cinema, during all of which the poor commentator did his best to make himself heard. I always remember the heavy wooden beams above the screen, with the rats running backwards and forwards becoming enlarged by the projected light and appearing as prehistoric monsters.

Anti-Japanese riots had occurred, and were expected again with the Japanese invading Chinese territory. There were not many

Japanese living in Hong Kong but there had been very serious trouble in 1931 when Manchuria was invaded.

I spent two days in the Queen Mary Hospital with unpleasant septic eruptions on my head and by this time I was getting used to good old Hong Kong complaints like prickly heat, dhobi itch, Montezuma's revenge and ringworm. From the veranda I saw my old friend SS *Ranpura* coming in past Green Island and later the word got round that one of the *Ranpura* passengers was a new sister who was coming on the ward. 'We'll soon sort her out' was the boast but we were all cowards and respectfully 'stood to our beds' without a crease showing on the bedclothes. It was my lucky day because the demure Sister Nan Mackie became my wife three years later.

The inspector in charge of Number 7 Police Station was nick-named 'Black Label' and he liked to make his regular visits to important places in the sidecar of a motor cycle, usually driven by an experienced police sergeant. It was arranged that I should have some unofficial instruction just in case I had to do this job. One afternoon I was driving on a quiet road on the Peak when I came face to face with Tommy King, the Inspector General of Police (IGP), driven by his chauffeur. I was not joy-riding and had another police sergeant on the sidecar, but the result was that I was put on the report and in due course appeared before the IGP charged with unauthorised driving of a police vehicle. At the disciplinary hearing, having handed over my revolver, I was taken in by a chief inspector and 'Black Label' who, to be fair, spoke in my defence. However, this cut no ice with Tommy King who found me guilty and a caution went on my record. The removal of the revolver was because, some years earlier, the accused had pulled his gun on the IGP and, having done this, upturned his desk at the same time!

Western District was an area of great contrast between poverty and wealth. At first, on night patrol, I would pick my way through the street sleepers – some there by choice but the majority by necessity – and immediately find myself in an area of affluence. From smart Chinese hotels, noisy revellers would emerge with their shrill but attractive ladies and get into expensive cars, private rickshaws, and the occasional sedan chair. Continuing west along

Queen's Road towards Kennedy Town, often in intense humidity, I had an arrangement with a shopkeeper to have a sarsaparilla drink on ice. Suitably refreshed, I went by the fairly steep Sands Street to Pok Fu Lam Road where I signed the book at the small police station.

My training was now complete and I had a few weeks at Central Police Station before crossing the harbour to Sham Shui Po with the rank of sergeant under Inspector Fred Portallion. Conditions were primitive at Central. We were four to a room with old-fashioned bathrooms but I was getting used to the Shanghai tub which was just like a huge pudding basin with a small hole in the bottom. The water was heated by a geyser and I quite enjoyed being nearly submerged in a crouching position. Our one piece of furniture was a large dressing table with drawers on one side and hanging space on the other. Without any great difficulty, this was taken with us from station to station suspended on ropes attached to bamboo poles with two bearers.

I quickly got into the routine at Sham Shui Po. There was a large book on the desk in the charge room known as the Occurrence Book in which everything was entered around the clock. Every complaint was investigated immediately. If a visiting superintendent spotted anything amounting to neglect, there was the inevitable notation: 'Please explain'. We worked ten-day shifts of 8 am to 4 pm, 4 pm to 1 am, and 1 am to 8 am. Night duty was essential so the man on day duty moved to fill these hours when an officer had his one day off in ten. It sounds a bit complicated but the result was there was very little day duty with free evenings. If an officer had to attend court the following day, his hours on patrol were reduced by one for every three spent in court! It was a hard life and as the hospital hours were nearly as complicated, the chances of Nan Mackie and I, who by this time were 'going steady', getting time off together were remote.

A monthly treat was either dinner at the Gloucester Hotel or at Tkachenko, a Russian restaurant in Kowloon. At the hotel, four of us would put on evening clothes and dine and dance, the total bill coming to about HK$40 which at $16 to the pound sterling was good value, considering my salary at this time was about £200 p.a. !

All stations had Indian police from the Punjab, either Sikhs or Mohammedans. They did not live together in the same barrack blocks and police regulations were very clear on the subject. Sikhs were allowed to gamble and drink alcohol but they didn't smoke. They didn't shave their hair and always wore an iron bracelet. Mohammedans were allowed to smoke, but I noticed that many cupped their hands and inhaled the smoke without the cigarette touching their lips. They didn't gamble, didn't drink alcohol, and their hair was cut in the smart military style.

As the Chinese and Indian constables went on duty, with their own sergeants, orders were given to patrol the beats from the left or the right, that is to say clockwise or anti-clockwise, so they were bound to meet. When things didn't quite go according to plan, an exchange of torch flashes at street corners generally brought the patrols together.

The 'chop' system was useful and it worked well. Each constable carried a small rubber stamp with his number on it at the end of a thin chain. The patrol officer had a report sheet on which the chop was stamped and the time noted. The system was foolproof, with the constable being met at least once during his four-hour spell of duty.

I passed my first two Cantonese examinations and was studying for my third which included learning to write characters. I very much enjoyed speaking to the ordinary Chinese, particularly the children with their good humour and ready smiles. Early in the morning, coming off night duty, it was fascinating to see the district come to life. Generally the nights were quiet with perhaps the sound of the 'night soil' coolies or the plaintive call of the vendor of 'Blind Man's Cake' walking in the middle of the road, or perhaps excited shouts from a late night *mahjong* party. There might also be an old woman with bound feet waving children's clothes at the end of a pole to drive away the 'devils' after the child had had a restless night.

Speaking of 'night soil' (the contents of cesspools, removed at night by bucket) I will never forget chasing a suspect on the waterfront and following him at top speed along the rickety central plank of a night soil barge. I shudder when I think of the possibility of falling off the plank. I did not get my man! During the chase my mind recalled the question which inevitably cropped up in Police Regulation examinations, namely the use of arms by police. The correct answer to the question included words I shall always remember – *'when in hot pursuit of a felon'*.

Police work is never dull and when things go quiet, expect a loud bang. One night I heard the heavy footsteps of an Indian constable running towards me with torch flashing. Together we hurried to the scene of a horrific crime in a knitwear factory, with blood and bodies all over the place. A young man had run amok with a meat cleaver after an argument over a small debt, and had killed several members of his family. What a sight! The station inspector and the Criminal Investigation Department were quickly on the scene. I cannot remember the outcome, but the assailant was a Mexican Chinese.

We had our fair share of serious and petty crime at Sham Shui Po with the usual routine of detainees being taken to court the morning after they were charged. On Saturday and particularly Sunday nights, with the court closed over the weekend, opium addicts got very restless and noisy in the cells, and to quieten them down it was necessary to administer a little opium water so that the station could get some sleep.

Trouble was brewing on the border with China, and Chinese soldiers were deserting in large numbers, many being detained at Ta Kwu Ling. The Sino-Japanese War was spreading to our border near Shum Chun which was in fact bombed by the Japanese. On two occasions Japanese troops actually crossed into our territory but retired at the request of our police force and military.

I was posted to Sheung Shui which included long night patrols along the border armed to the teeth and with Very light pistols. Complying strictly with police regulations, we wore long trousers and smeared oil on our hands and faces, not as a camouflage but to keep mosquitos away. Malaria was rife in the New Territories as I later discovered to my cost. It was not on duty but on a picnic at Sha Tin Heights when I actually saw the mosquito that bit me. A few days after the mosquito bite, in a police launch at Tai Po, I felt unwell as if a cold was coming on. That night, back at the station,

I had a bad night and was sent to hospital. It was malaria. I was given massive doses of quinine and felt as weak as a kitten. In the night I remember saturating a pair of bedsheets with sweat and all I could think of was bottles of Watson's locally made lemonade and orange drink.

During another emergency at the border, I was billeted in a railway box-car at Lo Wu bridge over the Shum Chun river, our border with China. We worked with a company of the Middlesex Regiment. The nights were cold and this was my introduction to cocoa laced with rum. I can recommend it. It was bright during the day and I remember patrolling the border on the bank of the river where some of the Sikh constables were in the river washing their tresses. The Sikhs had a good sense of humour and, shouting like children, they invited me in for a swim. It was a challenge, and to great cheers I joined them in my underwear. I am sure that their good spirits were due to this complete change of duty and being in the country air instead of plodding the beat in the town.

In 1939 Norman Gunning was transferred to the Water Police station at Tsim Sha Tsui to work on harbour duty, and then attached to Special Branch working on plain-clothes duty at Kai Tak. After the surrender of Hong Kong to the Japanese on Christmas Day 1941, Norman and Nan and their six-month-old son were interned in Stanley. After release and repatriation in 1945, Norman was one of the first police officers to be recalled to Hong Kong to help with the rebuilding of the colony. For his work in the hostilities he received a Governor's Commend.

1956: Crashes and Riots

Charlie McGugan

Two days' flight to Hong Kong by British Overseas Airways Corporation Constellation, and we arrived at Kai Tak Airport in Hong Kong on a brilliant, clear, October day. Police transport took us to the old Tsim Sha Tsui Police Station for temporary accommodation. The rooms of the old building each housed six or more expatriate inspectors. We were not impressed; in my case the accommodation was much worse than I had experienced with the Royal Air Force (RAF) at Little Sai Wan. On the way from the airport, we passed numerous cargo and civilian passenger aircraft 'mothballed' and stored along the perimeter fence. These had 'escaped' from China during the communist take-over of the Mainland and were awaiting disposal, sale or return to China.

We were required to report to Police HQ for an induction group meeting, followed by transfer to the Police Training School (PTS) on the south side of Hong Kong Island near Deep Water Bay. Buildings were military-style Nissen huts and facilities. The usual drill square was complete with Union flag and flag pole. Training period was six months. Because the HK Police was a paramilitary force, it followed that foot drill, arms drill and riot squad drill formed a large part of our training. The need for this for the majority of probationary sub-inspectors was dubious as most of the recruits had served in one of the UK armed services. However, balance was achieved by fairly large doses of law, civil and criminal.

At this stage, it was stressed that failure to pass the Cantonese language examinations by the end of our probationary period might result in termination of our appointment. Starting pay was about HK$960, around £60 per month. Even including accommodation, this was low for an expatriate living in Hong Kong.

Cold-weather uniform was smart, consisting of a dark blue tunic with black leather Sam Browne belt; .38 revolver; peaked cap; silver badges, trimmings and buttons; and a black leather-covered swagger stick with leather wrist strap. Summer uniform was khaki drill shorts and shirt; and khaki long socks with blue stocking tops. Badge of rank for probationary sub-inspectors was one silver star, but after completion of the three-year probationary period, this was changed to an army-style 'pip'. The silver star later caused me some merriment and a young American Shore Patrol army captain embarrassment, in the King Fu Bar in Wan Chai district. He had been causing some trouble and I was sent to sort out the problem. He saw my silver star and came smartly to attention. (A silver star in the US military indicates that the wearer is of 'field rank', major or higher.)

The passing-out parade, long awaited and anticipated, signalled the end of our time at PTS. Most of us however were a little disappointed with the chosen 'march past' music – *The Happy Wanderer* was somewhat of a let-down after the RAF march past music!

My first posting in 1956 was to the newly built No 7, or Western Police Station, a good mess, individual rooms and toilet facilities shared with your neighbour. Very satisfactory!

Duties, as explained to me by the sub-divisional inspector (SDI) (station commander) and the chief inspector (second-in command of the division), were a mix – parading and street supervision of the duty watch of some thirty to forty Chinese police constables (PCs) and non-commissioned officers; charge room inspector (inspector on duty, IOD) for eight-hour duty periods; and the most interesting and testing, executing 'dangerous drug' (DD) and 'women and juveniles' warrants.

At this time, opium use had declined markedly from the pre-war years and had been replaced by 'chasing the dragon' or smoking virtually pure heroin. This was sold in 0.05 gram packets at HK 50 cents (about three pence) and my diary records for the period March 1956 to April 1957, that I made the following drug seizures and associated arrests:

Possession of heroin: 39 arrests

Selling heroin: 59 arrests

Possession of opium pipes: 5 arrests

These duties were carried out in civilian clothes by a small armed squad consisting of myself, an experienced corporal and two or three constables. The work was interesting and demanding. Literally it was not possible to know what was around the next corner or up the next staircase.

While I was on IOD night duty in Western Police Station charge room, a prisoner hanged himself in a remand cell. The enquiry cleared me of any blame but I was ordered to attend the autopsy to impress on me the need for care of prisoners. The autopsy carried out in summer and in a room with no air conditioning was not an experience I would care to repeat.

A routine but unpleasant duty involved the searching of dead bodies to remove personal effects before delivery of the corpse to the mortuary. A degree of sensitivity was maintained by requiring male police officers to attend to male bodies and female police officers to search females.

A shocking incident from my diary:

> At 22.00hrs 22nd January 1956. Off duty, walking past Roxy
> Cinema Hennessy Road when Chinese female jumped or fell
> from 5th floor and landed approximately 10 feet from
> Sub-Inspector Reed and myself. Woman still alive phoned 999
> emergency unit and ambulance. Controlled crowds until they
> arrived. Went with DPC (Detective Police Constable) to woman's
> room, no foul play suspected.

Transfers between different police stations were considered a normal part of learning and I had my share. Western to Wan Chai, Wan Chai to Sham Shui Po and then Kowloon City. Sham Shui Po Police Station was an unhappy posting, partly because of the physical state and situation of the building. It was built during the early pre-war years in a noisy, dirty and crowded part of Kowloon. Sleep after night duty was frequently impossible, the quarters overlooked either a main road or the parade square. Foot-patrol duties were difficult and crime rates high. Severe street hawker problems led to blockage of traffic, pedestrian and emergency vehicle access and were a constant, and virtually insoluble, problem.

One happy personal memory remains; during a night patrol supervising rank and file foot duties, I was approached by a beat PC who asked for advice on his 'find' of a female baby apparently abandoned outside a public latrine. The child was unclothed, though wrapped in a small blanket, very cold and agitated. Orders for such cases (which were not unusual) were to take the child to the local hospital for examination and then to the Social Services Department for care. But I felt that this child needed immediate care and attention, so I took her to Miss Dibden, an English woman and ex-missionary at her care home in the New Territories. The child was welcomed, cared for and adopted by Miss Dibden. All the children that she took in were educated and found employment. This great lady subsequently retired to the UK and I believe took any children still in her care with her!

Lai Chi Kok amusement park in Sham Shui Po provided some light relief for a bored night inspector on foot patrol. Dancing shows by very mature chorus girls had to be visited to ensure that nothing indecent or unseemly occurred. I asked the sub-divisional inspector what constituted 'indecency or unseemly'. 'Pubic hair' he replied most forcefully, was not to be on show. The girls enjoyed embarrassing me as did the audience.

My short stay in Kowloon City was, by comparison, a holiday. Staff attitude to daily duties was reassuring and comfortable. The Kowloon Walled City, which had an unusual political status which ensured a 'hands off' attitude from most HK government services, warrants a story of its own.

At this time, the illegal immigrant situation from China was reaching a peak. I remember one night when I was on charge-room duty, a batch of about thirty refugees were brought in for booking and overnight security. One of the women aborted her baby in the remand cell; more work for the somewhat reluctant duty woman PC, until the ambulance arrived. Just another night of IOD duty!

My diary for this period records some items of interest:

There was the incident in which I attempted to rescue the occupants of a car which had gone into the harbour in Western. It appeared that the car had hit the water on its left side, buckling in both doors, then straightened up and sunk on its right side. The driver and passengers were initially probably still alive but I could not open the buckled doors or windows. I attempted to break windows but could not stay underwater long enough. The fire brigade arrived and dropped a steel hook on a heavy rope to me. I managed to break a window and hook into the door pillar. The vehicle and the bodies were then pulled up to the surface.

An extract from my police notebook follows:

Time of entry 03.00 hrs 14th May 1956. Private car HK3319 with 4 occupants went into the seafront near French Street at 00.05 hours on the 14th May 1956. When I reached the scene I handed my weapon to my Corporal and dived down to the car (water about 15 feet deep). The car was lying about 20 feet from the sea wall on its right side and sinking. I fastened a grapnel dropped to me by the fire brigade to the side of the car through the front window which was broken open and the car was then drawn to the side of the sea wall. I dived and fastened another rope to the front left wheel and the car was secured. The door was opened by Marine PC 4904 (right hand rear door) and four bodies, two Chinese males and two Chinese females were found inside. All were confirmed dead on arrival at Queen Mary Hospital.

Charlie McGugan attempts a rescue
(Courtesy Sylvia McGugan)

I was medically cleared for duty and some days later I was summoned into the office of the Assistant Superintendent, Western Division, who handed me an envelope, saying: 'Congratulations, here is something to hang on the toilet door.' It was a Commissioner of Police Commendation!

A week later, a Royal Air Force Auxiliary Harvard crashed near the top of the hill on Ap Lei Chau Island in Aberdeen. I attended the scene, accompanied by a very young colleague who was visiting me at the time. Upon approaching the crash area, I saw a large piece of bone covered by red ants. My colleague took this very badly and subsequently had a mental breakdown resulting in his repatriation to the UK. My police diary entry logged the time of my arrival at the site as 17.45 hrs on 21st May 1956 and reads:

> Arrived at scene of aircraft crash. Dispersed crowds. Nothing to be done. Aircraft type Harvard. Rudder turned to full port. Tail flaps full down. Pilot dead. Plane had apparently flown straight into the side of the hill. Pilot was earlier seen flying low over Repulse Bay beach and waving to the crowd. Suspect he was paying insufficient attention to flying the aircraft. Covered pilot with his parachute and awaited arrival of emergency services.

I was commanding a riot squad during the 1956 'Double Tenth' riots in Kowloon. This was a very interesting experience, not easily forgotten!

The squad which I commanded for the duration of the 1956 civil disturbances consisted of twenty police NCOs and constables. The unusual aspect of this squad was that they were not local (native to Kwangtung province) but from Shan Tung, or Wei Hai Wei, north of Shanghai. They spoke Cantonese but had a different accent. They were steady, mature and reliable, probably chosen because of my tender years and inexperience. The squad was armed with anti-riot 'Flight-Rite' tear gas missiles, Greener guns (shotguns) and personal Webley .38 revolvers for the rank and file, and for myself, my Colt Police Positive .38 revolver. The officer designated as my assistant, or aide-de-camp carried an American MI semi-auto carbine.

The reason for the issue of this very effective military weapon was not explained. What was clearly explained was that we were not to use these weapons except to protect civilian lives or to defend ourselves and then only after written and verbal warnings issued by a magistrate as detailed in the handbook *Guide to the use of firearms by police*. I can assure you that I studied this guide carefully before addressing my contingent.

Baton charges were necessary in and around Hung Hom, Sham Shui Po, Tai Hang Tung resettlement estate and Tsuen Wan to break up large gatherings. Arrests were made. A morale problem was solved by resorting to semi-legal action; I noticed the squad was restive and when I asked the squad sergeant for the reason, he replied 'cigarettes'. Being a non-smoker, I had not realised what three days without a smoke could do to seasoned smokers! The problem was that the streets were empty, no cash was carried by the squad and all the shops were closed. This was however soon solved by the sergeant banging loudly on the door of the nearest shop. The owner reluctantly emerged and upon receipt from me of a signed bill for 600 cigarettes, addressed to the Commissioner of Police, provided the necessary. I do not know if the receipt was ever presented or honoured. Food packages provided by the Garden Bakery were our only sustenance for three days – sandwiches, cold rice and an orange.

The disturbances lasted for five days after which the army was placed on standby. By the end of this period the civil authorities, in particular the police and the Fire Service were pretty well exhausted.

By September 1958, I had decided not to make a career in the HKP and took the open competitive examination for entry into the Executive Grade of the HK Civil Service. I was successful and after handing in my uniform and revolver at Kowloon PHQ, crossed the harbour to Hong Kong Island and on to the Colonial Secretariat in Garden Road for my recruitment interview.

Ping Chau First Aid

Peter Leeds

I left the Police Training School in Hong Kong in early 1952, and my first posting was to Marine Division. They had a modest fleet of second-hand boats, some of which had been well used in World War II. For the harbour there were a number of small wooden tugboats which had originated in Australia. For the open seas there were two 700-ton ex-Admiralty tugs, Lloyd's registered with the names *Empire Sam* and *Empire Josephine*, but in 1952 they were simply *Police Launch 1* and *Police Launch 2*. Next were two ex-Royal Air Force air-sea rescue boats, flimsily built with timber and plywood. These had three diesel engines, which, on the limited occasions when all three were working properly, could push them along at a respectable 21 knots. They were ill-suited for police work but not bad for impressing visiting foreign dignitaries. The only deep-sea boats were two ex-Admiralty motor fishing vessels which were reputed to have been used as mine sweepers. They could only manage a top speed of about 8 knots, and so were not noted for their capability in hot pursuit.

In those days, many villages in the New Territories had poor communications with the urban area and contact with officials was by boat or footpath. The Marine Police played a part in keeping in touch with the residents by visiting remote places and by making overland foot patrols.

On one occasion, I was on *Police Launch 1* and we were making a routine visit to Ping Chau Island in Mirs Bay. On the launch, we carried a first aid box which contained bandages, plasters, ointments, pills and potions which were used to treat simple injuries and ailments suffered by the villagers. We had little medical training but the villagers usually knew what they wanted.

On this visit to Ping Chau we were invited to go to a villager's house, where we found a woman, heavily pregnant, with an extremely swollen and suppurating leg. Hideous! One of the local treatments for heaven knows what, was to apply extreme heat to the sole of the foot. In this case it had gone terribly wrong.

This situation was clearly beyond our capability and it took some time to persuade the family that the lady must go to hospital. She was taken by *sampan* (small rowing boat) to *Launch 1*, which sailed off to Tai Po where an ambulance, summoned by radio message, took her to hospital. No member of her family would travel with her.

It was some weeks before we made our next visit to Ping Chau and as we approached we saw a man running down the beach and gesticulating. He climbed in to a *sampan* and rowed swiftly to our launch, climbed aboard and demanded to know what we had done with his wife!

A message was radioed back to Marine Police Headquarters. After a while a reply came back and we were able to tell the distraught husband that his wife had been discharged from hospital and was staying with her sister in Shau Kei Wan and, by the way, she had given birth to a baby boy.

The joyful father rowed ashore with incredible speed and we saw him run along the beach shouting the good news. A crowd gathered. We were invited to the village elder's house to join the celebrants. We appreciated their hospitality; they were not a rich community. The only disappointment was the drink offered, what we called 'the village elder's revenge': bottles of lukewarm Three Horses Beer.

A Dutchman in the the
Auxiliary Marine Police

Frank Goldberg

In 1956, I was the only Dutch expatriate employed by the Dairy Farm Ice and Cold Storage Company in Hong Kong. I soon discovered that my British colleagues had to sign up with the Navy, Army or Air Force Auxiliaries or with the Auxiliary Marine Police. They returned from their weekend duties and fortnightly 'holidays' with such exciting stories that I paid a visit to the Netherlands Consulate General to find out if I could perhaps also join. Lo and behold, a Dutch Royal Decree, dating from the Second World War, was still in force that allowed Dutch nationals in Hong Kong to serve under the British flag.

And so I became an auxiliary constable in the Hong Kong Marine Police, scrubbing decks, oiling machines and attending police and navigation classes. We also had to attend annual training camps in Aberdeen, driving there in our own cars. When our instructors told us that if we continued to park near the barracks they would give us parking tickets, our fellow 'auxies' who were also professional lawyers by day, told them that the police had no jurisdiction over crown land and were thus by law not allowed to fine us for parking there. Regardless, our instructors warned us that anyone who continued to leave his car anywhere near the barracks would be put on guard duty from 12 midnight to 4 am!

The camp weeks at Aberdeen were fun but marching in heavy boots was not my reason for joining the police force. Besides, some commands were completely unknown to me. When, years later, I was asked to march a squad of auxiliary marine police back to the barracks, all went well: 'BY THE LEFT, QUICK MARCH' and so on, until we reached our destination, with a 'SQUAD HALT' and 'STAND AT EASE'. There they all stood, facing me and soon realising that I didn't have a clue what order to call out next. Many had served in the regular army and, after thoroughly enjoying my misery, were also kind enough to whisper: 'Dismiss'. And 'DISMISS' I thankfully called out!

After several years of diligent study, I was deemed qualified to go out on the 70-foot launches for weekend patrols, taking over the duties from the regulars. For me this was always the ultimate experience. So it was that I proudly patrolled Hong Kong's harbour for the first time as an inspector, on Taiwan's 'Double Ten' Day, the 10th October 1961 – a holiday which was recognised by their supporters in Hong Kong.

The radio room advised me that a Chinese student on board the Peninsular and Oriental (P&O) liner *Orion* had committed suicide and directed me to go and investigate. Real police work at last!

The *Orion* was at anchor at Kowloon Bay. After climbing on board I was met by the first officer and a medical doctor, who took me to the unfortunate boy's cabin. Sure enough, he was dead. What to do? A decision had to be made, so I told the officers that I would take the body with me on my launch. 'Impossible,' said the first officer, 'the deck is full of passengers.' However, being a police officer and having made a decision, one had to persevere. So I ordered: 'Clear the Decks!' and all passengers were ushered inside the lounges and the curtains were drawn. Two sailors were summoned to bring up the body on a stretcher. We went in single file to the rope ladder: me in front of course, then the first officer and the doctor, followed by the two sailors with the body. It's hard to describe my feelings when I looked over the ship's railing only to find that the launch wasn't there. . . . The radio room (also manned by well-trained auxiliaries!) had given the crew another assignment, to which they had enthusiastically responded, leaving me stranded. . . .

Given the situation on the *Orion* I ordered a masterful 'About turn' and we marched back in reverse order, with me at the rear. The captain was by this time fed up with the delay and ordered the ship to weigh anchor. The passengers were allowed back on deck and there was I, standing amongst them sailing into Victoria

Harbour with the body for company, feeling very lonely and conspicuous in my new Inspector's uniform.

Finally, to add insult to my misery, one of the passengers tapped me on the shoulder and said 'I say, are you from the Cook's travel agents?'

As for the body, the SS *Orion* berthed at a pier on the Kowloon side of the harbour and there I could make a call from a public telephone to ask for a car with a body box. The van arrived and the body of the student, nicely rolled up in a blanket, was put in the metal box. So far so good, till one of the sailors mentioned that it was a P&O blanket and without further ado, they each took a corner and rolled the body into the casket and closed the lid.

Frank Goldberg and Victoria Harbour, early 1960s

A Day In the Western Police Station Charge Room

Charlie McGugan

The charge room, or report room, was the place where members of the public, on entry into the police station, would make their reports with regard to crime, or other requests for police assistance. It was also where officers would make their reports to the Inspector on Duty (IOD) on the results of inquiries or execution of any warrants, as well as the place where all arrested persons were brought for documentation and detention in cells.

The IOD was responsible for the proper operation of the room which included recording reports from the public, then initiating any necessary action and registering the result. He was responsible for all bail money, the security of exhibits received, and the lawful detention and security of prisoners in cells, as well as their well-being.

The following sets out the day of an inspector in the early 1950s to give a flavour of what might be dealt with in the report room. Each of these occurrences actually happened, not however on the same day.

Duty shifts were from 6 am to noon, noon to 6 pm, 6 pm to midnight and midnight to 6 am.

Awake at 5 am. Shower, shave and dress in full winter uniform with Sam Browne belt, cap and revolver (Police Positive Colt .38 with 5 rounds) and black leather-covered swagger stick.

Downstairs to parade ground to inspect the other ranks about to go on duty. Duty senior sergeant reports, beats are allocated to some thirty-four constables. The orders for the day and items of particular interest are communicated to them.

Beat duties dismissed to attend their allocated beats. Check available transport with duty transport corporal.

Relieve night inspector going off duty and similarly, junior police officers coming on duty to relieve the charge room staff. Check and sign for the charge room safe and holding cells. Thirteen male prisoners are accounted for but two appear to be suffering from drug withdrawal symptoms, and are sent to Queen Mary Hospital (QMH). Arrange for follow-up action on outstanding cases as necessary. Senior sergeant takes over report book entry duties and duty interpreter types daily report. Myself to inspector's mess for quick breakfast and back to charge room in time to greet sub-divisional inspector (station commander) when he makes his daily inspection. Duty reserve police constable (PC) on standby to follow up on any necessary inquiries.

Report Nº	Report	Time	Action
24734	Body in Harbour	07.10	Called Marine Police/Fire Service. Report 'not suicide' – CID to scene
24735	Wild animal escape & person injured	07.28	Called Emergency Unit (EU) & ambulance. Water buffalo escaped from Kennedy Town abattoir & gored bystander
24736	Pickpocket	07.25	Refer to CID 'Western'
24737	Obstruction by Falling scaffolding	08.05	Call Traffic/Fire Service & Public Works Dept. (PWD). No injuries reported
24738	Dead body to be searched	08.15	Call Duty Reserve PC for search. Body identified
24739	Traffic accident Reported at Pok Fu Lam Rd. Person injured	09.05	Refer to Traffic Division, Hong Kong Island (HKI) & call ambulance
24740	Captain of government dredger phoned report of recovery of suspected aircraft bomb from sea bed close to Kennedy Town praya	09.50	PHQ Bomb Squad/Marine Police, Marine Dept & Emergency Unit to scene. Further report awaited

Report Nº	Report	Time	Action
24741	Sgt Wu Tsin-on of EU HKI reported with his squad & vehicle for EU duty re report of bomb recovery by Capt. of Govt dredger	10.20	See report 24740
24742	Sgt 4881 requests assistance to bring suspect drug seller to station	11.10	Duty driver & Reserve PC to scene
24743	Fatal traffic accident reported outside 54 Connaught Rd West	12.30	Alert Fire Services/Ambulance & Traffic HKI
24744	DPC 1089 requested storage of seized cash in charge room safe	13.15	Enter amount into safe register & accept $16,205 from DPC
24745	Domestic disturbance reported at cockloft in 223 Jervois St, Chinese Female (C/F) injured	13.55	Call ambulance & duty PC to check
24746	Request from Cpl 286 for transport to assist arrest of 5 Chinese Male (C/M) in illegal gambling den	14.30	Call out Transport Cpl & Reserve Duties to support
24747	Cpl 553 reported to station with 6 illegal cooked food hawkers	15.10	Check food sale licences, confiscate mobile food stalls
24748	Dr Wong man-wai (QMH) phoned to report disturbance in QMH casualty ward	16.05	2 duty Uniform Branch (UB) officers to scene to investigate
24749	Report from Aberdeen Police Station of aircraft crash on Ap Lei Chau Island	17.45	Fire Brigade, ambulance, EU Unit & HK Auxiliary Air Force informed
24750	PC 1065 arrested C/M for illegal discharge of fireworks	18.08	Fireworks confiscated, C/M warned
24751	PSI Jones & Sgt 8210 arrested 6 suspected banishees (Persons previously banished from Hong Kong for criminal offences)	19.30	Transport and UB back-up to scene. 6 C/M no HK ID cards, detained pending deportation
24752	Fire at domestic hut at Mt Davis Rd; suspected drug link	20.10	Fire Services & CID to scene
24753	Dangerous Drug Squad (DD) Inspector Thomas requested transport to station after arrest of 3 C/M at unnumbered hut on Mt Davis Rd	21.20	Large quantity of DD seized & 3 C/M detained for further inquiries (see Report 24752)

Report Nº	Report	Time	Action
24754	Women & juveniles warrant executed at 21 Ko Kai. Insp. Williams arrested 2 C/M, 6 C/F (adults) & 1 underage C/F	22.15	CID & Social Welfare investigating
24755	C/F seen throwing packets of suspected DD from footpath into holding cell window	22.20	C/F arrested outside Western Police Station for passing suspected drugs to prisoners in custody cells
24756	C/F attempted suicide by jumping from roof of 107 Des Voeux Rd (W)	23.05	Ambulance, Traffic HKI & EU to scene
24757	Deceased body search of C/F	23.15	Body search by Duty Women Police Constable (WPC), Identity (ID) established
24758	Complaint by European female of noisy dogs in Pok Fu Lam Rd	23.20	Noted for action by night duty beat officers
24759	C/M arrested by PC 988 at Ko Shing Theatre for alleged indecent assault on C/F	23.30	C/M brought to station & statements taken from all involved. C/F underage (15), Social Welfare informed
24760	D/Sgt Lee on-wing requested C/M be held in custody cell awaiting charge 'Membership of Triad Society'	23.35	Fingerprinted, searched & detained
24761	PC 49 report main water pipe broken at Western Market	23.37	Call Public Works Department/Traffic HKI
24762	Unidentified junk reported offloading 10-plus people in Aberdeen Harbour	23.40	Refer to Marine Police/Aberdeen Police Station
24763	Report of shooting in Hill St	23.50	Police drug squad & Sub Insp. Peeler at scene. CID & ambulance alerted
24764	Duty PC in charge of custody cells reports 1 prisoner has attempted suicide by hanging	23.58	Attempt resuscitation, call ambulance, inform Chief Insp. Western
24765	Traffic accident Kennedy Town Praya	00.15	Call Fire Brigade, ambulance, Marine Police & EU HKI. Insp McGugan at scene
Off Duty		00.25	

Check List of Duties for next day:

8 am Riot Drill.

10 am Court (2 dangerous drugs possession cases).

2 pm Visit & check explosives stores.

4 pm Visit & check arms storage at Wing On Bank (request from chief inspector, Central Division, to check 2 Browning 12 gauge automatic shotguns, 1 Webley .38 revolver, 50 cartridges, 10 .38 rounds).

Central Police Station: 1956

John Turner

I was posted to Central Police Station in the summer of 1956, after the passing-out parade at the Police Training School in the lowly rank of probationary sub-inspector (PSI). At Central, I was 'welcomed' by the then divisional superintendent, a very youthful Ted Shave, who showed me to my quarters, a rather large room in C Block. The room had a small veranda which overlooked the very steep access road up to the station compound, and was linked to the adjacent Block B by a concrete walkway. There were three blocks of single inspectors' quarters, A, B, and C with A being for the more senior inspectors and C for the most junior.

Many of the residents of A Block, including Jimmy Hidden, Mike Davis, and Mo Hulbert, all apparently confirmed bachelors, had been in residence for some years and were not expecting to be moved. I, on the other hand, was informed that I would be moved to a 'superior' room in B Block as soon as a vacancy arose. The residents of the three blocks, twenty-five or thirty inspectors, were all served by one 'room boy', Ah Kit, who lived with his family on the ground floor of B Block. Ah Kit helped us all to survive our first few months outside the Police Training School and taught us the ropes. What a tale he could tell of the goings-on at Central! Young inspectors with me at the time included Bob Styles, Ivan Scott, Jock Atkinson and Ken Welburn.

The sub-divisional inspector was Mr Wong Wing Yin, nicknamed 'Mambo' Wong on account of his fondness for ballroom dancing, especially Latin American. Mambo wanted to be British and regarded England as home where he went on leave. He very seldom spoke in Cantonese, insisting on an interpreter whenever he interviewed Chinese officers.

Opposite B Block and adjacent to the entrance to the old Victoria Prison, was a large pre-war building, which served as Central Magistracy, where Mr Hing Shing-lo, the principal magistrate presided, dispensing instant justice to a mixture of unlicensed hawkers, opium addicts and wife beaters. Mr Lo wasted no time.

The charge room in the station was actually run by a sergeant who sat behind a high desk overlooking anyone who wished to make a report. He, and only he, was allowed to make an entry in the enormous red report book. I remember making an entry on one occasion but was quickly corrected by the sergeant. When the charge room became overcrowded, as it frequently did, those people waiting to make a report were placed in the large cage in the room, where they remained until they could be dealt with. The SDI's office was behind the charge room. However, Mr Wong seldom appeared outside his office.

In 1956, Hong Kong was overwhelmed by refugees from Mainland China who were fleeing the communist takeover of the country. They arrived in the tens of thousands, many of them turning up at police stations to be registered for a Hong Kong Identity Card. They would queue for hours outside the charge room, waiting their turn. Our knowledge of Cantonese was rather limited to say the least, although in our three-year probationary period, we were expected to qualify in both Standard I and Standard II language examinations if we were to become sub-inspectors. None of the refugees could speak English, and we were taught to ask them in Cantonese for their name, age, and place of birth. We struggled to understand and usually succeeded unless the person came from some obscure region in China and spoke a dialect which no one could understand. In such cases, we often invented personal particulars and passed on to the next one. Registration meant they would receive an identity card in due course, giving them the right to remain in the colony.

My first year at Central was fairly routine, and there was little in the way of excitement until the civil disturbances broke out on the 'Double Tenth' (tenth day of the tenth month, October) 1956, and I found myself in charge of an anti-riot platoon, consisting solely of policemen with wooden batons – little use when faced with an angry mob of stone-throwing rioters. The 'Double Tenth' was the National Day for Taiwan, the island to which Chiang Kai-shek and his army had fled following their defeat by the communists in China's civil war. An officious government resettlement officer had removed a banner celebrating the day and provoked a riot among nearby residents, most of whom were refugees from communism.

I, and my platoon, were sent from Central to the San Miguel Brewery in Sham Tseng, Tsuen Wan, in the New Territories, where the European staff were being held as hostages by Chinese workers. We succeeded in rescuing them and were then told to guard the brewery, obviously considered to be a vital point in those days, until relieved. Relief arrived some four days later. We had no rations of our own and were forced to survive on a diet of cuttlefish from the village shop, washed down by copious amounts of San Miguel beer! The riots eventually were subdued but not until more than fifty people had died, and there were thousands of arrests.

In the Central Police Station compound and next to the station charge room, was the headquarters of the Hong Kong Island District Emergency Unit. The personnel spent their time 'on standby', playing *mahjong* and waiting to be called out, when they would put on their white helmets, leap into their open-sided vehicle and speed off down the slope leading to Central District. There was a story that one night when on patrol, two constables fell asleep while on night duty, and actually fell onto the road when the patrol car went round a sharp bend!

Next to the Emergency Unit stood the Police Stores where Chief Inspector 'Granny' Scott presided. 'Granny' was a dour Scot who had an intense dislike of young inspectors. Woe betide anyone handing in their kit prior to vacation leave if even a single button was missing. This was a serious disciplinary matter in Granny's book. Not only would you be charged for the missing item, but also threatened with disciplinary action if there was any re-occurrence. As a result, most inspectors would appeal to the better nature of the barrack sergeant to persuade the Central Stores sergeant to accept the kit as correct. We called this the 'Ways and Means Ordinance'.

The large red brick building with its colonial-style verandas stood on the opposite side of the station compound and housed the Hong Kong Island District Headquarters, with Roy Turner, the district commander, and the Divisional Criminal Investigation Department (CID) with 'Paddy' Carter as the divisional detective inspector. The central divisional superintendent, Ted Shave, had his office on the ground floor of the building, together with Tommy Dow, the divisional chief inspector. Lowly uniform probationary sub-inspectors, such as myself, seldom had any dealings with these senior officers, except during official inspections. On one occasion though, I was surprised to receive Roy Turner's bank statement – the HSBC had apparently got our names mixed up. So the respite from my usual overdrawn status was illusory!

The Central Division and Hong Kong Island District Officers' Mess was located in the basement of the District Headquarters building. I had my breakfast and lunch there but only visited the upstairs on very rare occasions. It was usually frequented by the more senior officers, most of whom had a distinctly patronising attitude towards young sub-inspectors. It was 'get your knees brown' and 'what did you do in the war when we were in Stanley prison?' During World War II, Hong Kong was invaded by the Japanese and after the surrender, the Europeans and their families were incarcerated in Stanley Prison.

So, taking the hint, I and some of the other like-minded individuals – Bob Styles, Taff Hughes, Les Henson, and Jack English – would be found most evenings enjoying the delights of the Blue Heaven Nightclub which was in the King's Cinema Building about ten minutes walk downhill from Central Police Station. Here we all received a warm welcome from Louis, the manager, who, unknown to us at the time, was operating a large illegal casino on the floor above the nightclub and appreciated the security of having half the officers of Central Division wining and dining on the floor below. The club had a Filipino band, Tino's, and a gorgeous singer called Estella with whom we were all hopelessly in love but could not afford to pursue!

After a few months in C Block, I was upgraded to a room on the ground floor of B Block where I lived until early 1957. Then, I moved to Upper Levels Police Station where under Ron Dudman, the mess president, we enjoyed good food and company. Unfortunately this was not to last and at the end of the year, the Police Training Contingent, the anti-riot training establishment, was looking for volunteers and I was one of the first to go.

I look back on my time spent in Central as good days and quite unforgettable.

The Establishment of the Police Training Contingent

Ivan Scott

On 10th October 1956, a Resettlement Estate Officer unintentionally precipitated serious riots in Hong Kong by trying to remove banners celebrating Taiwan National Day.

Resettlement estates had a significant number of inhabitants who had fled from the Communist Revolution in China, and who supported the Kuomintang led by Chiang Kai-shek. Chiang and his army, defeated by the communists, had established themselves in Taiwan.

The resettlement officer was enforcing estate rules regarding the prohibition of the posting of notices, but not surprisingly, given political sensitivities, this was resented and rioting resulted which became violent and widespread. Over fifty lives were lost including that of the Swiss vice-consul's wife, when the couple were attacked by a mob whilst travelling in a taxi. Thousands of arrests were made and after several days the police restored order.

As a result of this terrible incident, it was decided that the police should review their training and equipment to enable them to deal more effectively with any future disturbance or riot. Assistant Police Commissioner, J.B. Lees and Chief Inspector L.F.C. Guyatt were appointed to conduct the review.

Changes in the structure of the internal security companies, their equipment and tactics were introduced.

Causeway Bay Road was closed to all traffic for the Riot Company demonstration. The company deployed from Roxy Roundabout to where North Point Magistracy is situated, with sections despatched to close side roads and columns for 'stop and search' of vehicles,

On a Sunday morning in 1957, at Victoria Park, Causeway Bay, an inspection and demonstration of three new platoon companies, before His Excellency the Governor of Hong Kong, Sir Robert Black, above, being briefed by Mr Vic Morrison, Divisional Superintendent, Central. Also present were Mr Edwin Tyrer, Assistant Commissioner of Police in command of Hong Kong Island (ACP/HKI), Sir Michael Turner Commandant, Auxiliary Police, and Mr A.C. Maxwell, Commissioner of Police. Probationary Sub-Inspector Ivan Scott was the platoon commander. (Courtesy of Ivan Scott)

persons and premises. On return, the sections and columns were re-grouped and the company returned to Victoria Park, amid cheers from local residents, bystanders and passengers on the top decks of the trams. His Excellency was most impressed with what he had seen and gave a directive to release funds for the creation of the Police Training Contingent, later renamed as the Police Tactical Unit.

Black Sleeves and Panda Faces – Traffic Days

Ian Stenton

Despite being considered by many colleagues as having been in Traffic 'forever', I did actually miss the years of the BSA motorcycle – as I did those of the Norton! However, I had owned a BSA M20 and many other large motorcycles myself in the United Kingdom, which is perhaps why I ended up in Traffic Division and on the streets for so many years of service.

The first Triumph police models with which I became acquainted were 350cc in a bluish silver colour and were swine. Started by a universal key (read screwdriver), the best were always taken by the traffic law enforcement *fokis* (staff) so the *bom baan jai* (inspector) got left with the fairly unreliable (read about-to-be-scrapped) machines. These usually had a defunct battery, so frequently had to be 'bump-started'. All very reasonable if one was in the police compound or on a downhill slope but when having to attempt this on a cross-harbour vehicle ferry with a slick and waterlogged floor, and whilst rolling in the harbour swells, it became mandatory watching for all car drivers and the accompanying third-class passengers. Oh, how they laughed!

The bikes in those days lacked power and therefore speed, and I was frequently passed by Kowloon Motor Bus double-deckers and other ramshackle vehicles. It was often a bit of a struggle to overtake some underpowered lorry belching out thick oily fumes in order to hand out a summons. It was thus that the famed traffic man's 'Panda' face look came about – goggles were essentially used by every bike man in those days and our white sleeves were invariably a greasy black at the end of a shift.

Anyhow, when over half of the original motorcycle fleet was laid up awaiting spare parts – the beginning of the end for the British bikes and about to be the start of the Japanese era – we started to get some newer, white Triumph models. The dizzy heights of now being a 'two pipper' (an Inspector with some seniority with two shoulder pips insignia) meant you were actually allocated one by the *che tau* (vehicle manager). The ignition key, not now a screwdriver, meant that the bike really was yours. It had a radio too, something the original did not, that could be relied on to work at least one per cent of the time so communication was now no problem. That is provided you were parked at the nearest store with a telephone.

These radios were a wondrous invention of the well-known British Pye electronics factory and were of a robust metal construction, replete with a mass of delicate valves specifically configured for duty on a motorcycle on poor roads in a tropical clime. Oh, how hilarious! An interesting feature of these radios was the telephone-style handset that was installed. This was felt by the HQ planners as being ideal for mobile use whilst wearing thick gauntlets and a crash helmet. But wait, the best is yet to come … the channel-switch box and the handset were mounted on a steel box inset on the tank in front of the rider. Hey, how convenient … until one either braked hard or otherwise came to a involuntary sudden halt. This of course helped explain the number of later-to-be senior officers talking in fairly high voices.

Further well-meaning, but equally pathetic designs by Communications Branch had both the radio set and the handset mounted on a steel tray to the rear of the rider – try changing channels on that at speed or in pursuit mode. The telephone handset with its cord and the mandated extra-thick long cabling ensured that even when stopped and dismounted, use could be described as somewhat inconvenient. Wearing a helmet and gloves – as required on the move – meant that, if at all, the conversation when moving was one-way, shouted into the handset, roughly guaranteeing that no message really got through when factors such as the banging of the handset on the helmet, interruptions due to avoiding obstructions one-handedly, speaking nicely to the passing motorists, and general traffic noise were taken into consideration. Need I say anything about attempting to listen to a handset through the thickness of a crash helmet?

Tests were done at the Police Driving School on the use of fairings, colour schemes and reflectivity, but these were deemed rather too ahead of the times and really rather unnecessary by the armchair experts ensconced in headquarters and so such experiments had to cease. Whilst indicators had to be accepted, albeit reluctantly, blue lights on motorcycles were not considered to be the way forward for safety or any other value – until the Japanese came along.

Briefly looked at were the larger Chinese-made machines, mostly combinations. These were direct copies of the Russian version of the BMW, the tooling of which had been 'liberated' from the Germans during World War II. They were generally felt by on-street men not to be technically quite up to what the Force now should move towards. Later, on tests, both rider and passengers were found to be terrified as they rapidly became aware of how totally ineffective the brakes were – as well as with aspects that on other machines had evolved rather a lot since the Second World War. Even HQ realised that perhaps these were not the machines for a modern, forward-looking police force.

As I noted, with the almost total lack of all things labelled UK 'spare part', the decision was taken to go Japanese. This first appeared in the shape of a Yamaha 650, a huge, extremely heavy, sway-back effort that had abysmal road holding. Indeed because of this, a special radio '10 code' was used which, roughly translated, meant *'I've fallen off my bike and am underneath it and can't move. The locals are stood around laughing, so come quick and help me!'* Some officers had assistance, some didn't, so were left waving feebly until a kindly passerby took pity on them. Great incentive not to fall off though! Fortunately, we then moved on to a better, lighter and more modern model.

This machine actually rode reasonably well – anything did after the 650 – and so was quite popular. By this time most riders had got used to the gear and brake pedals being on the opposite sides to those on the Triumph, but there were still times when inadvertent stops were made and sudden uncalled-for decelerations, with palpitations for any luckless motorists following behind . . . as well as for the rider himself!

Near the end of the service life of the first batch, there was a 'run off' between an upstart Honda and the well-entrenched Yamaha, which involved various traffic officers doing comparison tests. I recollect that to Sai Kung and back from Ngau Tau Kok Police Station on one of these proving drives, it took something like twenty minutes or less, within speed limits of course!

From thence came the much-loved Honda 650, the successors of which served faithfully over a long period in Traffic Divisions and the Force Escort Group, but slowly gave way to the BMW. Likewise, now with more professional Police Headquarters interest,

Traffic policeman John Murray on a Yamaha (Courtesy John Murray)

radios, personal traffic clothing and ancillary equipment also improved vastly. It still hurt when you fell off though.

In between the various 'large bike' sagas there were some smaller bikes on Hong Kong Island (HKI), allegedly accepted by Traffic Division HKI at the time due to lower cost (though that was fiercely denied). Somewhat unsurprisingly, the machines were neither up-to-standard for day-to-day working nor were they popular with the riders and so passed quietly and unloved into Traffic history.

Other small Hondas, Yamahas and even a few motley Ducatis too came along and into service as time passed. The Harley-Davidson was trialled as well . . . very, very briefly, being totally unsuited to our conditions and very agricultural in nature. At one stage, a considerable number of 350cc two-stroke Yamahas were bought by the commissioner and were actually used initially in 1971–72 at the Police Tactical Unit (PTU) for whole platoon training with the Saracen Unit (armoured cars) staff as the instructors/testers. This was to the annoyance of the PTU commandant and the local villagers who, along with the whole camp, were enveloped in thick malodorous smoke every morning during the parade and move-off by some fifty noisy motorcycles revving their oily hearts out!

Tokyo Olympics

Mike Watson

They say that if you can remember the 1960s, you really weren't there. I can certainly remember many events of that decade – the first man into space, the assassination of President Kennedy, the Beatles, the first moon landing and certainly the Hong Kong Disturbances of 1967, in which I was involved. However, my most single enduring memory of that period is my participation in the Tokyo Olympics of 1964, in which I represented Hong Kong at cycling.

I first arrived in Hong Kong in 1959 at which time the sport of cycle racing was in its infancy but growing in popularity. I became a founder member of the new Hong Kong Cycling Association (HKCA) and raced as the sole representative of the Hong Kong Police Sports Association, under whose banner I managed to win a number of Colony Championships at various distances and disciplines until I retired from racing in the early seventies.

Prior to 1964, Hong Kong had participated in only three Olympic Games in which only ten competitors were involved. However, with the Olympics coming to Asia for the first time, the Hong Kong Olympic Committee entered a team of thirty-nine athletes representing seven sports, which is still the fourth largest team to have represented Hong Kong. Cycling was included for the first time and the HKCA selected four riders, three from the South China Athletic Association and myself. Somewhat controversially, the Hong Kong Olympic Committee had not sanctioned the appointment of a team manager and we were told that this post would be filled by one of the two assistant managers of the Hong Kong delegation, although neither had any cycle-racing experience.

Before we left for Tokyo, the cycling team was selected to escort the Olympic Torch on what was the penultimate leg of its journey to Japan. Hong Kong was very lucky to have been chosen as a stop on the journey from Athens and we were to act as outriders to the athletes carrying the torch from the airport to the Star Ferry Terminal in Kowloon, where it was to spend one night before returning to the airport and the final flight to Tokyo. Unfortunately the exercise was not blessed with favourable weather and, when the aircraft carrying the torch arrived at Kai Tak, Hong Kong was in the throes of a typhoon, with strong winds and heavy rain, which meant that what should have been a pleasant task became something of a trial for both torch-bearers and escorts. While it was a well-publicised event, there were very few spectators and the few press photos which appeared simply served to emphasise the awful conditions.

Michael Watson (Courtesy M. Watson)

Overnight the Olympic flame was contained in an urn specially constructed by the Hong Kong and China Gas Company. However, the company's reputation was dealt a blow when it was later revealed that during the night the extreme weather conditions had extinguished the flame. It was, of course, re-lit and the true story was not widely known, but so much for keeping the flame burning between Olympics! Things got even worse when, on the following day, it was found that the aircraft had suffered damage during the storm and a replacement was found, only for it to develop engine trouble soon after take-off, forcing it to return to Hong Kong. By the time a second replacement had been found the schedule had been delayed by over 24 hours.

The Games were due to commence on October 11th and the main body of the team arrived several days before that to acclimatise and train before the competition. We moved into the Olympic Village, which was in the centre of Tokyo and close to the Olympic Stadium. It was at this point that the cycling squad was told that we would be spending only one night in the village before transferring to a town on the outskirts of the city where the cycling events would be held and where we were to be accommodated. It transpired that the team management had not known of this before we arrived and had assumed that all the athletes would be housed in the Olympic Village.

As we had not been allowed a team manager, such duties were to have been discharged by one of the assistant delegation managers, but that would have required him to travel back and forth between the village and Hachioji, a distance of about twenty miles. This was not acceptable to the team management and I was asked if, as the team leader, I would agree to discharge the duties of team manager for the duration of the cycling events. I had little choice but to agree, although I knew that this arrangement would be fraught with difficulty and not conducive to preparation for the most important competition in which any of us would participate.

Several days later we were bussed into the city to take part in the opening ceremony, which was nothing like it is these days, with all participants marching formally into the stadium and no cameras allowed, although this rule was ignored by some. Hong Kong had one of the best drilled squads in the stadium, as the Hong Kong Police had a good representation in the team, with Bill Gillies (shooting), Eric McCosh (hockey) and Mike Field (athletics), in addition to yours truly.

Hong Kong contingent at the 1964 Olympic Opening Ceremony
(Courtesy M. Watson)

The Games, which were formally opened by Emperor Hirohito, included 5,137 participants from 93 countries, competing in 21 sports. As an indication of how the Olympics have developed in 52 years, for the 2016 Games in Rio there were 11,303 participants from 207 countries, competing in 28 sports. Upon completion of the ceremony we cyclists were bussed back to Hachioji where we were to remain until the completion of the cycling events.

We had been entered in the 100 km Team Time Trial, a relatively new event in the Olympics, having first been staged in 1960. Four riders had been selected for the event, with a minimum of three required to complete the race. As we represented the smallest territory in the competition, with little experience in the event which was only occasionally raced in Hong Kong, we were not expected to trouble any of the stronger teams, given that at the time both road and track cycling was dominated by the European countries, not including Great Britain. Therefore our sole objective was to set a new Hong Kong record for the event, which was well within our compass.

In the days leading up to the event we trained twice a day, although my training was regularly interrupted by having to attend team managers' meetings, at which I was the youngest by at least twenty years and the only one who was also racing in the event. I struck up a friendship with the New Zealand manager, who was to prove helpful during the race by providing a team member to crew the following vehicle which all teams were provided with to carry bikes and spares in the event of a technical problem. Not that we had a spare bike, but we did have almost enough spare parts to build one! In the event we had no such problems and didn't have to resort to running repairs.

On race day it was raining, which was not a surprise as we had experienced wet weather almost daily following the opening ceremony. One thing I (and others) couldn't understand was why October had been chosen to stage the Games, when Japan is often cold and wet at that time. Most of the Games held in the northern hemisphere have been staged in the summer months and it was never explained why this wasn't the case in Tokyo. I note that, with the benefit of hindsight, the Games in Tokyo 2020 were scheduled for July/August (since postponed to 2021 due to the Covid-19 pandemic).

The weather became more of an issue than just the comfort of the riders, as later in the week when the track events got underway it became clear that the outdoor concrete velodrome was difficult to ride in the wet, with unnecessary crashes due to the slippery surface. So much so that on occasion the programme had to be changed to avoid the wet weather. We were not involved in the track events as Hong Kong did not have a velodrome and therefore we had no experience in track racing.

One interesting fact that arose from this situation was that we were told by officials and our team interpreter that Japan had a number of indoor velodromes which were used by the professional Keirin (motor-paced cycle racing) riders as a betting sport. Because of the separation between amateur and professional cycling these tracks were not made available to the Games organisers, which was a pity as performances on indoor tracks are always superior to those outdoors. It was also clear that the professional Japanese riders were of a higher standard than their amateur counterparts, a situation which also applied in Europe. Keirin racing was not introduced in the Olympics until the 2000 Sydney Games, by which time professional cycling was the norm in the Olympics.

Getting back to the racing, teams in the Team Time Trial were started at one-minute intervals and we were sent off towards the end of the field, as most of the strong European teams were in the top half of the start list, with the minnows of Asia bringing up the rear. This was fine by us as it meant that we were not caught very often by faster teams and we caught one team, which gave us a little confidence. We set a fast pace from the start, expecting to lose our weakest rider in the last lap as we had done in training, the result of having a team which was not balanced in terms of ability. In the event this is what happened, but what we hadn't bargained for was that the rider who was dropped was the one who had been strongest in training, which meant that the rest of us had to work harder to maintain our speed, which with just three riders proved impossible.

We eventually finished thirtieth of the thirty-three teams which started, beating Malaysia, Vietnam and India, but in a time which didn't break the Hong Kong record. This was disappointing, but it soon became clear that all teams had recorded slower times than expected, including the winning Netherlands team. This was eventually explained by the fact that the circuit on which we were racing was measured at 36.63 km, giving a total race distance of almost 110 km! Apparently the organisers had originally intended to start and finish the event at different locations but this had proved problematic, so the longer distance was maintained. This affected the winners more than us, as their average speed could have given them a new Olympic record over the correct distance.

After the race we stayed in the accommodation at Hachioji and watched the track events in the outdoor velodrome – weather permitting. This was also a time for people watching, as a number of well-known faces could be seen in the stands, many of them professional cyclists who had just come to the end of their season. However, for me the most memorable sighting was Crown Princess Beatrix of the Netherlands, who came to watch the Dutch team win a bronze medal in the 4000 m Team Pursuit and to whom I was introduced by the Dutch team manager. She became Queen in 1980 and abdicated in favour of her son, Willem Alexander, in 2013.

After two weeks at Hachioji, we joined the rest of the Hong Kong team at the Olympic Village prior to the closing ceremony, which was a much more informal affair than its opening counterpart. Hong Kong didn't win any medals at the Games but, as with the cyclists, the majority of athletes of whatever sport were there for the experience, which I am sure none of us will ever forget. My only regret was that being housed at Hachioji meant that I saw very little of the other Games facilities or other sports, except what was on television. In the sixties, this did not provide the coverage that is now expected at an Olympiad. We also saw very little of Tokyo, which was a pity as even then it was a dynamic and fascinating city, yet so different from Hong Kong.

Living in Hachioji also meant that I saw very little of the other HKP representatives once competition began, but the following is a brief summary of their performance in their respective sports:

Bill Gillies was the first police Olympian, who also represented Hong Kong at the Rome Games in 1960. He was a shooter who competed in the 50 m Free Pistol event in both Olympics. He was a pre-war officer who was interned in Stanley during the Japanese occupation.

Mike Field was the first competitor to represent Hong Kong at athletics in the Olympics. He ran in the 800 m, recording a time of 1:54.00 which stood as the Hong Kong record until the mid-eighties. He also ran in the 1500 m (at which distance he was also the Hong Kong record holder), recording a time of 4:02.60.

Eric McCosh was a member of the only team to represent Hong Kong at hockey in the Olympics. He played in six games, with the best result being a creditable draw with Germany.

I would just like to say how fortunate I was to be given the opportunity to participate in the Olympics and that it was a privilege to represent Hong Kong in the greatest sports event in the world.

I will conclude with a note on Hong Kong participation in the Olympics. Since 1952, the territory has taken part in every Summer Games except that of 1980, which was boycotted by many countries in protest at the Soviet invasion of Afghanistan. Hong Kong has also taken part in the last four Winter Games, in which four participants competed in short track speed skating. Hong Kong won its first medal, a gold in windsurfing, in Atlanta 1996 and has since won a silver medal in table tennis in Athens 2004 and a bronze medal in track cycling in London 2012.

Snippets of Empire

Jim Prisk

Growing up as a kid in Hong Kong in the 1960s was something that will always remain in my memory. In the period 1962 to 1966, my Dad's postings on his tour of duty as a *bom baan* (inspector) in the then Preventive Service (the forerunner of the Customs and Excise Service), meant that we lived on stations in Fanling and later Tai Lam Chung, both in the New Territories (NT).

Life there was everything you can read about now with regard to colonial service in the Empire – Dad working in the office downstairs, me playing football after school in the compound with junior Preventive Service officers on the station, large bottles of cold beer on the terrace at sundown, with cicadas chirping away in the background.

Once a month, my Dad would accompany his boss, the NT Chief Revenue Officer, George Welsby, on the journey by train down to Tsim Sha Tsui and then across the harbour to Preventive Service Headquarters, to collect and return with the men's pay which was in cash. For this duty both my father and George were armed, and George had this crazy fantasy of making an arrest of a would-be robber. So on the return journey, Dad would be in-structed to sit with the bag of cash by a deliberately opened window. Should any opportunist be bold enough to attempt to steal the bag, it was the plan that George, with revolver drawn and hidden behind a copy of the *South China Morning Post*, would make the arrest – if necessary using his weapon. Fortunately for Dad, this never transpired because apart from anything else, George was full of beer having visited the officers' mess, and Dad knew he was not a good shot anyway. The thought of George possibly using his gun filled my Dad with horror.

It was a tense time in the long hot summer of 1967 caused by widespread disturbances, initially arising from a minor labour dispute in a plastics factory but influenced by the Cultural Revolution then sweeping China. These had developed into widespread riots with a definite anti-colonial overtone. There were incidents on the Sino-British border, street demonstrations and a bomb campaign which lasted for several months and resulted in many civilian and police injuries and deaths. I used to walk along Conduit Road from my parents' quarters at Buxey Lodge to Glenealy Junior School to be greeted by the white school buildings daubed with slogans and 'anti-imperialist' banners.

Norman 'Bomber' Hill, the Police Bomb Disposal Officer, lived downstairs from us and we all knew of the long hours he spent carrying out his dangerous work during the bomb campaign. The bombs were improvised explosive devices, often in carrier bags or such, but nonetheless potentially deadly. There were also many hoax bombs but each suspected device needed to be dealt with cautiously.

One evening, having been out with my parents, we found a small parcel wrapped in Chinese newspaper in our mail basket in the hallway. Dad thought it sensible to get Bomber to come and have a look at it, which he did. Bomber sandbagged up the front hall and got dressed for work with his armoured suit, and we waited nervously inside the inner rooms for what would happen. Bomber appeared about fifteen minutes later to tell my Dad that the item might be mine. It turned out that this was an Action Man toy kit returned to me by a friend, who had decided to wrap it up in said manner as a prank – needless to say, with my parents' embarrassment at having disturbed our hero for nothing, I and my friend were not popular.

The privileged lifestyle we undoubtedly had was only really brought home to me when, as a young first-tour *bom baan* in 1982, I graduated from the Police Training School (PTS) and was posted to Wong Tai Sin Division, a place, despite its famous temple and my having grown up in Hong Kong, I had never previously visited. As the sub-unit commander, I was called to some fracas which had been reported during our overnight C shift in Wong Tai Sin Lower Estate. Entering one of the residential units in the old style 'H' blocks with Staff Sergeant Leung, I found some fourteen people of differing ages, gathered in the small one-room unit. I asked my second-in-command: 'Mr Leung, why are all these people here in the middle of the night?' I was given the scornful reply: 'Ah Sir, because they all live here.' Never was my naivety so obvious!

One afternoon in 1983, after a football match we had played at the Police Club at Boundary Street for the Galloping Gwailos and over a relaxing pint, Ron Brierly asked me what I thought of a lad called Marc Sullivan, who was a contemporary of mine at PTS in 1981. I replied, 'good bloke, good footballer, why?' It turned out that Ron was hoping to get Marc into Special Branch, especially for the football team, and duly recommended the transfer-in to his boss and team captain Jerry Skinner. Imagine the scene subsequently in the latter's office, when the prospective new Branch inspector turned up, looking by his very build, nothing like a footballer and telling Jerry that he liked rugby and tug of war, but was 'not very keen on football'. The name of the new SB Inspector was another old friend of mine called Martin O'Sullivan – RHKP career planning at its best!

13th February 1991. A parcel bomb had exploded in the front desk area of the Holiday Inn in Nathan Road. My team of Organised and Serious Crime Bureau (OSCB) officers and I were despatched from Police Headquarters to take over the scene and manage case enquiries. I set up my forward command post in the lobby bar, immediately opposite the scene. Whilst organising the arrival of forensic experts, the taking of statements and other matters of vital crime-scene organisation, the said command post was off limits to the public. Several hours later, a harassed American tourist at-tempted to order a beer at the bar, only to be told by hotel staff the bar was closed. When he queried this by pointing out a number of expatriates who appeared to be quaffing a cold Carlsberg at the bar, he was told 'Sorry sir, but they're policemen!' Incidentally we arrested the culprit within twenty-four hours and the miscreant was eventually sentenced to no less than thirty years imprisonment.

During the early morning hours one day in early 1991, my team as part of a large group of OSCB officers, raided the family premises of a gang of criminals. The main difficulty involved with arresting the gang, abed and unaware, centred around the fact that a reconnaissance had found that an eight-foot high metal fence, accessed by only one locked gate, surrounded the enclave. Given that we expected to find a large quantity of arms and ammunition in the premises, the professional expertise of the renowned Special Duties Unit (SDU) 'Flying Tigers' was enlisted to gain us the required access to the compound with the minimum of danger or fuss.

Thus at the required hour, in pitch darkness, I was standing outside the fencing with my OSCB officers and colleagues, whilst the SDU went ahead with their plan to access the fencing, enter the premises and subdue the gang in their beds. I watched the balaclava clad, armed to the teeth, SDU officers go through their routine when I noticed to my great surprise one of my detectives standing inside the compound. 'Ah Fai,' I hissed urgently, 'how the heck did you end up in there?'

'Dai Lo (big brother),' he replied, 'the gate was unlocked.' Cue, great bursts of muffled laughter, and much hilarity in the twentieth-floor Police Officers' Mess back at PHQ later that day! The gang members found this disclosure rather less amusing!

Monsoon Shipwreck

Charles H. Fisher

The northeast monsoon blows fairly steadily from September to February in Hong Kong but then, from April, the monsoon is unable to settle down and becomes the southwest monsoon. This period is known for its transitional weather, when the monsoon may blow from the northeast or the southwest.

In winter a large high pressure system is dominant over China. In the summer, pressure is low over China. So Hong Kong gets northeast winds in the winter, and southwest winds in the summer. The difficulties arise when the centres of high or low pressure are strong or weak, and how much they are moving around, which can be up to several hundred miles. Therefore in winter the northeast monsoon can blow from the northeast, north, or northwest. Similarly in summer the southwest monsoon can blow from the southwest, the south or southeast. The transitional periods may be early or late in the year and of varying intensity. But the general picture is predictable.

It was during this transitional period that the incident related below occurred. I was serving in the Marine Police and working twenty-four hours on duty and twenty-four hours off, with my opposite number Bill Renahan. Bill had been a regular in the Royal Navy whereas I had been only a national serviceman. On alternate shifts we commanded *Police Launch 28*, a seventy-foot launch. This was one of nine in the Marine Police fleet and had a crew of ten. We were based at Tai Po Kau adjacent to the Kowloon Canton Railway station.

On 4th April 1965, there was a lull in the northeast monsoon, and a thick fog had descended upon Hong Kong, predominantly in the Eastern Approaches. I was on duty on *Police Launch 28* when, at about 10.00 am, we received a report that a large vessel had gone aground, somewhere near Tai Long Wan in the northeast of Hong Kong. We made with all speed, about 10 knots, to the scene and found a Panamanian registered vessel, the SS *Nam On*, aground south of Tai Long Wan, near Tai Yue Ngam.

The vessel was hard aground by the bows, at the foot of almost vertical 150-foot cliffs, apparently undamaged. Steam was emanating from the forward winch. The sea was glassy with only a very gentle swell, but this was not causing the vessel to grind and cause further damage. I had no difficulty in taking the police launch alongside the *Nam On*, and spoke to the Chinese master who was from Taiwan. He told me that the crew numbered twenty-four, and that he, his wife, Chow dog and crew were all safe. He said that there was water in the forepeak but otherwise he thought the vessel was undamaged. He further told me that he had informed his agents in Hong Kong and had requested a tug to tow the vessel off. His Cantonese and English were poor, as was my Cantonese, but we managed to communicate all the basic problems. I had a couple of tins of Taiwan beer with the master, commiserating with him, and told him that 'all persons were safe, the tug was on its way and that his vessel could easily be towed off the rocks'. There was no apparent leakage of oil from the bunkers, the vessel having a triple-expansion steam engine with a single boiler. The master told me his radar had been out of order prior to the grounding. The prevailing current during the northeast monsoon sets southeast.

Eventually, at about 1 pm, the tug arrived, the MV *Golden Cape*, and the Australian master got the captain of the *Nam On* to sign the salvage certificate, known as 'No cure No pay', laid out a kedge anchor and awaited high tide before attempting to tow the grounded vessel off. The maximum height of spring tides in Hong Kong is about 8.6 feet and the *Nam On* had grounded during neaps when the tidal range is much less. The master of the *Golden Cape* was not too hopeful in getting the *Nam On* off. He was right, the *Nam On* did not shift one foot, even when using both the tug's engine ahead and the ship's engine astern (the *Nam On* still had steam from her, as yet, undamaged boiler), and heaving on the kedge anchor.

The tug, *Golden Cape* was only of medium size, and I thought if only the famous steam twin screw ocean-going tug the *Tai Koo*, with the equally famous master, Bill Worrall, had been in charge of the operation, then it would have been a relatively simple salvage job. Anyone interested in salvage should read Kevin Sinclair's book *No Cure No Pay*. Worrall was the master for twenty years of *Tai Koo* which, though ugly by nautical standards, had a wonderful crew who salvaged forty-two ships during his captaincy. His son and grandson have both served in the Marine Police.

The *Nam On* was about 2,500 net registered tonnage, four cargo holds, masting and derricks fore and aft to plumb the holds. The crew accommodation and bridge were amidships. The vessel was bound for Hong Kong with cement from Kee Lung in Taiwan.

By 4 pm the wind had got up from the northeast, as a cold front passed, and within half an hour, the sea began to get quite rough. It was certainly time for *Police Launch 28* to seek shelter. The master of the *Nam On* thought his vessel would be safe and did not request his crew to be taken off. An abandoned vessel has quite different legal salvage problems. The *Golden Cape* having failed to tow the vessel off, left the kedge and wire-cable in situ, and also ran for shelter. Myself, I was very pleased to seek shelter from the surge of the northeast monsoon at Tap Mun. By now it was blowing a gale, and the sea almost white, with streaks on the breaking side of the waves. The northeasterly monsoon was blowing at force six to eight and coming from the north or north-northwest. I informed Marine Police Control of the situation and my actions.

Next morning, 5th April, it was still blowing a gale from the north-northeast and we received a message from Marine HQ to the effect that the *Nam On* had swung broadside on to the rocks and that the crew needed rescuing! The engine and boiler rooms were flooded and the holds fore and aft were taking in a lot of water. It was far too rough for a seventy-foot launch to proceed to the scene, let alone attempt a rescue. Fortunately an Alouette helicopter from the Royal Hong Kong Auxiliary Air Force was called out to perform the rescue. The problems for the helicopter pilot were many. The vessel was adjacent and broadside on to the cliffs, there were two high masts on the vessel and the wind was gusting with wind shear near the cliffs.

I, with a party of Marine Policemen, drawn from the crew of the police launch, hiked over the hills from Chek Keng to Tai Long Wan (Sai Wan) to get as near to the wreck as possible, having equipped ourselves with heaving lines with the intention of using a breeches buoy system to rescue the crew. However, superb flying by the helicopter pilot, and picking up four persons at a time, he succeeded in landing everyone, including the dog, on the beach nearby. All persons were saved and no-one was injured.

We handed over all the rescued persons and the dog to the land based Police who had arrived from Sai Kung, who then dealt with them as shipwrecked mariners and passed them over to the Marine and Immigration Departments. My police party then returned to the launch, and went back to our base at Tai Po Kau before going off duty, somewhat late.

The next day, 6th April, when we came back on duty, we were told to see what was happening to the wreck of the *Nam On*, the wind and sea having abated. At dusk we were told to stand-by the wreck to prevent looting. A thick dense fog descended as the monsoon was again in transition. I decided to anchor in the lee of Tsim Chau Island nearby, and told the on-watch crew to listen out for any persons who might attempt to loot the *Nam On*. At Tsim Chau was a white-bellied sea eagle's eyrie on this very isolated small island; there is another eyrie at Mirs Point above Wu Ying Wan. We may have heard nothing from the wreck but these eagles were particularly noisy! The sound of the launch's generator must have drowned out any sounds from the *Nam On*. We weighed anchor at dawn, and it was still dense fog. Nearing the *Nam On*, scores of looters scrambled down into their fishing junks as they saw us approach. I thought – this is serious! I had been told to guard the wreck. The looters had also caused a severe fire in the midship section. To cover myself from a charge of 'neglect of duty', we were fortunately able to arrest two men, who were less agile and slow to return to their junk with their booty, which comprised some lead piping and two bottles of hair cream! All the others escaped and made off!

The two men engaged in looting were charged with 'Larceny from Wreck' and bound over by the magistrate to be of good behaviour. These two men came from Ko Lau Wan village opposite Tap Mun. The village representative, Mr Shek, a well-known opportunist smuggler, with whom we had an easy relationship, thanked us for being so kind to the two fishermen and we settled down and told our stories over a few beers in the local shop! Everyone was happy. The *Nam On* was eventually scrapped in situ, and there was very little pollution. The cargo of cement gradually eroded away.

So what of the helicopter pilot? I wrote a comprehensive report of the Marine Police actions, and the skill of the Royal Hong Kong Auxiliary Air Force pilot, and sent it off to Police HQ. I heard nothing more. No queries about my failure to guard the wreck! Subsequently I read in the *Government Gazette* that Squadron Leader Danny Cheung had been awarded the Air Force Cross. He certainly deserved it.

The transition between the northeast and southwest monsoons had been an exciting time for us in the Marine Police. No two days in Marine Police were ever the same and that was why it was such a pleasure to work in the Marine Division of the Royal Hong Kong Police.

SS Nam On *hard aground (Courtesy C.H. Fisher)*

A Harbourside Duel

Graham Harper

Having completed quite a few months at Western Division as my
first posting after Police Training School *circa* 1965, I found myself
zig-zagging somewhat between Des Voeux Road West and Gloucester
Road, climbing and descending lanes and steps, checking on beat
duties. Eventually I arrived at the harbourside and our commercial
wharves centre.

All was well, and I was enjoying a warm sunny day shift. I
walked, following the wharves towards the tram terminus and I
came across some coolie stevedores unloading rice grain sacks from
a ship. Following a coolie departing the ship's side for the nearby
godown (warehouse), I crossed the tram tracks and into a square.
These sacks were carried across the shoulders and backs of the
coolies – shirtless and glistening with the sweat from their exertions.
The sacks, I guess weighing some fifty pounds or so, held across
their shoulders with the strong support of their stevedore hooks –
fearsome looking long-bladed hooks, some two feet or so in length.

Nothing to report so far, though not for long.

Entering the square, it could be seen that a good crowd had
gathered, 150–200 strong it seemed. The occasional excited cries of
'Wha, wha!' arose in chorus from time to time as I approached. I
anticipated a breach of the peace, an affray or an assault, as I closed
in and began to break through this six or seven persons deep ring
of excited spectators to reach the centre stage. It was indeed all
happening.

A squat, heavily muscled and sweating coolie was wielding his
hook, very much now a weapon, and swinging it in pursuit of his
quarry, a slightly built and fortunately agile man who was dancing
out of reach terrified for his life. There was a heavy stench of

Chinese wine, emanating from the assailing coolie, who was not at all steady on his feet. He was checking his balance and taking a breather. He was nevertheless intent on pursuing vengeance upon his chosen victim for some reason.

As I had entered the ring, cries had immediately gone up *'Bom baan, Bom baan'* ('Inspector'), and I drew the attention of the surging crowd. Just for the moment the threat of violence abated.

Assessing the situation, I decided to draw my revolver.

Will he shoot, will there be a kill, an arrest perhaps? I sensed the questions which arose among the crowd.

Our coolie recommenced action and with another shift of his feet closed in on his quarry. He swung his blade as the terrified victim danced away elusively.

Should I first fire a warning shot in the air, or go for the assailant's thigh, risking perhaps a miss and the prospect of injuring one of the spectators? The atmosphere was charged.

It became necessary to unbutton my Sam Browne belt as someone behind me was pulling the shoulder strap about and making it difficult to maintain my balance. I unbuckled the Sam Browne from the rear, thus freeing myself. Meanwhile, our coolie swung

Illustration by Graham Harper

again and the agility of the intended victim refocused crowd attention. Our coolie, slow on his feet, unsteadily checked himself.

Maintaining restraint, I was relieved to see that our beat PC had appeared on the scene and after a quick appraisal of the situation, had disappeared back through the crowd to find the nearest telephone to call for additional assistance.

The crowd continued to surge, to bay for action.

It can only have been a short time although it seemed an age before the distant sound of approaching police sirens alerted me to imminent assistance. The Emergency Unit (EU) contingent broke through the throng and surrounded the by now tiring hook-wielding coolie.

This incident was now in the hands of the EU Duty Inspector, Neville Broomfield, and I happily replaced my revolver in its holster. I buckled up my Sam Browne belt and liaised with him, eventually reporting back to Western Division Police Station. The necessary report book and personal notebook entries were made and the beat constable debriefed with my compliments. I found myself off-duty. Shift ended.

A San Miguel, or two, was surely enjoyed later on that night.

A Thai Catch

Graham Harper

Early in 1966, I found myself posted to Marine Police Division, and shortly thereafter to the Marine Police flagship, *Police Launch 1* (PL1) which was assigned to Green Sector, the eastern waters of Hong Kong. After some three months or so, I took command of the night shift and initially conducted routine licence inspection of Hong Kong fishing junks.

At about two o'clock one morning, PL1 dropped anchor in an island cove off the Ninepin group of islands, and set a minimum crew, with lights extinguished and on radar watch.

At about three o'clock, a single radar return appeared, settling apparently in a 'hove to' position close to the boundary with China waters. Night vision binoculars indicated an unusual foreign fishing vessel, a Thai trawler according to our Marine Police silhouette guide notes. We kept watch for another hour or so, when this vessel then proceeded into the centre of the northeast-southwest fishing

Police Launch 1, Sea Lion, *early '70s*

lanes where Hong Kong junks trawled back and forth over a three nautical mile stretch.

Alerting Sergeant Lee Hing Man, a fully armed and equipped Marine Police section was then raised from their bunks. As dawn's first light approached, this mystery vessel left cover of the fishing lanes, and headed towards the Sai Kung Peninsula where it dropped anchor. Not long afterwards, some interesting activity was observed.

A smaller vessel detached itself from the Thai trawler and made its way onto the rocky shoreline of Town Island and sent a small landing party. PLI's ship's dory was lowered and Sergeant Lee and a well-prepared boarding party dispatched. At about the same time, a quarter to six, a Morse report was radioed to Marine Police Headquarters. It was our suspicion that illegal dangerous drug activity was taking place.

After a short delay, PLI engines were activated and we nosed quietly northeasterly out of our rocky island cover and sprang a surprise as our armed boarding party detained the Thai vessel, and arrested both the crew, and their island landing party – now in the act of its second delivery of what was indeed drugs.

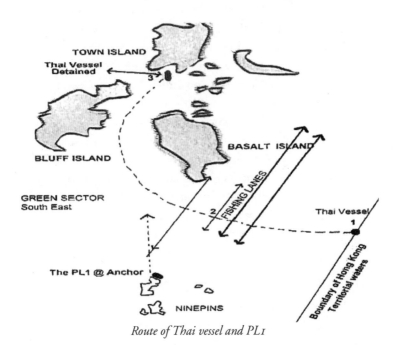

Route of Thai vessel and PL1

In historical terms this drug seizure probably was the Hong Kong Marine Police's biggest drug haul ever – caught 'red-handed'. From memory, this was itemised as some 1,380 lbs of bagged prepared opium, one small 10 lb box of pure DH (diacetylmorphine hydrochloride, or heroin), one small box of opium processed into blocks (looking like cork), and one small tin of barbiturates (thought to be for the use of the crew).

At Marine Police Headquarters, on receipt of our Morse message, the duty inspector had notified the divisional commanding officer who in turn had informed the Narcotics Bureau.

It happened that there was an international police narcotics conference taking place in Hong Kong at this time – an annual event involving regional police forces. The Narcotics Bureau alerted the Thai Police delegation at their hotel. Arrangements were made to fly their representatives with some Narcotics Bureau officers to the scene in the Hong Kong Auxiliary Air Force Alouette helicopters. Confronted by such an impressive array of senior Thai and Hong Kong police officers, coupled with the seizure of the drugs, the Thai crew 'sang like canaries'.

Later that morning, we towed the Thai trawler into the Marine Police detention area within the Yau Ma Tei Typhoon Shelter and our three days patrol shift was over. We adjourned to the bar and had a celebratory drink, the first round being on Chief Inspector Sandy Chalmers, the Sector Commander. Much enjoyed by all.

This account is based on a forty-year-plus memory. At the time it attracted little publicity in the press or indeed within the Force. It also does not feature in Iain Ward's excellent histories of the Hong Kong Marine Police. It may be that Narcotics Bureau chose to keep this incident quiet and not to publicise it, so as not to jeopardise future operations arising out of this case.

The 1967 Riots and the Dockyards

Duncan L. Macrae

Mr Duncan Macrae is a close friend of a number of members of the Royal Hong Kong Police Association. He joined the Tai Koo Dockyard in Hong Kong as a section leader in the Ship Drawing Office in 1962. He retired in 1987 as deputy managing director of the Hong Kong United Dockyard Ltd, this company being the result of a merger between the Tai Koo Dockyard and Engineering Co. Ltd, and Hong Kong and Whampoa Dockyard Ltd in 1973.

In early 1967, I was working for the Taikoo Dockyard and Engineering Company in the capacity of chief ship draughtsman, cosseted well away from the hustle and bustle of the busy shipyard.

Earlier that year, there were signs of unrest in industry throughout the colony, mainly resulting from the overspill of the Red Guards' Cultural Revolution in Mainland China. Things came to a head on 6th May, when disturbances at a factory in San Po Kong led to a number of arrests. During the rest of May, widespread industrial disputes required curfews to be imposed, mainly in Kowloon. This, in turn, led to large communist-led demonstrations in Garden Road and in the vicinity of Government House. Tear gas was used to subdue the rioters. It was obvious that the colony was in for a rough ride.

Taikoo Dockyard, in company with many shipyards worldwide, had a high percentage of left-wing and communist supporters among its 3,500 strong workforce, supplemented by some 2,000 retained contractor's employees at busy times.

At the end of May and in early June, the yard's productivity was brought to a halt by strike action affecting all departments. Fights broke out between left- and right-wing workers. The communist element commandeered the yard's fleet of Lister trucks and patrolled the 52-acre site singing nationalist songs. They were armed with steel spears, with sharpened points at the 'working end'. When peace returned, all confiscated weapons were required to be handed over to the Royal Hong Kong Police Force. I secreted one of the spears in my changing locker and it now hangs proudly in the library of my home in Ballater, Scotland. Meanwhile, the situation deteriorated and on 3rd June the General Manager, Mr James Cassells, along with two senior expatriate staff members, were surrounded and held prisoner by the rioters.

The dockyard had an expatriate staff of ninety-two, about seventy of whom were Scottish. The prisoners were rescued by our 'heavy gang' – ex-Clydeside Shipbuilders – some hours later. There was no resistance!

(Our daughter, Fiona, was born on 13th June, 1967, when the riots were gathering momentum. I had some difficulty getting my wife through the anti-government riots in North Point and Causeway Bay en-route to Matilda Hospital on the Peak. I have always said Fiona was born during a riot and has been a riot ever since.)

Obviously action had to be taken. A meeting of senior managers was convened and it was decided that the yard would be closed the next day. All expatriate staff were instructed to report for duty at 6 am. Notices were posted on the locked main gates in King's Road and on the west gate – to the effect that the yard was closed for re-organisation. All workers and Chinese staff would be advised, as soon as possible, when and if they could return to work. As a precaution, some 200 armed members of the Royal Hong Kong Police Force were ensconced and hidden in the basement car park of the main office building. As it happened, no real trouble resulted from the closure, only some minor demonstrations outside the gates. On reflection, perhaps we were somewhat naive thinking that the workers did not know what awaited them should they breach the gates.

The next task was to weed out the good from the bad. We contacted a few senior local staff we could trust, all done by word of mouth, and advised them they would be picked up by the dockyard launches at Queen's Pier in Central District.

This was one of the lighter moments of the riots as the non-engineering expatriates could not contain their mirth while watching their former chief seagoing engineering compatriots attempting to manoeuvre two of the boats of the dockyard launch fleet out of the narrow slip-way into Aldrich Bay.

Eventually they were all at sea. The dockyard had detailed record cards of every Chinese staff member, time worker, and pieceworker, some 3,500 cards in all. The cards were all laid out on the drawing boards in both the Engine and Ship-Drawing Offices, to be scrutinised by expatriate departmental heads and trusted senior Chinese staff. The process took about three twelve-hour days. During the seven days that the yard was closed the expatriate staff were allocated specific duties. As usual, I was lucky and acted as chauffeur to Mr Cassells in his new Jaguar. During this time, I conveyed three members of the expatriate staff for hospitalisation. They were no longer able to cope with the increasingly difficult situation. For recreation, we had memorable swimming races in the 787-foot-long drydock.

During the closure, the Dockyard Security Force, led by three expatriate ex-RHKP members, was out of action. I lived at the time at Braemar Terrace, a complex of sixteen terraced company flats on the hill above King's Road, in North Point. If I remember rightly two of our expatriate staff were on duty rotationally for four hours each night. We heard disturbances in King's Road below us, including gunfire, but our quarters were never approached. A further complication was a shortage of water. Hong Kong relied heavily on Mainland China to supply the colony's reservoirs. On July 13th, water supply was limited to four hours every fourth day. The dockyard and the Taikoo Sugar Refinery had their own reservoirs above Braemar Hill and Shau Kei Wan Road at Quarry Bay.

Back to the 'weed out'. Exactly five days after we closed the gates, most staff and workers were sent a letter advising them to return to work at 8 am on a specific date. The 'baddies' were sent a letter advising them that their services had been terminated and asking them to report to the Government Labour Offices in Spring Gardens where any monies due to them would be paid.

The dockyard re-opened for business. We had nipped 'our riot' in the bud, and what a difference it made. All our employees went about their business in a joyful and happy manner, it was as though a dark cloud had been lifted – and so it had!

The dockyard's commercial performance was not seriously affected by the riots, although a substantial number of workers, in many hundreds, were dismissed. New recruits were soon trained to fill vacant posts. In fact, the benchmark of 100 dockings per year in the Dockyard One Graving Dock was first surpassed in 1967 when, despite civil disturbances and industrial disputes, a total of 104 docking operations were carried out.

I conclude with a few personal recollections with regard to 1967.

On 24th May, 1967, when I was chief ship draughtsman, I was suddenly and unexpectedly promoted to assistant shipyard manager. From my comfortable and cosseted hide in the Drawing Office I was thrown into a cauldron of unrest and anarchy. The reason for this sudden promotion was that the shipyard manager had resigned to seek a safer life in Canada. Mr Willie Brown was appointed shipyard manager, and I became his assistant.

At the time of the riots I was group scoutmaster of the 36th Hong Kong (St John's Cathedral) Scout Troop. We met in the Cathedral Hall at the bottom of Garden Road on Friday evenings. I travelled there on a Vespa scooter provided by the dockyard for patrolling the yard. During the riots I was heavily disguised to hide my race. Following the meeting my fellow scouters and I would repair to a Malaysian curry house in Happy Valley for refreshments. On one occasion we were pursued by an unruly mob intent on blood. We reached our destination unscathed. The proprietress immediately locked the door and led us out through the back kitchen from where we made our escape.

When I was in the drawing office, my No. 1 was a brilliant draughtsman by the name of Tam Mo Pun. Unfortunately, Tam was also a brilliant communist and an active instigator during the riots. In view of this he received a two-year prison sentence.

On release, Taikoo could no longer employ him and he worked for a Mainland Chinese ship repair company in Kowloon. Later on, he established his own naval architect's consultancy. I used to meet Mo Pun at the occasional cocktail party – his introductory line was 'I used to be a communist but now I am a capitalist'!

In July 1986, after twenty-five years in the colony, it was time to go home. The phone rang, and I recognised the voice. It was Tam Mo Pun. He and his family invited my family to a farewell dinner at one of Hong Kong's best hotels – and this was a man I had sent to jail some nineteen years earlier.

The riots of Hong Kong in 1967 were a great experience. It brought out the best, and the worst, in us, both Asian and Caucasian, at times working in harmony. Bomb attacks were almost a daily occurrence until the end of December. The cost to the colony was fifty-one lives. Fifteen were killed by bomb explosions, including two members of the police, a British Army sergeant and an officer of the Fire Services: and eight police officers were killed in other incidents.

I still have my first edition of the 'Wee Red Book' of quotations from Chairman Mao Tse-tung, published in Beijing (Peking) in 1956. It served me well eleven years later, when produced at the appropriate time.

A Lo Wu Incident – 1967

Chris Fraser

Most police officers in Hong Kong never had to fire a shot in anger, including myself in many years in Special Branch (SB). However, I did draw my revolver on one occasion in 1967.

I was at the time in charge of the Special Branch office at Lo Wu, the rail crossing point between Hong Kong and China. The Special Branch staff were still operating 'watch lists' from a large Black Book, working alongside Immigration Department staff.

Gradually the tempo of the Cultural Revolution across the border, in what is now the metropolis of Shenzhen – or in Cantonese, Shum Chun – began to sour. Shum Chun was then a village of agricultural workers who tended the rice fields, and did some fishing. The atmosphere on the bridge which crossed the river dividing Hong Kong from China became more tense. The frequent '10,000 People Marches' which took place on the China riverside bank, with participants shouting in unison 'Down with British Imperialism', 'Down with US Imperialism', 'Down with Soviet Revisionism', did little to reassure the staff manning the government offices on the Hong Kong side of the border. When the 'Man Bing' militia began to fire ball bearings from catapults at targets on the Hong Kong side the situation began to deteriorate, particularly as People's Liberation Army Border Regiment guards on the bridge stood aloof and did not interfere. This was the pattern throughout China at the time, with the PLA personnel confined to barracks or standing by while their materiel was stolen by Red Guards or rival worker factions.

I telephoned Special Branch Control in Police Headquarters on several occasions to report what was going on, but no advice or reaction was forthcoming. When the Lo Wu complex began to be invaded daily for short intervals by Man Bing shouting their slogans, I decided we had to take our own action to safeguard the Special Branch documents in the office at the rear of the complex.

Concurrently, the Kowloon–Canton Railway (KCR) engine drivers who bravely continued to cross the border to pick up freight wagons bound for Kowloon were forced to shout 'Long Live Chairman Mao' and anti-imperialist slogans whilst on the China side. Their engines were decorated with 'Big Character Posters' such as 'Hang Trench' (His Excellency Sir David Trench who was the governor of Hong Kong at that time), 'Burn Gass' (Sir Michael Gass, the colonial secretary), and 'Slice up Godber' (the senior police officer who was lauded for his role in battling rioters and

The bridge over the Shum Chun River. The white tower
with the red star is the Chinese authorities' building.

KCR engine with communist slogans

communist elements in the urban areas, but who was arrested and
convicted of corruption in the 1970s).

The Special Branch sergeant came up with an idea, after consulting
his friend in the KCR, and we arranged for an engine to be on
standby at Sheung Shui Railway Station, outside the Closed Border
Area, to come to the rescue should the incursions become more
serious. The Special Branch documents were placed in a large
suitcase which I brought from home, and were spirited off on the
engine to the safety of Sheung Shui.

The situation continued to deteriorate for quite some time
before eventually a British Army Gurkha military presence was
established. On one occasion, I was caught unawares when the Man
Bing under their aggressive and by now familiar leader, charged
straight through Immigration into the compound where the Special Branch office was located. My colleagues had wisely locked
themselves inside with whatever documents they had, not realising
(I hope) that I was still outside. The Man Bing leader rushed
towards me, wielding an iron bar and shrieking the usual slogans,
aiming to strike. So I drew my revolver and pointed it at his chest.

He stopped abruptly and opened his shirt wide, shouting: 'Go ahead and shoot!' and pointing to his chest. This was a tricky one! We were trained to never cock our weapon in case of an involuntary discharge, but this was an occasion when I ignored the rules and in order to show I was serious, made a show of cocking the revolver. There was a standoff for a short time, and then he retreated shouting abuse, and praising Chairman Mao. At this point the door of the Special Branch office opened and I was ushered inside. Thus was avoided what could have been a famous border incident with international consequences had I opened fire or had he struck me.

Eventually, the Gurkhas did arrive and patrolled the bridge and immigration complex area, although in the early days when there was no officer present, the soldiers did not seem to have any orders and therefore did nothing when the Man Bing cautiously approached them. This changed though after a militiaman armed with a homemade zip gun came up to a Gurkha on the bridge and shot him in the neck, causing a flesh wound. The Gurkha moved not a muscle at the time but their officers then finally realised that there was a real threat and the immigration setup was properly protected from then on and the invasions stopped.

The original bridge crossing point at Lo Wu still stands but has been superseded by a new bridge and complexes on both sides, and the Hong Kong Special Administrative Region authorities still operate a 'border' scenario with the Mainland. Few there still remember the violent days of the Cultural Revolution, or if they do on the China side, prefer not to mention it.

Serve the People

R.A. (Bob) Steele

On the 3rd December 1966, the main story on the front page of the *South China Morning Post* was the talks on the cruiser HMS *Tiger* between the United Kingdom's Prime Minister, Harold Wilson, and Ian Smith, the leader of Rhodesia, over the future of that colony. The front page also carried a sidebar headed, 'Macau Leftists Resume Demonstrations'. That article described a noisy and sometimes violent demonstration at a 'read in' of the quotations of Chairman Mao Tse-tung, the leader of the People's Republic of China, at Government House in Macau.

There was no way I could have known that this seemingly insignificant Macau incident would morph into something which would loom large in our lives in the eighteen months to come. For 3rd December was also my wedding day.

A year or so earlier, in November 1965, somewhat unusually for an officer not long into his first tour,[1] I was serving in Special Branch and living in the single officers' mess at Western Police Station on Hong Kong Island. Like many urban stations *'Chat Ho Chai Kwun'* (No. 7 Police Station) was not the most salubrious area, being towards the western end of the Hong Kong tram line, and containing dockyards, godowns and dried fish shops. Western District, *Sai Ying Pun* in Cantonese, was populated by stocky, muscled stevedores wielding fierce-looking billhooks which they used to unload the sacks from the lighters ferrying cargo between large

---

[1]   The first tour of duty for an expatriate officer was usually three and a half years and then some six months' home leave in the country of origin. After three years, subject to passing exams and being of good behaviour, one was confirmed to the pensionable establishment and promoted from probationary inspector to inspector.

ships in the harbour and the shore. The pervading odour on a good day was a mixture of dried fish and harbour water.

One evening, the birthday party of one of our mess members brought to this urban Shangri-La a number of Queen Alexandra's Royal Army Nursing Corps sisters (QAs) from the British Military Hospital (BMH) at Bowen Road on Hong Kong Island. Among them was a tall girl with long dark hair named Janet Smith.

Over the next year, Janet and I found we had much in common. My father had been a surgeon in the Royal Army Medical Corps (RAMC) and I had been brought up in and around military hospitals. We discovered my father had known a number of senior QA majors serving with Janet when they were very young lieutenants, and the commanding officer of the BMH was Colonel James Miller MC, who also knew my father.

Colonel Miller stood *in loco parentis* and we had to attend a dinner at BMH, Mount Kellett, on the Peak on Hong Kong Island with Colonel and Mrs Miller so I could be vetted for my suitability as a partner for one of his officers. It was the only dinner I have been to where the ladies 'retired' at the end of the meal leaving the men – Colonel Miller and I – to our port and cigars. I must have passed the vetting for Colonel Miller gave Janet away at our wedding.

In those days, first-tour officers had to seek permission from government to be granted 'married privileges' – essentially a government married quarters and a marriage allowance. It so happened that there was a dire shortage of single officer's quarters for police and thus we were given a married quarters at 12 Green Lane Hall, at the top of Blue Pool Road in Happy Valley, three months after we were married.

Janet would have to resign her commission on marriage but six weeks before the date, the Army changed the rules and Janet was permitted to remain Lieutenant Steele née Smith, the first married QA. While we were delighted at the time, it was to cause problems later.

December 3rd dawned bright and clear and we pitched up at St Margaret's Church, Happy Valley: my best man, Peter Lennett, I and my guard of honour in winter-blue uniform with swords. Janet, princess-like in traditional white and Colonel Miller in RAMC dress blues with medals to give her away, arrived in the Commander British Forces' official car. So there we were, waiting at the altar rails – no priest! Father Tom, the British Forces Roman Catholic Chaplain, had been held up on the way back from Kai Tak Airport and arrived somewhat late. In those days there was no Cross Harbour Tunnel and Father Tom had to use the vehicular ferry from Jordan Road, which as ever, was busy. I think this flustered him somewhat as he did forget the bit about 'just cause and impediment' but, as we were quickly reassured, this did not in-validate the marriage!

Off to the QA Officers' Mess at the BMH with its panoramic views over the harbour for the reception at which, I might add, no beer was allowed. Janet's matron had already lost two of her officers to Hong Kong policemen and was not enamoured of the amount of beer drunk at receptions. As it turned out, our best man and the Maid of Honour had concocted a rather potent but innocuous tasting punch from a recipe of Janet's father, which having been made the night before, continued to ferment to something like a 80-proof Ribena.

Our wedding night was spent at the Mandarin Hotel – Bruce Forsyth was playing dinner theatre. Early next morning we were woken by the phone. It was Peter Lennett. 'Had I heard about Macau?' (We had planned and booked the Bela Vista Hotel in Macau for our honeymoon.)

'Yes,' I replied, 'we are all set to go.'

'You can't,' he said, horrified, 'have you not heard the news?'

I did not like to say that I had better things to do on my wedding night than sit glued to the radio! It transpired that the 'read in' at Government House had escalated into general rioting and we were forbidden to travel there.

And that was it – our honeymoon was spent at 12 Green Lane Hall, rather than the old-world charm of the famous Macau hotel; or would have been if I had not been called back to work. Though I did not know it at the time, our wedding took place almost exactly half way between what became known as the Star Ferry Riots in Hong Kong in April 1966, and the start of the Cultural Revolution–

inspired disturbances in Hong Kong in May 1967, that became known as the 'Confrontation'. And so it began.

British Hong Kong was between Communist China under Mao Tse-tung and Nationalist Taiwan under Chiang Kai-shek's Kuomintang (KMT). Each considered themselves the 'true' China, and Hong Kong tried hard to strike a balance between the two, though, in 1950, the United Kingdom had recognised the Chinese Communist Party (CCP) as the legitimate government of the 'one China'.

It was important for peace and order in Hong Kong that institutions supporting either side were not allowed to use the colony to openly continue their political struggles. Consequently, the Hong Kong government was at pains to ensure that, in spite of permitting the existence of trade unions, organs of the press, and schools, supporting (and supported by) either the CCP or KMT, their political enmity did not spill over into disturbance in Hong Kong. Much of the work of Special Branch was in pursuance of this aim – supplying the intelligence necessary to maintain internal security – its Chinese name meant 'Political Bureau'.

The Double Ten riots in October 1956 resulted in fifty-nine deaths and some five hundred injured. Subsequently there was a complete review of the Hong Kong Police's internal security structure and practices. The flying of either Nationalist or Communist flags remained sensitive issues for many years thereafter.

These disturbances also resulted in the formation of the Police Training Contingent (PTC), the forerunner of the Police Tactical Unit (PTU). The aim was that as many members of the Force as possible, both officers and rank and file, would pass through PTC and be trained in riot drill and internal security tactics. This provided a large trained cadre able to regroup into security mode from normal watch and ward duties at short notice as and when required.

Between 5th and 9th April 1966, a series of demonstrations and disturbances took place in Kowloon. Towards the end of 1965, the Star Ferry Company had applied to the government for an increase in fares; 10 cents for the upper deck of the ferry, and five cents for the lower, as I recall. Not a great deal, but a fare hike of 50 per cent all the same. There was much press comment and a petition raised by Urban Councillor and social campaigner, Mrs Elsie Elliott,[2] against the increase attracted some 23,000 signatures. The fare increase was approved nonetheless.

On 4th April, a young man, So Sau-chung,[3] wearing a jacket emblazoned with the words 'Hail Elsie', began a hunger strike at the Star Ferry Terminal on Hong Kong Island in protest at the fare rise. So returned the following day and attracted a growing crowd, obstructing the turnstiles to the ferry. After due warning, he was arrested. Later that day, Special Branch information indicated that there was to be a demonstration at the Star Ferry in Tsim Sha Tsui. This was permitted by police but the demonstration grew and 'processed' around Kowloon causing disruption to traffic and general noise and nuisance. As dawn broke on 7th April, the demonstration began to disperse under the watchful eye of the police.

Anticipating further demonstrations as night fell, the Force went into 'Emergency Structure' and a number of riot companies were formed. Over the next three nights there was serious rioting, disorder and destruction of property in much of Kowloon. The Army was called in to aid the civil power and eventually the disorder subsided, but not before one person had been killed, some fifty injured and much damage done to property both public and private.

Most of those taking part were young people and there was no evidence of political or triad involvement. The consensus now is that much of the impetus for these disturbances came from social problems regarding housing, education and health facilities – problems subsequently recognised and addressed by the government.

That winter, the Force as a whole studied the April riots in an effort to learn lessons and to improve preparedness for, and response to, serious breaches of internal security.

2   The post-disturbance report did not deal kindly with Mrs Elliott who was
     accused, wrongly in my view, of inciting the disturbances. Some twenty years
     after these events, as commander of Kwun Tong Police District, I had a
     number of dealings with Mrs Elsie Tu, as she was by then, and found her to
     be an honest and straightforward social reformer. She was awarded CBE in
     1977 and died aged 102 in December 2015.
3   Who later became a Buddhist monk.

In April 1967, a run-of-the-mill trade dispute broke out at the Hong Kong Artificial Flower Works factory in San Po Kong, Kowloon. Trade union disputes were not unusual and there had been others earlier in the year. However, in May 1967 this dispute turned violent. Activists from the pro-communist Federation of Trade Unions (FTU), taking their cue from the Great Proletarian Cultural Revolution then taking place in China, sought to 'mediate' in the dispute by using the 'Quotations of Chairman Mao'. Workers and students from pro-communist schools, egged on by inflammatory articles in the pro-communist press, took to the streets.

There were mass demonstrations outside Government House and other strategic locations around Hong Kong, and they took on a distinctly anti-colonial flavour. Hong Kong compatriots could not be seen to be less 'patriotic' (i.e. pro-China and pro-Mao) than their counterparts in Macau. Communist publishing houses in Hong Kong like the Commercial Press rushed out editions of the 'Selected Quotations of Chairman Mao Tse-tung' in small red covered books, which became known as the 'little red book'.

The two main pro-communist newspapers, the *Ta Kung Pao* and *Wen Wei Po,* carried lurid stories and pictures of 'police brutality' against demonstrators. Public buildings were plastered with anti-colonial and pro-Mao posters and articles from the communist press. An 'All Circles Anti-Hong Kong British Persecution Struggle Committee' was established by pro-communist elements to co-ordinate 'the struggle'.

Those policing the demonstrations often discovered demonstrators carrying their own bandages and bottles of 'blood' to adorn themselves with at the appropriate moment when the press and television cameras were on the scene. There was much abuse hurled at the police who were accused of 'persecution' of the Chinese compatriots. Europeans were called '*paak pei zhu*' – 'white-skinned pigs', and the Chinese officers '*wong pei gau*' – 'yellow-skinned dogs' or 'running dogs'. Insults like these tend to amuse the Brits and being called a 'white-skinned pig' became something of an accolade. So much so that neck ties were made depicting white-skinned pigs and yellow running dogs, and 'red fat cats' representing the wealthy

Chinese demonstrators who would turn up in their expensive cars, alight, wave their red books for the cameras, and then be whisked away again. This tie was worn with some pride by Europeans, Chinese police and government officers alike.

There was no doubt however, as to the anti-foreigner tenor of the demonstrators and though I personally never felt particularly intimidated or threatened when wearing plain clothes in the street, I was not sorry to be carrying my personal sidearm. There were a number of incidents where Europeans, male and female, were jostled and intimidated and had to be rescued by uniformed officers. Though there is an apocryphal story of one enterprising European who, when approached by a hostile crowd of 'Maoists', produced his HSBC passbook in its red plastic cover and waved that aloft to the cheers of the crowd who assumed it was 'the little red book'. Thereafter, we all carried our HSBC passbooks.

These demonstrations carried on through June and into July causing considerable disruption to the life of the colony, and severely taxing the Force whose steadfastness and loyalty never wavered in spite of much threat, insult and provocation. At the end of June, a general strike was called by the FTU. The Hong Kong government realised that this situation could not be allowed to continue for much longer and it was decided that plans would be drawn up to mount raids on various communist premises from which the disturbances were being organised and directed.

This task fell to the Military Intelligence Officer (MIO), assisted by myself. An MIO had been attached to SB for many years as liaison between the British military and the civil Police. In 1967, the MIO was one Major H.G. ___ .

H.G. was a larger-than-life character both in size and personality. In those days, even in the height of summer, we wore suits to work and H.G. would sit at his desk, a large florid man in shirt sleeves and red braces with a big Browning .45 automatic in a shoulder holster. But he was calm, efficient and a delight to work for. I was a very young inspector in those days and H.G. taught me much about the methodical organisation of large quantities of informa-tion into suitable forms for briefing officers. He also taught me the benefits of maintaining a calm, unruffled demeanour in the face of high stress and pressure. We worked very long hours, seven days a week for a considerable period of time and the portfolio of folders on all the communist premises grew and, more importantly, were frequently checked to ensure they were up to date. Thank you, H.G.

As it happened, our work was completed none too soon, for things turned rather unpleasant as the mass demonstrations became increasingly violent and then escalated into a bombing campaign with the indiscriminate placing of real and hoax Improvised Explosive Devices (IED). There is still speculation about the rationale for this change to what was, to all intents and purposes, an embryonic armed struggle. Over the border in China, the rampages of Mao's Red Guards had also become more violent and it has since been speculated that instructions had come from the ultra-leftist groups in China.[4] Then came the Sha Tau Kok incident.

On 8th July 1967, several hundred 'demonstrators' crossed the border from China to Hong Kong at the border village of Sha Tau Kok. The border ran down Chung Ying Street in the village and the demonstrators, including members of the People's Militia (a sort of police/civil defence organisation) attacked the Hong Kong Police post there with stones and 'fish bombs'. Police tried to disperse the demonstrators using tear gas and baton shells but, in the words of a statement to the House of Commons, 'came under fire from several points, including automatic fire from Chinese territory. Five police [three Chinese and two Pakistani] were killed and 11 wounded.'[5] One Chinese militiaman was also reported killed. The Army was called in and two companies of 1/10 Gurkha Rifles with kukris drawn, reinforced by Life Guards armoured vehicles, relieved the post without having to open fire.

This incident shocked us all in Hong Kong and no-one knew if it was a precursor to an attempt by China to take back Hong Kong. It wasn't, but the event may well have inspired Hong Kong compatriots to take on a more militant and violent role.

4   *South China Morning Post;* '1967 ringleader Yeung Kwong "just followed orders"', Gary Cheung, 1 July 2001.
5   Hansard Commons, 10th July 1967.

Through all this, Janet was still working at the BMH in Bowen Road and understandably the military were often on standby, and 'confined to barracks'. My working hours were erratic to say the least and so we weren't seeing very much of each other. Knowing that the first thing I'd do when I got home was to go to the fridge for a cold drink, our fridge at Green Lane Hall became a sort of 'dead letter drop' where we would pass messages reassuring each other that we were alive and well.

The first IEDs started appearing soon after this and the Hong Kong government brought a number of emergency regulations into force. Unlike Macau, the Hong Kong government was not about to agree to the demands of the Maoists. Certain pro-communist newspapers were proscribed and their editors arrested. Communist schools such as the Heung To and the Pui Kiu were closed. Fireworks were banned to prevent the black powder they contained being used in IEDs.[6]

Raids on communist premises began, including one on Kiu Kwan Mansion in North Point with the assistance of a Royal Navy helicopter from HMS *Hermes* which landed police on the rooftop of the heavily defended building. Inside was found a number of live IEDs, much bomb-making equipment, makeshift weapons and a fully equipped hospital with an operating theatre. That was not in our briefing folder on the premises! The Army, acting in aid of the civil power, often provided cordons around premises that were being raided. There was a widely circulated story that an irate European tried to drive through a cordon operated by the Gurkhas thinking that the 'stop' order did not apply to him and got a bayonet through his shoulder for his trouble.

One response to the Police activity against the compatriots in Hong Kong was the sacking and burning of the British Legation in Peking (Beijing) and the imprisonment of Reuters' correspondent, Anthony Grey. Sino-British relations hit something of a low point.

---

6   Every Chinese celebration from religious festivals to opening of shops was
     accompanied by the 'crack' of firecrackers. Long strings of these red 'bangers'
     would hang from buildings, to be set off at the appropriate moment.

The commencement of the bombing campaign led to a number of leading pro-communist personalities being arrested and detained on warrants under emergency regulations. A number of us were formed into two-man investigation teams – one expatriate with one Chinese inspector. I was teamed with a good friend, and for a period of some three months we were involved very deeply in the search for those planting explosive devices. Most of those arrested to whom we spoke were sure that we Brits were on our way out and I was sometimes surprised by the level of venom directed towards my Chinese partner. But in the main I got the impression they thought the bombing campaign was a mistake and that it was the work of a few ultra-militant Red Guard types.

This job, together with the move of the BMH from Bowen Road to King's Park in Kowloon, led to some anxious moments for Janet and I, and ultimately to her leaving the Army. There was considerable disruption to the life of the colony caused by the bombing campaign. I was not happy that the Army was unable to provide transport for Janet to travel from our flat on Hong Kong Island to the hospital in Kowloon. Previously, when the hospital was in Bowen Road, the Army sent transport for her, but though the journey was more difficult, being across the harbour, and longer, there was no transport. Further, it was not a secret that I was investigating 'Chinese compatriots'. After the assassination of Lam Bun, a journalist who had spoken out against the bombing campaign (his car was stopped and set on fire with him and his cousin inside), my Chinese partner and I were strongly advised to vary our daily route to the detention centre. It was not beyond the bounds of possibility that Janet could become a target too. So after some correspondence and discussion, the Ministry of Defence felt that she should leave the Army.

We were both very sad at this. Janet loved the work and I was immensely proud of her. Also she was about to be promoted to Captain. I was outranked on marriage and about to be so again – her three pips to my two! And the money would have been useful, especially as it was not counted for Hong Kong tax purposes. In the end however, we both felt it to be for the best, and at least we would see something of each other when I was home.

The bombing campaign continued, but it began to be counter-productive for the communists. The public outcry, muted at first, began to swell when, towards the end of August, two small children were killed by an IED wrapped to look like a gift and hung on the railing of a street in North Point, Hong Kong. The assassination of the journalist Lam Bun, as already mentioned, in a particularly gruesome manner, further turned the people of Hong Kong against the compatriots.

By September, the number of IEDs was growing smaller. Police action against the bombers had largely been successful. And as public antipathy towards the compatriots grew, so did the support for the police and the Hong Kong government which had stood firm in the face of adversity. But it was not quite over yet.

Janet and I were driving down Hennessy Road in late September, 1967, when we heard a loud explosion. We knew what it was of course, but only later found that an IED had exploded outside Wan Chai Fire Station, killing Station Officer Aslam Khan. And in November, Senior Inspector of Police Ronald McEwan of Traffic Division, Hong Kong Island, was killed in Yee Wo Street by an IED. The IED was in the road and was causing serious traffic congestion and, thinking that it may well be a hoax as had often been the case, Ron was cautiously tying a string in order to pull it away from a safe distance, when it exploded. Ron was a decorated officer who had rescued several people during Typhoon Wanda in 1962. There was considerable angst in the Force in the aftermath of Ron's death as *The Star,* an English-language tabloid, published a graphic picture of Ron's body on its front page. Much effort was expended in ensuring his grieving family did not see it.

Normal life gradually returned to Hong Kong. The disruption to the generally peaceful life of Hong Kong and the stories of the horrific violence perpetuated by the Red Guards in China, turned the people of Hong Kong against the Maoists. And it was not just the stories of violence in China – bodies with hands tied behind their backs, sometimes with barbed wire, evidence of executions, were floating down the Pearl River into Hong Kong waters, to be recovered by the Marine Police.

Overall, fifty one people were killed during the Confrontation; ten police officers, an Army bomb disposal officer, a fire officer, four bombers, twelve civilians and twenty three rioters. Hundreds were injured and some five thousand persons arrested. The exact number of IED planted is not known but estimates indicated some 8,000 of which about 1,500 were genuine.[7] Property damage ran into millions of dollars, and many people sought to emigrate. Why China did not press on and seek more forcibly to recover Hong Kong at that time, is not clear to me. Modern scholarship seems to indicate that Foreign Minister Chou En-lai (Zhou Enlai) instructed comrades in Hong Kong to cease and desist. The Sha Tau Kok incident was thought to have been instigated due to an excess of zeal on the part of the local authorities in Shum Chun (now Shenzhen).

During Confrontation, Hong Kong people were forced to choose between supporting a violent and radical revolutionary movement in China and the Hong Kong government. Overwhelmingly they chose the Hong Kong government and I have no doubt that this was in large measure due to the firm stand taken by the government and the steadfastness and professionalism of its officers at all levels, and of the Hong Kong Police. In recognition of its contribution, the police were honoured with the title 'Royal' by Her Majesty the Queen. Her Royal Highness Princess Alexandra became the Force's Honorary Commandant General.

In 1997, sovereignty of Hong Kong was relinquished to China and interestingly, in 2001, and not without some comment at the time, Yeung Kwong, Chairman of the Federation of Trade Unions and leader of the 1967 'Struggle Committee' was given an honour by the administration of Hong Kong for his 'outstanding contribution to the labour movement and labour welfare in Hong Kong and his dedicated community service'. A former editor of the pro-communist *Wen Wei Po* commented that 'Yeung made the mistake in implementing the orders of the ultra-leftist Mainland officials but the major responsibility was not his'.[8] Yeung died in 2015.

---

7   *A Modern History of Hong Kong*, Steve Tsang, pp. 183 et seq.

Princess Alexandra, RHKP Honorary Commandant General,
at a Police Training School parade with David Hughes

The events of 1966 and 1967 led to the government realisation that there was a large gap between the governed and those governing, and that serious social problems in housing, education and health needed to be addressed. This led to the formation of a City District Officer scheme in each district of the urban area, mirroring the organisation which was extant in the rural New Territories (and also in many other colonies). This was a success and brought the government much closer to the people, providing an outlet for complaints and early warning of discontent. There grew an increasing sense of belonging to Hong Kong among large sections of the population, and the idea of a 'Hong Kong Belonger' or 'Hongkonger' was born.

It is ironic to think that the independent mindset of Hong Kong people now, which sometimes causes difficulty for both the governments of Hong Kong and China under the 'One Country – Two

8   *South China Morning Post;* '1967 ringleader Yeung Kwong "just followed orders"', Gary Cheung, 1 Jul, 2001

Systems' structure, had its genesis in the pro-communist unrest of 1967.

By April 1968, almost four years after I had first arrived in Hong Kong, Janet and I were able to return to the United Kingdom on 'home leave'. It had been an eventful tour. We sailed home on a Dutch cargo ship from Singapore to Rotterdam. Six weeks of sun and sea, and the honeymoon we missed eighteen months earlier. The only worry was that I recognised the bo'sun in charge of the Chinese crew on the ship as a leading light in the pro-communist Hong Kong Seaman's Union. I was very circumspect about my job in Hong Kong!

The Cultural Revolution at Sea

Frank Goldberg

As dutiful Auxiliary Marine Police Officers, we always carried out our work with great enthusiasm, but we were never too sure if we were really such good policemen. On patrol, we were once ordered to check a fishing junk at sea. After we boarded the boat, the skipper produced a paper that stated he was not to leave the harbour of Cheung Chau Island under any circumstances. So we escorted the boat back to Cheung Chau and reported our 'catch' to the local police station. They congratulated us on a job well done and we asked what would be the consequences for the junk owner. When we heard that the man would get a fine, we felt sorry for the poor fisherman and his family and so made a quick collection on board and handed the money to the most surprised Chinese fisherman.

When we went on fortnight's patrol, we were under orders to intercept any vessel in an endeavour to stop illegal immigration, so obviously when we spotted a motor vessel closely following the coastline of Lantau Island without any navigation lights, we signalled her to stop. The navigation lights were quickly switched on, but the skipper continued on his way. So we signalled again, went alongside and I stepped on board, where a well-dressed crew member in a smart white uniform asked me if I wanted to speak to the owner. As it was evening and rather cold, I had put on a red sweater over my uniform, so was not properly dressed at all, but being on board, I could hardly refuse, so he took me to the aft deck, where I met . . . Sir Michael Hogan, the chief justice of Hong Kong, who kindly asked me if I needed to see the navigation papers of his guest on board, the commodore-in-charge, the senior Royal Navy officer in the colony. After saying this was not quite necessary, I sheepishly returned to the patrol boat to find that all of my crew mates had instantaneously disappeared from sight at the first sign of my encounter with the top brass!

At the debriefing at the end of our tour, I was wondering if it had become known and if so, would I get a reprimand for being dressed more like a pirate than a policeman. However, all that was said, was 'and I'd like to congratulate you on the courteous way in which you addressed Lady Hogan. . . .'

As a result of unrest caused by the Cultural Revolution in China in the mid-1960s, the Auxiliary Police was mobilised and I was able to take a small part in a very interesting period in Hong Kong's history.

Information received indicated that the dock workers in Hong Kong were prepared to continue their duties during the Cultural Revolution, provided they could be sure that there would be sufficient police around to guarantee their safety. The harbour being of vital importance to Hong Kong, this resulted in the most impressive measures taken by the government. It was decided that, as a show of force, all official vessels would be painted black and given police numbers. And this happened within days. The Department of Commerce and Industry boats, Immigration, and even the Fire Service boats, continued to carry out their roles, but then as Police Nos. 88, 92, etc. As the Auxiliary Marine Police consisted of only European nationals, we could not provide extra crew to man these boats, but a uniformed policeman was put on the stern in full view. The harbour was black with 'police' vessels and the work continued.

During this time, a report came in that the Chinese crew had taken over command of a British merchant vessel at sea. Somehow the British captain and first mate had managed to steer the ship during the night into Hong Kong harbour, where they anchored and radioed for help. I went on board and rescued both British officers from a rather hostile crew. I fortunately had my Webley .38, so having the upper hand in firepower I took as a souvenir a large portrait of Mao Tse-tung, which the crew had posted on the officers' cabin door. How very relieved and thankful the officers were to be back on British territory!

The mobilisation also changed my personal life. The San Miguel Breweries had contacted me in 1966 and offered me a job as marketing manager to set up a distribution system with driver/salesmen, as I had done previously for the milk and ice cream deliveries at the Dairy Farm Company. When the Cultural Revolution threatened the security of Hong Kong, the San Miguel Breweries head office in Manila were not sure what the outcome would be and quickly started to replace European employees with Chinese. So my job became rather insecure, not least because I was also away from my office for weeks on end at the Marine Police HQ. I was therefore happy to be offered a job with the Hong Kong Trade Development Council in 1968.

At the end of the Cultural Revolution troubles in Hong Kong, I was very pleased and honoured to receive the Colonial Police Medal for Meritorious Service, which, after getting approval from the Dutch Embassy in London, was gracefully awarded to me at Government House on behalf of Her Majesty Queen Elizabeth.

In addition, I was also immensely touched by the gift from the members of my unit. It was a silver tankard bearing the inscription:

FRANK GOLDBERG
For leadership
from the lads of Marine Division
Hong Kong Auxiliary Police Force
May 1967

Thirty Years of Policing Hong Kong

Richard Tudor

I was incredibly lucky in my thirty-year career in the Royal Hong Kong Police, between 1967 and 1997. It covered a period of great political, social and financial upheaval and saw the Force change from a very paramilitary organisation to a modern, metropolitan police service, albeit with a hard edge if necessary. I served in a wide variety of operational posts, including the Uniform Branch (UB), Magistrates Court, Criminal Investigation, instructing at the Police Training School (PTS), the anti-terrorist Special Duties Unit (SDU), Airport Station and the Frontier Patrol Detachment on the border before finishing as District Commander, Kwun Tong. I have never worked in Police HQ, which was a blessing, since I frequently was my own boss. I am proud to have worked with some very talented, industrious and often fearless men and women, especially in SDU but much of that experience must remain for me alone to remember.

I have chosen to relate only a few, mainly light-hearted incidents arising out of serious situations, but I know I will never regret boarding the plane to Hong Kong in 1967, escaping from the drudgery and boredom of the civil service in England.

Love at First Sight

During a final farewell evening in my local pub, the Green Tree in Bath, I received plenty of lurid, inaccurate comments and descriptions about Hong Kong, related by ex-servicemen and other reprobates. Such comments included, 'a terrible rat-infested place', 'hot as hell', and 'fabulous Oriental smells', as well as 'wonderful girlie bars with Chinese, or were they Japanese, hostesses, who give you the pox?'

I stumbled home for one last night before catching the train to London the next morning, 6th April 1967.

I subsequently met up with the eleven other British men who were to be my companions on the flight and to form Probationary Inspectors Courses (PI Courses 37 to 39) at the Police Training School (PTS). Among them was a tall, ex-Metropolitan copper with a distinctive Somerset accent who I swear was the officer I had met in the street, months earlier, when asking the way to Stag Place, Victoria for my initial interview. He had replied: 'What do you think I am, a tourist guide!'

After twenty-four hours flying via Rome, Delhi and Bangkok we emerged into the fetid air of Kai Tak Airport and were bussed to the Police Training School in Aberdeen. In our exhausted and somewhat rich-smelling state, a result of nylon shirts and winter sports jackets, we were subjected to an hour-long, degrading initiation ceremony, too tired, disorientated and confused to realise that the drill pig 'staff' were our age and from the senior probationary inspector's squad, and not mature, experienced instructors. Exhibiting impressive stamina after travelling halfway round the globe and with no sleep for forty-eight hours, we accepted an invitation to join the senior passing-out squad for their party in the officers' mess provided we did not try to chat up the ladies. Resuscitated by my first couple of San Miguel beers, I noticed a group of attractive European women arriving allegedly from Special Branch in Police Headquarters. Was it love at first sight?

Full of Dutch courage, I ignored dark looks from senior squad members and asked an incredibly beautiful girl for a dance. By the end of the evening we were inseparable and I escorted her gallantly through the darkness, breathing the unique odour of the duck farm abutting PTS, to a road where I confidently hailed a taxi to take her home, despite not having any idea of where I was or where she was going. We have since been together now for fifty years. So much for exploring the exotic pleasures of the Orient!

Could Have Shot Him

Following truncated training under 'quarantine' conditions at PTS, because of the 1967 riots, we were let loose onto the streets of Hong Kong in October 1967. I was posted to Central Division where a campaign of bombings by leftists kept us busy day and night. I spent my shifts cordoning off suspected improvised explosive devices (IED) and escorting the legendary 'Bomber' Hill as he examined and defused them. More often than not he blew them up with controlled explosions just big enough to reduce passing American tourists, who tended to ignore police cordons whilst shopping, to tears.

More frightening were the fanatical leftist prisoners I guarded in the custodial ward of Queen Mary Hospital who, apparently immune to injected anaesthetics, had to be subdued by police guards and fearless male nurses as they tore thick government blankets to shreds and scratched communist propaganda onto the walls with bare nails. Police officers died on the streets that autumn but despite exciting gambling raids, chasing drug traffickers across rooftops, and other encounters, I never had occasion to draw my revolver throughout my first three-and-a-half-year tour.

However, a routine, verbal exam on the use of firearms was mandatory for all probationary inspectors and I had been duly summoned to the divisional superintendent Central's office. Expecting a severe test, I was bemused to find myself distracted by the drumming of giant fingers on an enormous desk as a plump superintendent asked me to describe a scenario when I would be justified in drawing my gun. 'On foot patrol in a back alley in the middle of the night I am confronted by two chopper-wielding triads who make to attack me,' I confidently replied. Raising a chubby palm in my direction, my interrogator who had spent most of his career behind a desk, said, 'Too hasty young man, I would first look around the alley for a piece of wood or bamboo to defend myself with.' Dumbfounded, I left the office wondering if I had a future in the Force.

I only relate this tale because of what happened to me some five years later. It was 1973 and I was in CID Shau Kei Wan, having been called out to a triad gang fight in a housing estate. We found rival 14K and Wo Shing Wo triad gangs had fled, leaving swords, choppers and blood on the road, no doubt carrying their wounded with them. As I drove my coughing, unreliable Volkswagen Beetle home through the dimly lit streets at 2 am, I glimpsed a youth walking furtively along the road ahead of me, apparently armed with a two-foot-long sword, flashing in the moonlight. A member of one of the warring triads I thought. With foolhardy bravery, I jumped out of my car and drew my revolver. I called out in my best Cantonese: 'Stop, put down your weapon!' The young man kept walking towards me, disappearing repeatedly behind parked lorries only to emerge again as the distance between us narrowed. I repeated my warning but still he came on brandishing the intimidating weapon. When he was about ten feet from me, my tortured mind was telling me to shoot him before he attacked. Pointing my revolver shakily at his chest I screamed, 'Stop!' He dropped the weapon at my feet and stood still until I made him kneel down before handcuffing him. I examined the weapon which turned out to be a length of aluminium window frame with a piece of cloth wrapped round as a handle. The frightened youth spoke English and explained he worked at a nearby factory and carried the makeshift weapon to protect himself from robbers on his way home. His story checked out and I later released him.

I could have shot him. Had I done so, would I have been justified? Despite many dangerous encounters in the rest of my career I have seldom had to draw my weapon since then and never opened fire except in exercise scenarios.

Sedan Chairs

In 1971 I returned to Hong Kong from my first vacation leave, disenchanted by the depressing winter of strikes and growing unemployment in the UK. Posted to the Anti-Corruption Office in Central, I joined a small team tasked with investigating the Prisons Service. While some of the detention centres and prisons on Lantau seemed more like spartan holiday camps, the high-security prison in Stanley was a different matter. Staff were suspected of conspiring with triad inmates to import and traffic in dangerous drugs. It became apparent that we would need informers on the inside. To this end, we arrived at Stanley one sunny, cold morning to interview a triad office-bearer notorious for his influence, violence and business acumen. I was curious to make his acquaintance, such was his reputation.

The door to C Block opened and a cortege of grubby humanity entered carrying a rather effete, pale young man on a makeshift sedan chair! We conducted our interview with this psychopathic, yet magnetic personality, but gleaned little useful information. We left wondering what on earth we had just witnessed.

Different triad societies, identified by unique tattoos, were housed in separate wings in the prison to prevent unrest. I have no idea what became of our informant but I have no doubt that he was a high-ranking triad who contributed to the smooth running of Stanley Prison. Ten years later, I was reminded of the Stanley encounter as I joined a team of runners carrying a six-stone woman round the Peak in the annual sedan-chair race. It was the most masochistic and exhausting exercise I had ever done, and I wondered if that triad had made his minions run him round the corridors of Stanley Prison?

Michael Jackson

In 1988, I was divisional commander Tsim Sha Tsui when Michael Jackson, at the height of his fame, visited Hong Kong. His team of minders had negotiated for him to film with an anti-riot Police Tactical Unit (PTU) platoon within the confines of the station compound. My regional commander (RC) had stipulated that we were not to allow our families to the station to meet the global superstar and also made it clear that he was no fan himself. Michael and his manager hid in my office between shoots. He was polite and inquisitive about police work and admired our uniforms. A knock at the door and who should appear but aforementioned RC beaming 'Michael, still here, could I have your autograph and perhaps a photo together?'

Michael Jackson, 1988 (Courtesy Richard Tudor)

Before leaving my office Michael perused pictures on my desk and picked up a framed photo of my two little girls. He then uttered the words, 'Why didn't you bring them to meet me, I love children!'

Hanoi

While serving as district commander Airport in the early 1990s, I was involved in a government programme to repatriate Vietnamese refugees using ageing Hercules aircraft hired from Indonesia. There had been rumours of crashes in the Sumatra jungle and it transpired that government servants were not covered by insurance for these journeys outside Hong Kong. My wife was not keen for me to go and I had led her to believe that I would not. Nevertheless, I felt I had to lead by example. Consequently, on the day of the first such flight, I led a group of airport police and security branch officials and we strapped ourselves in along the stripped-out fuselage, guarding about forty nervous Vietnamese men, women and children. They were classed as 'voluntary returnees' but some didn't seem too keen to return to their homeland.

As we approached Hanoi, I was aware we had been circling for some time so I went up to the spacious cockpit to see what was happening. I was horrified to see an Auxiliary Air Force officer studying an ancient *road map* of Hanoi in order to guide the pilot to the runway!

To convince the local authorities that the returning refugees were doing so voluntarily, the police element of the escort party were not allowed off the aircraft. Therefore, a blanket was hung over the tail exit and the returnees fed through it to waiting Vietnamese military personnel. Our cover was blown when, to our amazement, enthusiastic hawkers thrust tourist mementos such as ceramic elephants through the curtain into the plane in return for tins of much-sought-after Coca-Cola.

Meanwhile, unbeknown to me, my wife had telephoned the Airport Police Officers' Mess asking where I was, only to be told: 'He is in Hanoi.' The Deputy Regional Commander Kowloon West who took her call recoiled from her response! I undertook a couple more trips before going on annual leave and my deputy, a future commissioner of police, K.S. Tang, took over command. Whilst in the UK in 1994, I was distressed to learn that one of the repatriation flights had crashed in Hong Kong. Were airport police led by K.S. Tang aboard? My horror was tempered when I discovered the crash had occurred after the flight had returned from Hanoi and all HK personnel had disembarked. It had crashed on take-off for the journey home to Jakarta, killing six of the twelve Indonesian crew. That was the end of the Hercules flights.

The Border

In 1993, I was due to take over the post of Senior Superintendent Border from the legend that was Vince Chapman. He of hectic long-distance hill walks with his faithful dogs. We agreed to meet for a patrol of the Sha Tau Kok Peninsula to familiarise me with illegal immigration routes. Inevitably it turned into a hill race.

Vince didn't wait or make small talk. After two hours of clambering up and down rough ground, I was hanging on grimly when Vince sat down on a gravestone for a rest. He looked a little grey around the gills and gradually slid to a horizontal position, grudgingly admitting he may have overdone it the night before. It became clear he was in serious trouble, probably having a heart attack. I made him comfortable and told him I would go for help, having no radio or one of the new-fangled mobile telephones. I ran off up the path to a remote village a mile away where a grizzled old Hakka woman showed me to an ancient Bakelite telephone. I persuaded the regional police controller to send a helicopter to the graveyard where I imagined Vince was breathing his last. I got back in time to meet the incoming helicopter but Vince was nowhere to be seen. Had he crawled to a more sheltered spot, out of the baking sun and collapsed? On board the helicopter, we searched the area following the footpath. Eventually a mile away, we spotted Vince below striding purposefully through the undergrowth. As the helicopter landed near him, I jumped out and urged Vince to board the rescue vehicle. He refused outright, so I joined him for the trek back to our cars at Wu Kau Tang. The aircrew were not impressed!

Vince made it back and drove himself home to recover. Meanwhile, I set off for a scheduled farewell party at the Sek Kong Vietnamese refugee camp for which I had responsibility. Over a very welcome ice-cold lager, I was relating Vince's misadventure to a group of fellow officers when who should appear but Vince, determined to catch up with a few beers. He was a man who didn't want to admit defeat.

A week later, he nearly got his revenge when, on a recce of Robin's Nest, a hill overlooking the border fence, we were caught in a violent thunderstorm. Vince was intent on making it to the hilltop. With incessant, blinding flashes of lightning around us, I shouted through the wind, 'We must get down now!' and set off. He reluctantly followed and we jogged down through torrential rain. Once again Vince had no radio and his driver had returned to base leaving us with a long, bedraggled walk back. I admired Vince but was relieved when he retired, leaving me to run his beloved border stamping ground.

Vince thought I was a wimp about the thunderstorm but I had developed a healthy respect for lightning since an incident in 1984. I was on a training run with a fellow SDU officer, Charles Kong, on the road through the Sha Tau Kok Peninsula when a thunderstorm suddenly engulfed us. In driving rain, I leapt over puddles, imagining that by jumping to each crack of thunder I would not be struck by the almost simultaneous flashes of lightning. Charles laughed and we made it back to base unscathed. I switched on Radio Hong Kong in my office only to hear that two Gurkha soldiers in an ambush position on the hill directly above the road where we had been running, had been struck by lightning and killed.

Maotai

Liaison visits were an important feature of border policing in the mid-1990s with the looming handover of the sovereignty of Hong Kong to China. It was our turn to visit the People's Liberation Army (PLA) in Shenzhen and they always proved very sociable and liberal with their alcohol of choice, *maotai*, virtually tasteless but probably 100 proof. They delighted in trying to get expatriate officers inebriated in drinking contests with toasts to anything that occurred to them. In order to preserve my liver, I enlisted the help of a large, South African PTU officer with the constitution of a bull, to join our delegation. After the business of intelligence sharing on illegal immigration issues and plans for possible joint operations, we sat down for lunch and the usual round of toasts. With my Afrikaans officer cheerfully slugging cups of *maotai* in response to raucous toasts, it occurred to me that our hosts never seemed to get the worse for wear.

Chinese waitresses topped up the cups from two teapots and with my suspicions aroused I asked that our drinks be replenished from the teapot the PLA were using. Furtive glances were exchanged between the waitress and the PLA leader as I sipped my drink – sure enough it was water!

No wonder we always staggered home across the Lo Wu bridge. Future liaison visits featured only Chinese tea.

Hello Sailor

Keith Braithwaite

I joined the Hong Kong Police in April 1967, following two-and-a-half years walking the beat in London. Service in the Metropolitan Police Force, considered by some (and certainly itself) in those days to be the best Police in the world, was an education for a young nineteen-year-old from Somerset. I was attached to both Gerald Road and Rochester Row Police Stations and one of the beats of the latter covered the Crown Agents building where I saw and eventually responded to an advertisement to join the Hong Kong Police.

Walking the beat in London was an eye opener for a country boy and really enjoyable. However, one of my most enduring memories concerns the firearm policy of the Force at the time, particularly relating to the manner in which armed constables carried out their 'guard' duties outside one of the large number of embassies in Belgrave Square, where a perceived threat existed.

The PC who was given the task of guarding the premises on a two-hour rotating basis was issued with a revolver and six rounds. In those days there were no radios available to give to officers. As far as I recall, neither I, nor any of my colleagues, had received any firearms training. This was probably the reason that we were instructed by the duty sergeant, on pain of death, to place the revolver in one pocket of our greatcoats and the rounds in the other, and also to make ourselves conspicuous outside the embassy. Now what, you may ask, was supposed to happen in the event of a sudden attack? But woe betide any of the guards who, when the patrol sergeant arrived frequently to check, had not ensured that the rounds were kept as far away from the revolver as was possible. How times have changed!

This and a number of other issues made me question the validity of the efficiency and reputation of the Metropolitan Police and were instrumental in me applying to join the Hong Kong Police. Another very important factor in making up my mind was the thought of getting on a plane for the first time and seeing the Orient, a part of the world I would never otherwise have been able to afford to visit.

Probationary inspector (PI) training in the HKP normally lasted six months, but due to the political upheavals, with riots and a subsequent bomb campaign, our squads, PI 39 and 40, were reduced to four months training and then sent out to perform as best we could. As it happened, most of us did well and went on to have very successful careers.

During the 1960s and early 1970s, the north shore area of Wan Chai, made famous by the 1960 film *The World of Suzie Wong*, was at times awash in a sea of black and white. I refer, of course, to the invasion by thousands of United States Navy and military personnel on rest and recreation from the rigours and traumas created by the Vietnam War.

United States warships were 'dry' (no alcohol on board) and so by the time the sailors had arrived in HK they were up and ready for the exotic delights that Wan Chai had to offer, situated only a few hundred yards from Fenwick Pier where they landed. There, practically everything to satisfy their desires and vices could be purchased. Wan Chai certainly did not disappoint the hungry appetites of the matelot. In addition to the bars and restaurants, there were many brothels, massage parlours, drugs, gambling dens and even 'blue' movie parlours available. These latter, illegal, establishments were moved constantly by operators to avoid the interruption of business by police.

Many touts roamed the streets but those most in the know as to where the 'action' was taking place were the rickshaw boys and bar girls, the latter whose constant refrain of 'You buy me drinks?' echoed throughout the bar area.

The policing of the district came under the command of Wan Chai Police Division whose sub-divisional inspector at the time was the redoubtable Bill Boyton, much feared by the local populace and subordinates alike. His unenviable task was to attempt to keep a lid on the illicit activities being conducted in the area. This was not easy, given the demand created by the sheer volume of cash-rich visitors from US and other foreign ships arriving in the harbour.

In an effort to gain more accurate intelligence as to precisely where illicit vice activities were being conducted, Bill had obtained two genuine US Navy uniforms (there was a rumour that two seamen were languishing in the Wan Chai cells at the time wearing very little!). Anyway, two bright-eyed and bushy-tailed probationary inspectors, myself and Ben Munford, who had acquired quite a reputation for himself at the Police Training School for being a left-arm and left-foot-forward marching drill exponent, were to don these uniforms and patrol the Wan Chai streets in an undercover operation. This was a really exciting assignment and Ben and I jumped at the chance, because in the normal course of events, undercover and surveillance by *gweilos* (Caucasians) was a nonstarter for obvious reasons and opportunities to perform such duties were few and far between.

Our mission was to gain intelligence as to the precise locations of any nefarious activity, not to take action, but to report back verbally to the station. So, off we sauntered with a jaunty gait down Lockhart Road amongst the swarms of what we thought were identically clothed US sailors. All went very well for the first hour when we had seen a couple of blue movies in some local's front parlour, been offered some heroin, a massage and taken by rickshaw to a working brothel where we gave our excuses and departed after noting the address. So we were quietly pleased with ourselves as we walked back towards the station, not knowing that Bill had in fact been following our progress by trailing us on foot in plain clothes. Of course, the rickshaw trip put paid to that, despite his best efforts at keeping up, and he had lost us.

As we made our way, Ben and I were confronted by a group of US Shore Patrol personnel, who stopped us and asked us to which ship were we attached. Apparently, we did not have the name of our ship on our shoulder flashes. We, of course, had not thought to research into which ships were in port and our west country English accents attempting to sound American did not impress our inquisitors, who became very suspicious. Their suspicions were increased further no doubt when in response to the question: 'Who won the last Super Bowl?', we suggested hopefully: 'Mississippi Pirates' (or some other equally silly non-existent team). We were then pounced upon and frogmarched back to Shore Patrol Headquarters at Fenwick Pier, despite our protestations. Meanwhile Bill had given up searching for us and returned to Wan Chai whereupon he was informed that two US sailors had been seen being manhandled by the Shore Patrol in Lockhart Road. Putting two and two together, he hotfooted it round to Fenwick Pier to check and ensure that he was not going to be short of two sterling young officers. I imagine that visions of having to explain this to the Divisional Superintendent Roy Moss the following morning also weighed heavily on Bill's mind and aided in his speed of foot.

Upon our arrival at Fenwick Pier, Ben and I had begun to realise that it was about time to reveal our true identity. Visions of us being detained and thrown in the brig on a warship prompted us to state who we were. Initially this was not accepted by the US officer in charge until a very sweaty Bill Boyton arrived and identified himself. The US Shore Patrol were not familiar with our police warrant cards, so it took a further couple of telephone calls to the Wan Chai Station to confirm our bona fides, whereupon we were released.

As far as I am aware no other similar undercover operations by HKP personnel were ever repeated, but in future years when working in the Narcotics Bureau, I did participate in a number of operations conducted jointly with the US Naval Criminal Investigation Service, when undercover US personnel were ferried into HK to do exactly as Ben and I had done, but more convincingly and productively. However, it was nice to know that we had been pioneers in this regard!

I must admit though, that during moments of reflection, I have often wondered what it would have been like to have cruised the South China Sea as a guest of 'Uncle Sam'.

'Luck Be a Lady Tonight'

Ian Lacy-Smith

This is a story of how a detective police constable (DPC) and I seized opium and morphine with a street value of HK$4 million, by being in the right place at the right time, and despite a lack of radio communications or back-up. The encounter could have gone seriously wrong but with luck and a modicum of skill, at least by my DPC, we prevailed and obtained a successful conclusion.

During my second tour of duty in Hong Kong when I was serving as an inspector between 1966 and 1970, I was attached to the Narcotics Bureau of Criminal Investigation Department (CID) at Police Headquarters. After about a year of researching files, producing bulletins for Interpol and other administrative tasks, I was assigned an investigation team comprising a detective corporal and three detective constables. We were under the command of Acting Senior Inspector G.C. 'Big Bill' Morgan and the Superintendent, Operations, Gordon Riddell. Senior Inspector John Thorpe, who in due course went on to be the director of Special Branch, was in charge of surveillance and when the case I'm relating broke, the bureau as a whole was under the temporary command of Senior Superintendent Murray Todd.

On Saturday morning, 24th August 1968, I and three other investigation team inspectors were called into Mr Riddell's office for a briefing along these lines: 'A large shipment of drugs from Thailand is believed to be imminently delivered by boat in the Sai Kung area of the New Territories. A group of foreigners have arrived in Hong Kong to collect their payment from a local crime syndicate, but they have been holed up in a Kowloon hotel during the passing of the typhoon. Before the storm, they had been seen being escorted to various possible landing places including in Sai Kung and Clearwater Bay. For a few days, I arranged uniformed road blocks in strategic places to deter the movement of the drugs out of that area but I have now taken them off and am replacing them with your plain-clothes teams, each patrolling for six hours for the next twenty-four hours. With any luck they will be lured out. Ian, you will patrol from 02.00 to 08.00 hours tomorrow morning. Prepare accordingly and good luck. I will be on standby at my flat.' As we left I said to the boss: 'I hope you're not a heavy sleeper, sir, because I'll be giving you the good news at about 04.00 hours.' He just grunted and I was only joking but it was around 03.15 hours when I actually telephoned him!

My team's corporal was on leave but I decided not to call him back because I had been more impressed with the ability and experience of one of my DPCs, Li Fong, who, incidentally, was to progress to the well-earned rank of detective station sergeant. Mr Riddell had not called back my immediate commander Bill Morgan from leave either.

So it was up to Li Fong and myself, in my MGB sports car, and the other two DPCs in an old banger, to make the most of an early Sunday morning patrol. I couldn't think of anything else for each of us to carry but our service Colt .38 revolver, a pair of handcuffs, notebook, pen and an electric torch. Hand-held mobile phones were far in the future, and the Force's 'Motorola' radio system or even an old field telephone could not be set up at short notice. I was a little concerned about the lack of communication with my other two DPCs (whom I will name Ah Chan and Ah Wong) if we were to split up. In the circumstances I decided not to be separated for long and anyway, the chances of anything happening in the meantime were pretty remote, weren't they?

As instructed, Li Fong, Ah Chan and Ah Wong arrived at my Kowloon quarters at 01.30 hours and I said I would fully brief them when we reached the junction of Clearwater Bay Road and Hiram's Highway. In 1968, the latter was a narrow metalled road constructed post-war by the Army. It ran northwards and unlit for some five miles through farming land to the area of Tai Mong Tsai via Pak Sha Wan (Hebe Haven), Sai Kung and Tai Wan villages. Clearwater Bay Road is still the main road from East Kowloon to the bay of that name, ending at a car park about six miles south of Hiram's Highway. I had never driven beyond Sai Kung before but near Tai Wan is a concrete pier suitable for shallow-draft boats. That is where I later discovered the drugs had been landed.

When we arrived at the road junction, I instructed Ah Chan and Ah Wong to park in a place where they could note the number plates of all vehicles passing them in either direction along Clearwater Bay Road. I told them to use their headlights if necessary, and make a note of anything unusual, while Li Fong and I patrolled the whole length of Hiram's Highway. 'We won't be long,' I said, 'and then we can decide what to do next.' Off we went into the dark, not seeing any vehicles or anything unusual until, at around 02.30 hours and a mile past Sai Kung village, I saw the lights of a vehicle approaching about half a mile away and so I pulled into a passing bay to let it go by. It was a light-coloured saloon car and just before it reached us I raised my headlamps from dipped to full. This caused the driver to brake slightly before carrying on his way, during which pause, Li Fong would have had a good look at him. The driver was travelling on his own.

I had just pulled out to carry on with our patrol when I saw the lights of another vehicle approaching, so I reversed back into the passing bay to repeat the observation procedure. This time it was a light goods vehicle and when I again raised my headlights there were three men in the front looking either dazzled or startled. I let them carry on but thought it was a bit early for farmers or delivery men to be here. Suddenly Li Fong exclaimed: 'I think I know that man in the car. He came to Narcotics Bureau recently but as a companion of someone else, not to give a statement.' That was good enough for me to pull out with a squeal of tyres and chase after the goods vehicle. Fortunately I had no trouble in bringing it to a stop after I had cut in front of it. Li Fong jumped out first. We showed our warrant cards and Li went to the rear of the vehicle. Very quickly he returned with the message, 'Lots of opium, sir. The smell!' Whereupon I pulled out my revolver and held the three men at gun-point. Li Fong directed them to alight and squat down while he cautioned and handcuffed the men together. So far so fantastic, but it was to get even better.

Commercial vehicle stopped by police in remote area of Sai Kung
(Courtesy Hong Kong Police)

Next, I had to get Ah Chan and Ah Wong to the scene and then report the news to Gordon Riddell. Up at the road junction I found both DPCs snoring their heads off, but never mind that for the moment. 'Get down there,' I said, pointing down the road, 'a mile past Sai Kung, and help Li Fong with three arrests and a load of opium. I'll see you after I've phoned the boss from Sai Kung Police Station.' On the way to the station I said to myself, 'Please God, look after Li Fong until the troops arrive.' This was with good reason because I did not know how many more gangsters might be in the area. There was to be one more, a complete idiot as it turned out.

Around 03.40 hours, a pumped-up and excited Gordon Riddell puttered to the scene on a small motorbike from his flat at Silverstrand just a few miles away. I described our seizure and three arrests and mentioned the man in the first car who I thought had been leading the way. 'Well,' he said, 'that's fine anyway, now for the others we have had under surveillance and I'll get the photo and fingerprint guys here as well,' and off he went to telephone from Sai Kung Police Station. When he returned he told me that he had ordered the arrest of two Malaysian and three Thai men whom he hoped were still in their hotel rooms in Kowloon, and also one local Chinese male seen during surveillance. We now expected to charge four locals and five foreigners with serious drug offences.

This total was to reach an unexpected number of ten whilst we were still at the scene. Even now I find it hard to understand how anyone could be so stupid as to return to a scene with police present, even if he had been ordered to do so. Yes, it was the same driver who had been seen by Li Fong when passing us in a car ahead of the goods vehicle.

This is how one Chau Sau-tai came to be arrested. It was getting light as dawn was breaking at about 05.00 hours and I was examining one of the cartons of drugs, when to my amazement I saw the same light-coloured saloon we had seen earlier, slowly approaching our hive of activity. When I waved to the driver to stop he did so, quite unfazed, and our conversation went as follows in Cantonese:

'Good morning, sir, can you tell me why you are here so early in the morning?'

'I'm looking for a friend as we arranged to go swimming. What's the matter?'

'I think you know. We are all police. Get out, you're under arrest and I now caution you for being in possession of illegal drugs.'

Chau did not reply. He could hardly have admitted that he was there to find out whether the goods vehicle had broken down. As already mentioned, there were no mobile phones in those days, which was awkward for my team, but for Chau, the lack of communications was calamitous and led to two lengthy jail sentences.

I then handed Chau over to Li Fong, hoping that the shock of his arrest would panic him into revealing his paymasters. I knew this was unlikely but it was still possible at this early stage. I realised I could make a 'constructive possession' charge against him really stick if I could establish a link between him and one of the three in the goods vehicle. This was achieved later when we found an address book at Chau's home with the name and address of the driver of the goods vehicle in it. We also found his own details in an address book belonging to that same driver who had further-more hired the saloon car in his own name so that Chau would not be implicated. All very careless and avoidable. The four men were duly convicted at the Supreme Court for possession of 640 kilograms of raw opium and 49.674 kilograms of morphine hydrochloride destined for the heroin trade. Three were sentenced to seven years imprisonment and the fourth to three-and-a-half years. But all four were also convicted with the five foreigners for conspiracy to import dangerous drugs and all nine defendants were sentenced to six years imprisonment. The local Chinese arrested with the foreigners was acquitted in the committal proceedings preceding the two Supreme Court trials.

Evidence against the five foreigners largely centred around the surveillance, during which they were seen visiting a fortune teller whom they asked to foretell when the drugs would arrive in Hong Kong. This was after the typhoon had delayed the shipment from Thailand and they wanted to know whether there would be a happy outcome. They were also seen before the storm being driven to the Sai Kung area but I cannot be sure whether Chau Sau-tai helped with the driving, though he had certainly been seen with them, and was therefore an important link between them and the seizure.

Another important link between the foreigners and my seizure came my way in the shape of a mere slip of paper with ten numbers on it. It had been found inside the passport of one of the Thai men arrested and I concluded that the numbers were the weights in grams of ten of the blocks of morphine. Tucked in with the hundreds of packages of raw opium were fifty blocks of morphine, and each one weighed close to one kilogram, total weight 49.674 kgs. The exact weight of each block in grams was written on its wrapping and I found there were fifty different such numbers ranging from about 990 grams to 1010 grams. As there were five foreigners, would each have a fifth share in the morphine alone? Almost certainly, I thought, because when I examined my own list of the fifty numbers I was delighted to see that the ten numbers on the slip of paper were amongst them and not duplicated. My one-fifth share each of morphine theory was therefore strong enough to be put to the jury and must have added to the case against all five foreigners.

I concluded luck was certainly a lady for me that night, but Li Fong's memory was really the key. Some of the traffickers could have covered their tracks but did not do so, and will have rued their carelessness and stupidity over several years in prison. Fortunately, surveillance was tight before the arrests and everyone in our team had been working professionally. Those of us involved in the operation, including Li and myself, were rewarded with Commissioner's Commendations. Fifty years on and technology being what it is, it would probably need even more luck to achieve such a successful result. It was all the more satisfying then to have been able to do so and make a small dent in the terrible drugs trade.

The drug haul (Courtesy Hong Kong Police)

Midwife Duty

William C. Trotter

On leaving Police Training School in March 1956, I was posted to Western Division. I was in my very first week on night patrol, and on my own, because my mentor Ron McEwan (who was later killed in the line of duty in the 1967 Disturbances) was unwell and unable to accompany me. Suddenly, I was dragged into a building in Third Street by a terrified Chinese man, who, holding my belt, pulled me up a flight of stairs and into a cubicle. There, lying on a bed, was a young woman obviously in an advanced state of giving birth.

I had a fair idea of how babies started but no idea of how they came in to the world. All I could think of was that hot water came into the equation somewhere and after the young man had brought me a bowl, I looked at him and he looked at me, in the mutual realisation that neither of us knew what to do next. With that, two things happened simultaneously. First, the baby started to come, and next, an older Chinese woman rushed through the door, sized up the situation, and promptly threw me my hat and bundled me out of the door. I stood on the pavement outside, a quivering jelly, and it was a few minutes before I could trust my shaking legs to move.

This experience frightened me, as I came to realise I could have done more harm than good. Next day I went up to the Matilda Hospital and met with the sister in the maternity unit and explained what had happened. She gave me a two-hour lesson on the essentials of childbirth and what to do in the event of a similar situation in the future. Surely this could never happen again!

On 24th September 1968, it did happen again. I was then an assistant superintendent, acting as Superintendent, Traffic, HQ. I was also company commander of the Kowloon Police Headquarters internal security company. At 01.30 hours one morning, during a joint police/military exercise, in Kowloon, which involved a mock riot in Gillies Street, near the Hung Hom Ferry Concourse, I received a radio call from an army unit nearby, saying a young woman was about to give birth on the pavement and could anyone help.

I answered their call, set up some blankets from the army vehicle for the woman to lie on and more blankets draped over railings to give some privacy. There was a young girl with the couple and I asked her to bring hot water, towels, scissors and string. I then delivered a baby boy, to the delight of everyone, including the Commissioner of Police, Ted Eates, who turned up in the middle of the activity. He asked if I knew what I was doing and I assured him I did. The mother and newborn were taken to Kwong Wah Hospital, where, as the *China Mail* reported, all went well. It was a good news story at a time when we needed some good press. The Police Welfare Unit arranged for the baby boy's future education.

About a month later the governor was dined-in at the Gazetted Officers' Mess. His Excellency the Governor, Sir David Trench, said to the commissioner that he would bet ten Hong Kong dollars that I had not actually carried out the delivery, but he was assured by the commissioner that I had, since he had witnessed it. Whereupon, the governor instructed his aide-

Superintendent Bill Trotter—he delivered the baby.

A police superintendent early today delivered a baby on a Hunghom pavement in the middle of a mock riot.

Mother and child were rushed to Kwong Wah Hospital. This morning they were both "doing fine".

It is the second time in his 13-year career with the Hongkong police force that Superintendent Bill Trotter has been pressed into emergency midwife duty.

And Supt Trotter, 34, said from Traffic Office, Hongkong Island, today: "It was all in the line of duty.

Trouble

"We were taking part in a combined police-military exercise in Kowloon, and we had staged a mock riot in Gillies Avenue, near the Hunghom Ferry Concourse.

"Suddenly we saw a couple who appeared to be in trouble, so I went to have a look.

"It was obvious that the woman was about to have a baby—so there was only one thing for it, and that was to do the best we could at the time.

"There was a little girl with the couple, and I sent her off for some dressings, towels, and hot and cold water.

"It was 1.30 am but the girl showed a lot of sense, and she managed to get the stuff we wanted.

Difficult

"The delivery was a bit difficult, but we managed, and the next thing I knew in all the confusion was that an ambulance had arrived.

"By that time, the mother had had the child — a little boy — right there on the pavement."

China Mail, 24th September 1968

de-camp to hand over ten dollars to the commissioner.

Many years later, long after I had left the Force, I was interviewing suitable people for a vacancy in my department in a large multinational company at which I worked. Discussing this particular applicant's background, it turned out that he was the army officer who had made that first radio call about the baby! What are the odds on that?

Bizarre Justice

Roland Dibbs

One evening in 1970, a taxi-driver came to Sai Kung Police Station, where I was sub-divisional inspector (station commander) and reported that a man had hired his taxi in Kowloon and told him to drive to Tai Mong Tsai village which, at that time, was the end of the metalled road.

The driver said that the man made him get out of the taxi and perform a sex act on him. He said that the man then got into the taxi and drove off after which he, the taxi driver, made his way to the police station.

Whilst he was making his report, a team of Customs and Excise (C&E) officers came to the report room with a man they had arrested for using industrial diesel (which was taxed at a lower rate than that for private vehicles) in the taxi he was driving. The first taxi-driver immediately said that the man the C&E had arrested was the one who had stolen his taxi. When asked if he was sure, he replied that he was absolutely certain, not least of all, because the man was wearing football boots!

It finished up with the original taxi-driver being charged by C&E with using industrial diesel in his taxi; the man brought in by C&E was charged with a series of offences involving assault and taking a vehicle without the owner's consent.

If only all cases could have been solved with such ease.

The Agency of Last Resort

Peter Halliday

'The basic mission for which police exist is to prevent crime and disorder. . . .' So said Sir Robert Peel in 1829 and this dictum has stood the test of time. Nevertheless, 'basic' is the operative word. A more practical mission statement these days, if not since the dawn of recognisable modern policing, is that the police is all things to all people. We are supposed to be able to help in any and all circumstances, hence the received wisdom that the police is the agency of last resort.

There is simply no accounting for the infinite diversity of reports that members of the public make to the police. The majority are routine and unexciting but as with life, there is always the unexpected. Indeed, reports to the police span the entire spectrum of the human condition.

Hereunder are two in which I was personally involved. They are at the opposite extremities of the spectrum to which I have just referred.

The Case of the Missing Boat

Typhoon Rose scored virtually a direct hit on Hong Kong on the night of 16 August 1971. It was the most violent and intense cyclone to hit the territory since Typhoon Wanda in 1962. Sustained winds near the centre exceeded 140 miles per hour.

On the morning after – the 17th – I was on duty in the Marine Harbour Police Station at Marine Police Headquarters, Tsim Sha Tsui, when a man came in and asked to see an officer. He appeared relaxed and was certainly well mannered and polite. I was unoccupied at that moment and beckoned him to the end of the counter, across which we then conferred.

I asked him what the problem was and he said, as accurately as I can remember: 'We have lost our boat.' Note that he used the term *teng* (craft), not *suen* (ship).

At that time, dozens of reports were coming in of large numbers of foundered fishing and pleasure boats, and so I associated the man's statement with this type of craft. I said that we would record details and endeavour to find it over the coming days.

The man listened patiently and then said: 'It's quite a big boat.' I was still thinking small and made some sympathetic reply. Not to be put off, the man said: 'It really is a *big* boat.'

Something in his tone of voice rang a warning bell and I said: 'OK, exactly how big is it?'

'It's about 240 feet long and 2,600 tons. And there are people on it,' he replied.

God Almighty! I thought. 'Tell me exactly what this ship is!'

'It's the Hong Kong-Macau ferry *Fat Shan*.'

I knew all about the *Fat Shan*, having travelled on it. Over the next few minutes the story came out. The captain had offloaded all passengers and cast off from the Macau Ferry Pier on Hong Kong Island the previous morning, saying that he was going to anchor

The wreck of the Fat Shan, *19 August 1971*

somewhere and 'ride out the storm'. Nothing had been heard from the ship since.

I contacted the Marine Control Room and briefed them. The resident Royal Naval minesweepers and Marine police launches were alerted and the search began. As it turned out, this was of short duration as four survivors had managed to swim to Ma Wan Island in the Western Approaches and had hailed a passing craft, whence the authorities were informed.

The *Fat Shan* had anchored in the Rambler Channel the previous day, off the northeastern tip of Lantau Island. It had reportedly dragged its anchor/s, collided with two other ocean-going cargo ships, and capsized.

Eighty-eight crew members went down with the ship.

I was not involved with the investigation into the disaster and the resulting inquest. I was put in charge of the identification of the bodies at the Kowloon Public Mortuary, but this Dante's Inferno is another story.

The Case of the Mysterious Hole

By 1972, I had 'come ashore' from the Marine Police and been posted to the Tsim Sha Tsui Police Station. (Physically, I moved only some 10 yards or so from the Marine Harbour Station! They were co-located.)

I was in the report room one afternoon when a most irate individual came in. Indeed, he was beside himself. I steered this erupting volcano away from the main milieu and asked him what was the matter.

'Those _____ rascals have knocked a hole in my wall!' he shouted. We established that his 'wall' was the wall of his high-rise apartment in Mody Road. Not unnaturally, I started thinking in terms of 'burglary with breaking.' Nevertheless, this did not quite ring true particularly when he told me that the wall was the *outside* wall and that nothing was missing.

I decided that the matter required an on-site investigation and I accompanied the complainant back to his apartment. It was quite a number of floors up. Sure enough, under the large window in the sitting room of his small flat was a neat rectangular hole through which fresh air now flowed. The villains had considerately swept the floor clean of debris, which was more intriguing still.

Having examined the 'scene,' the next step was clearly that hallowed police investigative technique known as the 'neighbourhood canvass'. None of the tenants on that floor could help, so we went down to the management office.

It did not take long to assess the individual on duty as being intellectually challenged and questioning him was akin to pulling hen's teeth. However, he ultimately agreed that earlier that day he had let some workers into Mr _____'s flat 'to install his new air conditioner. They said that they will come back later.' At this statement I thought for a moment that Mr _____ was going to go into cardiac arrest. 'What air conditioner?!' he screamed.

The perceptive reader will guess the rest. The staff in the management office had directed the workers to the wrong floor.

Suggesting very firmly to this individual that the management office make good the new unglazed window in Mr _____'s flat, I left them at it and made a dignified withdrawal.

Riding Out Typhoon Rose

Iain Ward

Typhoon Rose was one of the worst storms to hit Hong Kong in the last fifty years. Winds gusted between 130 knots (150 mph) and 150 knots (172 mph) and some 12 inches of rain fell during the storm. Over 150 people were killed (no one knows the exact number) and nearly 6,000 rendered homeless. Thirty-seven ocean-going ships were wrecked and 300 fishing vessels either sunk or irreparably damaged.

In August 1971, I was in command of Police Launch No. 1, *Sea Lion*, command vessel for Eastern Waters in Hong Kong. She was 111 feet long, weighed 250 tons and had a crew of about thirty. The number fluctuated because of the additional role she had at the time as the fleet's basic training vessel for those of all ranks joining the command. This was an experimental project initiated by Jack O'Meara, the then Chief Inspector Marine.

For this reason, the 'permanent' crew was quite small, about a dozen of us. The original commander when the project started was Senior Inspector Lau Kai-fat, former commander of the Marine Police Training School, and I was attached as his second in command because of my qualifications and experience from my previous service in the Merchant Navy. Between us we picked our deck sergeant, Li Hing-man, the bosun, the three senior coxswains and the senior engineers. The chief engineer and the cooks came with the ship! Everyone else on board was brand new to the command and would spend a month or two with us before moving on to other postings in the fleet. In fact, Lau Kai-fat himself only lasted a couple of months in charge before Jack O'Meara found he couldn't do without him at Marine Headquarters and I was left (very happily) as both OC Launch and assistant sector commander; a unique position for a two-pip inspector at that time.

In the days before the typhoon struck we had, unusually, been deployed in the western area of Victoria Harbour to prevent the intimidation of cargo workers on ships by communist activists (a big problem at the time). We couldn't conduct our usual training exercises there because we were on constant standby for callout but we were aware of Typhoon Rose in the offing (typhoon signal No. 1 had gone up on the 14th August) so we had used the time to get out the typhoon moorings and train our young marine policemen on the handling and maintenance of heavier gear than they normally dealt with day to day. *Sea Lion* was well equipped in this respect, being issued with special composite mooring hawsers (known as 'hurricane hawsers' in the Royal Navy) made up of doubled eight-inch natural fibre ropes combined with three-inch wire tails so that she could be made secure in a more restricted area than that needed to swing freely round a buoy. We would not have this luxury: Aberdeen Harbour, where our typhoon moorings were located, was one of the world's most crowded, being home to some 20,000 fishermen and boat people aboard 3,000 junks on an ordinary day, let alone when there was a typhoon in the offing.

Despite our preparations, we weren't very worried about Rose to start with; she appeared to be heading well south of Hong Kong. I don't remember being particularly worried even when No. 3 signal was hoisted on the morning of August 16th, although I requested permission to leave Victoria Harbour to lay in extra rations 'just in case'. In fact I just wanted the crew to have a chance to go for a *yum cha* (snack) after what had so far been a pretty boring trip. So off we went to Sok Kwu Wan on Lamma Island, where most of us headed off to the nearest tea house. Our cups were barely raised to our lips when the duty *fei din* (radio operator) came panting in to say that No. 7 signal had just been raised and that Typhoon Rose was now heading directly for Hong Kong. On the way back to the ship I met my cook, Lee Shing-on, with a huge bundle of noodles that he had bought at the local store; something that we were all to be very grateful for later.

At Aberdeen Typhoon Shelter we were the senior vessel for both South and East Sectors as our sister ship PL2 *Sea Tiger*, the command launch for South Sector, was in dock. There were altogether four police vessels there that day: *Sea Lion*, PL28 *Sea Roamer*, PL29 *Sea Rider* (70ft patrol launches) and MD29, a 67ft Marine Department vessel painted in Marine Police colours and on full-time loan to the fleet. The combined crews added up to nearly 70 men. PL28, PL29 and MD29 were all South Sector vessels and soon after we arrived at Aberdeen, Colin Reigate, the South Sector commander, came out from the local operations base on PL25 (a 20ft harbour patrol boat which was later sunk by the typhoon) to check their moorings. The other East Sector vessels (two 70ft patrol vessels and the Sai Kung Harbour patrol launch) had already found safe havens up on the east coast, so I was able to concentrate, with the able assistance of Li Hing-man, on snugging our own ship down for the trial to come.

We had lowered our dory (a useful heavy work boat) on the way into the typhoon shelter, so were able to make fast with slip-ropes between our designated mooring buoys fairly easily (or rather between *Sea Tiger*'s buoys, as there were at least a dozen fishing boats already made fast to ours). We then (very carefully) lowered the starboard anchor into the boat, broke the chain cable and shackled it to the ring on the buoy. The anchor itself was then hoisted back aboard and lashed down on the afterdeck. The heaviest of the composite mooring hawsers was then led through the bullring at the bow and shackled to the buoy, the pins on both shackles being moused with seizing wire.

At the stern, composite hawsers were led from each quarter and shackled in the same way to the after buoy. Once their lengths had been adjusted so that all the hawsers were taking an even strain, the wire turns round the bitts were lashed in place with light line and the starboard anchor cable walked back on the windlass until the catenary almost reached the bottom of the harbour (to dampen 'snatch' strains on the bow cable). We then hoisted the boat and lashed that down as well before walking round to check that all the awnings and anything else that might be at risk was safely stowed or securely lashed in place. The last things to be securely stowed below decks were the light machine guns from the bridge wings and the heavy 0.5-inch machine gun from its mounting on the main deck; we certainly weren't going to need those over the next few hours! I now felt we were about as ready as we could be and Li Hing-man and I went for a beer in the wheelhouse while the cooks prepared an early supper for everyone. It was to be the last beer we were able to enjoy for quite a while.

As the day wore on, the gusts of wind grew stronger, mainly from the east so that to start with we were protected from the worst of them by Brick Hill. Our launches were moored in a line abreast, all pointing roughly north with our sterns to the new sea wall across the harbour entrance and the open sea beyond. Thus, as the wind backed towards the northeast after the No. 9 signal was hoisted at 9.10 pm, the full force of the gale was channelled down Wong Chuk Hang valley to strike us on the beam. The gusts became almost continuous, impossible to stand against as they picked up spray from the harbour which combined with the driving rain to smash against our windward side like huge white hands. With nothing much to do except trust in our moorings, it could have been frightening for our trainees had it not been for Sergeant Li and the other old hands in the crew who did a marvellous job keeping up their morale and finding 'essential' work for them to do.

By the time the No. 10 signal was hoisted at 10.50 pm the whole typhoon shelter was a maelstrom of white water and spray, and the gusts on the beam were heeling the ship over to port quite worryingly. Pleasure craft were being torn from their moorings and came spinning past us out of the darkness and then on towards the coast of Ap Lei Chau Island, while the fishing boats that were relying on their anchors were beginning to drag and becoming a potential problem. Luckily, we had some big fenders and we lashed them along the gunwales in strategic places, a difficult job in the conditions and no doubt made more awkward by my order that everyone with duties on deck should wear a lifejacket.

The winds steadily got worse and sometime after midnight there was a power cut ashore which took away all our points of reference. Our moorings appeared to be holding well however and the crew was in good heart, the biggest worries in my mind being the danger of a fishing boat smashing into us and the heeling of the ship under the wind pressure on the starboard beam. This took the form of sickening lurches as the gusts hit us, and as they increased in strength and frequency the vessel often didn't have time to return to the vertical before the next one hit.

Finally, at about 1.30 am, a series of gusts hit us that pushed the ship over to about 15 degrees. She hung there, then lurched further – and then further. I was in the wheelhouse with a coxswain, a trainee and the radio operator and our wonderful cook, Mr Lee, who had just brought us bowls of noodles which had been placed on the ledge by the bridge windows. I remember looking *up* at the starboard wheelhouse door and then watching the bowls of noodles leaving their ledge and hitting the port bulkhead several feet away instead of the deck. At that moment I really thought she was going to go over.

But she didn't. She suddenly straightened up and the heeling stopped. A moment later I found out why, as the lookout posted on the afterdeck came running to report that the after moorings had gone. I checked the forward moorings with the Aldis lamp and saw that the mooring hawser was bar-taut but led straight down into the water – there was no sign of the buoy. For the moment I couldn't work out what had happened; the buoy might be dragging or damaged or both. All around was still utterly black with no visible reference of any kind, but there was no doubt that our position had changed as the wind was now on the bow and still blowing at hurricane strength. The fishing boats around us were in chaos, smashing into each other and moving *en masse* towards us as the wind drove them. It was quite a worrying moment.

The ever-dependable Li Hing-man appeared and I asked him to take a party and drop the port anchor underfoot in case we lost the forward moorings while I checked the situation aft. There the situation was even more confused. Again there was no sign of the buoy and the mooring hawsers, which were still taut, led straight under the counter. At the time, because of the report that the after moorings had parted, I concluded (incorrectly) that they must have snagged the propellers in some way, which meant that we daren't use the engines to lessen the strain on the forward moorings. But

I didn't have long to think about it before another problem reared its head. Having originally been moored on our port beam, PL29 was now almost directly astern of us with a mass of big fishing boats rolling and battering at her port side. She was already dismasted and as I watched I could see all the awning stanchions and the big engine room vents being smashed by the fishing vessels' high poops.

Li Hing-man came to report that the port anchor was down and from the feel of the cable he could tell that we were holding position. This was good news but we didn't have long to enjoy it because at that moment many of the fishing vessels that had originally made fast to the other government buoys broke free and bore down on us, driven by the screaming, deafening winds that were still blowing well in excess of 100 knots. Half a dozen of them hit us, in most cases glancing blows because of our change in attitude to the wind but still causing damage to the gunwales and facing plates around the upper deck. Two of them managed to grapple on to us and in fact stayed with us until dawn, but the rest carried on and slammed into PL29's starboard side. In moments the wheelhouse was smashed in and I began to seriously worry about the crew. None of them were in view; they were obviously holed up in the engine room and in the forward crew accommodation below deck. At least the hull seemed to be holding up under the battering which gave us time to deal with the next problem: PL28.

Our change in position had actually been caused by our typhoon buoys dragging, although the succession of events after that had been so swift that we had not had the time to properly assess what had happened. One effect of the dragging had been that our stern buoy had got entangled with PL28's forward buoy and pulled it out of position so that the strain on the launch's moorings was intense. Also she was now as vulnerable to the fishing junks being blown down on us as PL29 (remember that through all this the wind was at hurricane strength, visibility was virtually nil and the rain torrential, flying at us horizontally with the force of bullets).

Her OC, Sergeant Wong Yin-sum, acted swiftly and decisively, cutting his stern moorings with the galley chopper and using his engines to swing the launch parallel with us so that we could get lines aboard and haul her alongside to make fast on our port side. Our trainees got a lot of practical rope work experience that night.

By about 2.30 am the winds were still gusting as strongly as ever but there was the occasional lull when wind strength would drop to 50–60 knots or so. PL29 was still being battered and we could see that the whole roof of the forward superstructure in way of the radio cabin and the OC's cabin was starting to lift off. During one of the lulls someone opened the foredeck escape hatch from the crew's quarters and waved, and I decided to seize the moment to try and evacuate the crew. As she was directly downwind of us we were able to get a heaving line across to her and used that to transfer a heavy mooring line which her crew made fast to the big brass bitts on the foredeck. We then used our afterdeck capstan to haul her closer by main force; in hindsight I shudder to think of the strain we were putting on the gear but I could think of no better way to do it in the circumstances. We then took the whole crew off over our stern with a lifeline on each man as he made the transfer. Once they were all aboard and accounted for we slacked the mooring line off but kept it made fast. I also posted a couple of men to keep a constant eye on her; she was in an awful state but she was still afloat with fishing vessels all around her and I was very aware that she had a full outfit of stores, arms and ammunition aboard.

We then at last had time for a cup of tea and some of Mr Lee's excellent noodles – as, indeed, did the crews of PLs 28 and 29 and quite a few of the fishing families from the vessels made fast to our starboard side (Mr Lee performed wonders that night and I later put him up for an official commendation). Happily, everything held together for the rest of the night although we had to keep battened down for several more hours. But the wind slowly subsided and No. 10 typhoon signal was replaced by No. 6 at 4.40 am. It in turn was replaced by No. 3 at 9.15 am. Come the dawn we were able to work out what had happened: our moorings had in fact held perfectly and came off easily when we slacked them off to replace them with slip ropes. It was the typhoon buoys that had shifted; torn from the sea bed by the sheer force exerted by the 'supreme winds' when they took us on the beam at the height of the storm.

And boy, were we glad that they had!

Postscript: The coming of the dawn and the lessening of the typhoon winds were not, of course, the end of the story for the tired members of *Sea Lion's* crew. The seas outside Aberdeen were still huge, and we had a long list of distress messages that had come in during the night (and were still coming in) to check out. In some cases we were able to help; in others all we could do was collect the bodies. The aftermath of any typhoon leaves a long shadow and the effects of Rose were more far-reaching than most. Our story is just one of the many that came out of that long, long night.

Grass-Roots Diplomacy

C.R. Emmett

In February 1972, US President Richard M. Nixon visited China. The visit came after years of negotiation and marked China's slow and cautious emergence into the world community. Mao's Cultural Revolution was pretty much over, but a few rowdy scrap-ends remained. On the Chinese side of the Hong Kong border, people wore ill-fitting Mao tunics and trousers, and there were fiery billboards extolling the virtues of the great helmsman and the invincibility of the masses. Loudspeakers pumped out scratchy music to workers tilling the fields.

At the border village of Sha Tau Kok, the Hong Kong Police and the British Army performed daily patrols down Chung-Ying Street, literal translation: China-England Street. The street did not look much, it is just a few yards wide but the border ran right down the middle. Guarding the Chinese side was a solitary People's Liberation Army soldier. He carried a Kalashnikov assault rifle and wore a one-size-fits-all uniform of green britches, Mao tunic with red collar tabs, and a soft cap with a red star above the peak. The Chinese soldiers looked intimidating but they were very disciplined and the Chung-Ying Street patrols would pass without incident. Still, the mood in the village was tense. Sometimes, children threw fireworks at our patrols, and workers on the Chinese side frequently shouted abuse. Just five years earlier, during the 1967 Disturbances, disciplined gunfire from China had raked the Sha Tau Kok police post and killed five Hong Kong policemen.

The border fence ran from Sha Tau Kok in the east to Deep Bay in the west. It was a rickety, chain-link affair that took no account of centuries- old ancestral land boundaries. As a result, the Shum Chun People's Collective worked land on the Hong Kong side of the border while some Hong Kong farmers worked land on the Chinese side. It was all totally illegal but in a display of pragmatic reality, the Hong Kong government installed gates to make the daily commute a little easier. The arrangement worked fine but rather than walk to the gates, many farm workers made shortcuts by cutting holes in the fence. Each month the police had to survey the fence for damage. This was a good excuse to get together with the army and carry out another joint patrol. The fence patrol meandered along a narrow border road through pleasant countryside. A dirt road ran along the Chinese side and the PLA manned little guard posts every quarter mile. The Chinese soldiers were doubtless pretty bored so when they saw the patrol, they made a show of cocking their Kalashnikovs and shouting defiance at the forces of imperialism.

As Nixon and Mao raised their glasses of *maotai*, I was starting a six-month attachment to Sha Tau Kok sub-division. The station commander was a chief inspector, known as the sub-divisional inspector. Above him, at Frontier Division Headquarters, was Senior Superintendent Stan Flower, the man in charge of all border policing.

I had been at Sha Tau Kok for about a month when I did my first fence patrol. A constable and I boarded a police Land Rover. An army sergeant and four soldiers boarded an army one-tonner and together, we took off for Lin Ma Hang village. The walk back to Sha Tau Kok took less than an hour and apart from noting down a few holes in the fence, there was nothing to report. As we neared Sha Tau Kok, the army sergeant slipped and dropped a flare pistol. It was only a moment or two before he realised it was missing but by the time he turned to retrieve it, a Mainland farmer had nipped through a hole in the fence, picked it up and darted back into China. For a while, he stood swinging it round his head and baiting us with some pretty scathing remarks.

As soon as I got back to Sha Tau Kok's police post, I reported the incident to the SDI who immediately called the boss, Stan Flower. Stan should have passed it up to Police Headquarters. Instead, he collared a Mandarin-speaking sergeant, hopped aboard a Land Rover and fifteen minutes later was getting a briefing from the SDI. Stan, the SDI, the sergeant interpreter and I went down to the border fence. There was a Chinese soldier on the other side of the fence and our sudden appearance piqued his interest. He came closer.

'Excuse me, Sir,' Stan called.

'*Wei – Tongzhi,*' the sergeant translated. He used the Mandarin word for 'comrade', instead of 'sir'.

The Chinese soldier blinked. His jaw dropped. This was new stuff.

Stan Flower raised a hand like someone greeting a friend at a railway station. 'Sir?'

'*Wei – Tongzhi.*'

The Chinese soldier did not answer. Instead, he took a step back, cocked his Kalashnikov and levelled it at us.

Stan was unruffled. He explained that a British soldier had dropped his flare pistol, which was not an offensive weapon but rather a safety device. We would very much like to have it back, he added. From the Chinese soldier, silence. Stan repeated himself several times. At last, the Chinese soldier spoke. The sergeant interpreter put his head close to Stan's. 'He says, "Wait".' The soldier turned and scurried away. Shortly afterwards, he returned with three others. They all wore the same baggy uniforms with no badges of rank. One was older and the others were very deferential to him.

Stan repeated the request.

The Chinese soldiers said nothing but the older one gave a barely perceptible nod then they turned and left. The next day, a Mainland farmer came to the Sha Tau Kok village police post and handed back the flare pistol. He said his mischievous son had picked it up as a joke and he hoped there were no bad feelings.

Today, this kind of contact would be normal but in 1972, China was the great, closed empire. The American Secretary of State, Henry Kissinger, had spent years building a tenuous relationship with China. If Stan Flower had reported the incident to Police Headquarters, from there, it would have made tortuous progress to the Foreign Office in London who may, or may not, have decided to open negotiations. Instead, a Hong Kong policeman and a Chinese soldier conducted a common-sense act of grass-roots diplomacy.

A Salty Solution

Roland Dibbs

In the early 1970s, I was the sub-divisional inspector (SDI or station commander) of Sai Kung where the High Island Reservoir was being constructed. In conjunction with the scheme, the village at the western end of the proposed reservoir, which would be inundated, was in receipt of very generous compensation for the residents consisting of new flats, shops and cash compensation for trees and plants.

Another village, which was in the centre of the area to be inundated, was refused compensation because the villagers had moved from another village at the eastern end of the peninsula, which was not inside the area to be covered by the reservoir. The District Office had informed the villagers that they were not entitled to compensation because they could move back to their original village.

One morning, two young officers from the District Office reported to the police station that when they had approached the village, they had been pelted with rags soaked in urine. I went to the village, accompanied by a sergeant, and questioned the women, who admitted the offence. They were arrested and conveyed to the station where they were charged with common assault. They were bailed to appear at the magistracy the next morning, where I expected them to be bound over or receive a small fine.

However, later that morning, their husbands came to the station and said their wives had been sentenced to a month's imprisonment. A meeting was set up with the district officer (DO) but the villagers would only deal with the police and refused to speak to him.

I then contacted the chairman of the Heung Yee Kuk (a New Territories association which tried to look after the interests of villagers) and asked if he could assist. In response, he provided a lawyer who had recently returned from ten years practise in the UK. I met with him and he proposed going to court the next morning to ask the magistrate to reconsider his previous judgement on the grounds that the women had not been represented and had not realised the severity of the offence, to which they had pleaded guilty. The next morning, at the court, the magistrate agreed and set the case down for a further hearing a month later.

I, in the meantime, had discovered a memorandum in the dusty archives at the police station, written by a DO about twenty years previously, which included a résumé of each of the, then, ninety villages in the Sai Kung area.

In respect of the village at the eastern end of the peninsula, from which the villagers had moved, he had written 'the village and surrounding area, because of its proximity to the open sea, had become inundated with salt and could not therefore be cultivated . . . it would take a philanthropist of unlimited means to return the village to an inhabitable state.'

I conferred with the lawyer and he agreed that when the case resumed, he would plead the women 'guilty' but I would be asked to give evidence in mitigation, introducing the DO's memo in evidence.

The magistrate agreed, although he expressed some surprise at my appearing for the defence when my name was on the prosecution charge sheet.

In the event, the magistrate sympathised with the villagers' situation and bound the women over to keep the peace, recommending that the case be brought to the attention of the District Office.

This was done, and in light of the memorandum, the village received the same level of compensation as the other village being inundated.

The villagers went home happy and I achieved my purpose in keeping the peace in circumstances which could have erupted into a violent situation.

The '633' Squad

John Murray

Having left Police Training School (PTS) in mid-October 1973, we were all to do a spell in the Colony Special Duty Squad. This was an anti-drugs and gambling squad which had no boundaries as to where it acted in the territory. It was also under no obligation to tell anyone where it was about to strike. Superintendent Ko Chun led us and his deputy was Chief Inspector Jim Main. This unit was much better known as *'Luk Saam Saam'*, which is Cantonese for 'Six Three Three'. It was so named after the exploits of the fictional WWII Royal Air Force '633 Squadron' from the British film of the same name. It was an exercise to get us used to policing the colony and doing the paperwork necessary to take people to court.

We were briefed for the first time by Mr Ko, who left us in no doubt as to what he expected from us. It was going to be hard work, with many periods of observations, acting on tip offs and intelligence, and many long hours carrying out operations. He was not kidding. At the briefing we were divided into teams of three. We also arranged a series of rendezvous points at various strategic locations throughout the colony and we referred to them by a number.

After an initial couple of days to settle in and study available information, we were ready for our first raid. On 23rd October, we raided second-floor premises at No. 61 Russell Street in Causeway Bay where there was an illegal gambling operation. After using an axe and crowbar to gain entry we arrested ninety-one people and seized a large amount of money and gambling paraphernalia. At Wan Chai Police Station we were not very popular. The cells were quickly overwhelmed as were all available rooms that were reasonably secure. Each prisoner had to be documented, searched and personal property listed and signed for. A charge sheet then had to be prepared as well as a bail sheet. All the exhibits had to be listed and stored away. We got off duty at 8.00 am and the officer who had been chosen to lead the raid, Chris Beck, had to be at court that morning. Two of the prisoners pleaded guilty as they were from Singapore and did not want to return for a later court appearance. All the other eighty-nine pleaded not guilty and so a full case file had to be prepared. It was a pretty big one when it was completed.

On our next raid, we had information that there was a reinforced metal door on the only entrance, so we turned up with a Stihl chainsaw. Dave Madoc-Jones was put in charge of it. When we got the go-ahead to hit the place, we all piled into a lift and went up several floors to our destination. Dave was a bit worried that the saw might not start quickly enough when we got there, so he had started the engine at the bottom and we stupidly had got into the lift with him. By the time we got out, the lift was so full of smoke that we staggered about coughing and spluttering and trying not to be sick, unable to hear anything due to the ringing in our ears from the two-stroke engine. By the time we had used the saw to gain entry, the money from the gambling establishment had gone out of the window and down the stairwell. Luckily we managed to recover it. Another successful raid. But only just!

A few days later, after being briefed by Chief Inspector Perkins in Kowloon, Dave Fairley and I went looking for pornographic literature at a bookstall in an alley opposite Bristol Avenue. We decided to pretend to be off-duty soldiers. After only a few moments, the bookstall proprietor offered us some pornographic magazines and then, to our surprise, asked us if we would like to see some films. We ad-libbed and readily agreed. So, after a phone call, he took us to a dingy apartment on Nathan Road where another man indicated to us to sit on an old settee and demanded thirty dollars from each of us, which we paid. We then watched four pornographic films screened using a noisy old 8mm projector. Video recorders were just coming onto the market at that time. We were then shown our way out. It was the first time in my life that I had seen pornographic films and I was very surprised at the extremely candid content. Later that day we obtained warrants and hit the bookshop and the flat where both men were arrested and the offending material seized.

As the officer responsible for these arrests, I was at court the following morning at 9 am, and after they were found guilty, I had to return to the squad where we were briefed for another gambling raid, this time in the Yau Ma Tei area of Kowloon. Just after 10 pm we hit No. 87 Woo Sung Street armed with a warrant and again arrested a large number of suspects and seized a large quantity of gambling material. That night it was the turn of the staff of Yau Ma Tei Police Station to be put out. I finally got off duty at 4.10 am, a very long shift. On this occasion Mr Ko had arranged for a reporter from the *South China Morning Post* to accompany us and our nocturnal activities duly appeared in that publication.

We then had a rather lean time for a week during which time every suspected premises we visited resulted in nothing being found. However, on the afternoon of 5th November, me, Dave Kendal and Julian Turnbull were checking out a few addresses in the Western District of Hong Kong Island when we saw two men walk out of an alley. They were rolling down their sleeves and rubbing one arm. We all knew what was going on, so without a word being spoken we went into the alley and behind a wooden partition we found eight men squatting down in a line. Each had one sleeve rolled up and at the head of the queue sitting on a box was a man with a syringe. Beside him, on a table, were the drugs and other equipment which was used. The eight squatting down were easily arrested. The man with the syringe tried to run for it but got nowhere. They were duly taken to Western Police Station where they were charged. This was a lucky break, simply being in the right place at the right time.

Over the next few weeks we upset most of the police stations in the colony when we arrived with large numbers of prisoners and vast amounts of exhibits. The three of us who were married men also upset our wives, by on many occasions leaving home at 8 or 9 am and not returning until the small hours. When we weren't at work we were sleeping.

On 13th November, we raided a premises in Causeway Bay where opium was being smoked. My job on this occasion, after entering, was to draw a plan of the inside of the premises to record where the occupants had been and the location of the smoking equipment. Ten people were arrested inside and they were all extremely drowsy from the opium. They had to be gently guided from the building. The place must have been used as a 'divan', as an opium den is correctly called, for a long time as the walls and ceiling were chalky white with the smoke from the opium pipes. The other officers were constantly coming and going with prisoners while I sat drawing my plan when I suddenly felt very weak and rather intoxicated. The next thing I remember is lying outside, where I had been pulled by my colleagues, in order for me to get some fresh air to recover from breathing the narcotic fumes. There were no after-effects. After a while, I completely recovered and carried on with the job, but not inside!

Later that month we carried out a raid that became quite famous locally and could have had political consequences. This was the drugs raid that we carried out in the Kowloon Walled City.

At this stage I must give a quick history lesson in order that the reader may fully appreciate what a momentous occasion it was.

In 1842, the Island of Hong Kong had been ceded to Britain following the First Opium War, but not at that time the Kowloon Peninsula. Part of Kowloon was ceded to Great Britain after the Second Anglo-Chinese War in the 1860s but in 1898, by a convention signed in Peking, the territory of Hong Kong was extended to include the remainder of Kowloon and a land area up to the Shenzhen River, the latter subsequently being called the New Territories. A very small part of Kowloon, a village referred to as the Walled City and which had been a Chinese administrative centre, remained Chinese territory. This was so that China could keep a vested interest in what was once their land, and their ships, including warships, could continue to use the village waterfront. Over the course of the years, land reclamation took place and this little piece of China was left completely surrounded by British territory. For very many years, certainly while civil war raged in China, no Chinese official was appointed to administer it. The reason for its existence became obsolete but although China ceased to supervise it, Hong Kong laws and customs were not enforced.

The Kowloon Walled City as it was called, was thus a completely lawless place and who knows what went on in there which the outside world never got to know about. Despite the name, it had lost its wall long ago. Hong Kong building regulations did not apply here so there were high-rise buildings crammed closely together with alleyways between them just wide enough for someone to walk along. The contrast between that place and the surrounding area under Hong Kong jurisdiction made the Walled City stick out like a sore thumb. At ground level there were many trading premises, but the majority of them were dentists, run, apparently, by dentists qualified in China, but not qualified to practise in the colony.

It was not uncommon for a fleeing criminal to disappear down one of the dark alleys in order to escape from the pursuing police, who did not follow. In fact, to sum up, it was a disgrace that it was there, but unfortunately it was and there was nothing that could be done about it, or so everyone thought up to that time.

So it was against this background that we were briefed by Superintendent Ko regarding a trial raid at a premises used to smoke heroin, or 'chasing the dragon' as it was more colloquially called. He assured us that the governor of Hong Kong, Sir Murray MacLehose, had sanctioned the raid and that it was his intention to see the reaction by China. In other words, our real mission was to probe the water and see if any of the ripples got as far as Beijing. We all looked around at one another and I could see that one or two of our team had already been affected by the ripples and we hadn't even touched the water yet.

Later that day, armed with a warrant that had no legal standing in the Walled City, we made our way quickly, in single file, through a maze of narrow streets. We passed astonished residents who quickly got out of our way, until we got to the place that was named on the warrant. The door was not even closed, after all they were hardly expecting anyone in authority to call. In we went and arrested several men in the act of 'chasing the dragon' (smoking heroin). Sufficient evidence was seized in order to prove the case against them and out we went, following the same alleyways that we had come down. I think that at this stage everyone's biggest fear was of becoming separated and getting lost. We had acted like a snatch squad but the operation had been well executed and our prisoners were duly convicted the next day. Of course, looking back, there had been more to this than we had seen ourselves. The magistrate who heard the case must have been briefed about it in order for him to accept jurisdiction to try the case and the divisional commander at the Kowloon Police Station where we took the prisoners must have been told to accept them.

About a week or so later we were told that the Beijing reaction to our raid had been nil and this therefore opened the way for further raids, although not by us, thus ensuring that it was not quite as lawless as it had been. We had been the thin end of the wedge, so to speak. Eventually the place was demolished after consultation with China, but even then it took until the early 1990s for this to happen.

After two months carrying out these duties we were disbanded so that the next group leaving the training school could take over from us and we were posted to various police stations throughout the colony. However, what we had learned stood us in good stead for later as most of us would be required, on our own initiative, to carry out raids as part of our normal duties.

I was posted to Wan Chai, a bustling area which was known for its bars, restaurants and nightlife, and more. One raid that I carried out there sticks in my mind. I received some information that there was a brothel operating among the many, many rooms in a block on Jaffe Road. I gathered a small team together and we changed into plain clothes. We had the necessary authority and so went straight to the property which we found to be open. So taking that as a green light, we went inside. There we found a dingy, poorly lit room full of small tables with chairs. There were several men sitting at various places drinking tea. There were teapots on tables as well as cups, bowls and the like. I was taken aback. This was not what we expected. There did not seem to be anyone in charge, just men drinking tea. I wondered if perhaps it was illegal alcohol, but having sniffed a few teapots decided that it wasn't. The officers on my team spoke to the men but they were just here to drink tea they said. All very implausible and there was something not right.

As I was thinking what to do next, a hidden door in one of the walls opened and an attractive girl entered, almost naked, carrying a tray with a teapot and cups on it. She saw us and stopped dead in her tracks. We, in contrast, were galvanised into action and were through the hidden entrance in seconds where we found another room fitted with cubicles. A man sat at a small desk and his jaw dropped as we pushed past him. This was our opportunity and we needed to secure evidence of what was going on. We were able to look over into the cubicles and see that in every one that was occupied there was a man and girl engaged in some form of sexual activity. As the shouts of alarm began, men and girls tried to escape in various stages of undress. However, we had closed the door so we had a captive group. The participants of this episode duly appeared in court the following day.

Incidents in Traffic Division

John Murray

I reported for duty with the Traffic Division, Hong Kong Island, on Monday, 2nd September 1974. I was lucky because I had already twice passed my motorcycle test in the United Kingdom. Once in a private capacity and again after a police motorcycle course which I took whilst serving as a police cadet with the Durham Constabulary. We had ridden old BSA motorbikes on that course and the only thing I had to be careful about was that, on the Yamaha which I would be riding in Hong Kong, the brake and gear pedals were the reverse of the BSA. No problem though. The next day, at the Police Driving School at Ngau Tau Kok, after more tests I was authorised to drive motorcycles, Land Rovers and light saloon cars.

Hong Kong Island traffic problems were severe. There were far too many vehicles on the road for the inadequate amount of road space, particularly at rush hour, into and from the Central District. This area was officially the capital, called Victoria, but everyone called it Central.

From Central there was only one practical road leading up the hill to the main residential areas of Mid-Levels and the Peak. It was called Cotton Tree Drive and it was a steep hill with double white lines in the centre all along its route, indicating overtaking was not allowed. This was the route used by the more affluent members of society to get to the two areas mentioned. During the evening rush hour, everyone was heading south, up the hill, desperate to get home and frustrated by the gridlocked traffic, which at best went at a snail's pace. Near the top of the hill there was a parapet, a sort of observation platform, where we kept a tow truck to remove breakdowns from the road. This is also where I stood, together with other officers, keeping a watchful eye for anyone attempting to cheat in the wacky race to get home. If I saw anyone breaking any traffic law, I would direct an officer to pull them in and they would be reported. Quite often it would be an expatriate who would commit an indiscretion and I would deal with them. They all knew me. My wife, who worked at the Bull and Bear pub in Central, told me that it was common for people leaving work and popping in for a quick drink to ask her if I was on duty and would groan if she confirmed it.

There was another group of drivers who learned to dislike me. They were the public light bus (PLB) drivers. These vehicles were fourteen-seater minibuses, all cream with a red stripe, which plied for hire everywhere. There were thousands of them. On many roads they were forbidden to set down or pick up passengers but they didn't care. I decided that this would be a crusade of mine and I targeted them to such an extent that they gave me a nickname, 'lo foo sha', the tiger shark, and I lived up to the name.

One evening, there had been a horse-race meeting at the Happy Valley Racecourse and I was patrolling the surrounding streets on my motorcycle, with other officers to try and keep the traffic moving. It was always chaos after these meetings. Ahead of me I could see that the traffic was at a complete standstill and horns started blowing as tempers became frayed. I sped off to see what the problem was and at the head of the jam was a PLB picking up passengers in a prohibited area. It would have been pointless to stop and report him, as this would have kept the traffic at a standstill for even longer so I pulled alongside and waved him on. He looked at me and continued to pick up his passengers, taking their fares as they got on board. I banged on the side of his cab and indicated that he should drive off but he again ignored me. Meanwhile the horns sounding behind us became a cacophony as the drivers became more frustrated. Right, I thought, that's it! I pulled my motorcycle in front of him to prevent him driving away and got off with the intention of arresting him for causing a wilful obstruction. I asked him several times to 'lok che' (to get out of his vehicle), but he still ignored me. I pulled open his cab door and tried to pull him out but he wrapped his arms and legs around the steering column. The tugging and shouting went on for a few moments with me now absolutely determined that he wasn't going to win. Meanwhile, his passengers were abandoning ship and running away.

I eventually got him out of his vehicle but he continued to struggle. As this was happening I became aware that we were surrounded by an awful lot of unhappy people and I saw that there were quite a few empty parked PLBs. The bus drivers had come to assist their comrade. Blows started to rain down and my prisoner must have collected just as many as me as we swung round and round, with him still trying to get away. I was in a tricky situation but out of the corner of my eye I saw that we were only yards from a restaurant, which had double glass doors. Seeing this as a refuge, I used my prisoner as a battering ram to push through the throng and through the swing doors of the restaurant, but our velocity was such that we continued on until we fell onto a table full of food. This collapsed under our weight leaving several seated diners frozen with fear. We continued our fight, rolling in rice, noodles and I think sweet and sour pork on the collapsed table. After a very short while, fellow traffic officers arrived and the situation was resolved with my man being taken to Wan Chai Police Station where he was later charged. I left a sergeant to apologise to the restaurant owner as I went back to base at Central Police Station to go off duty. I wonder what the laundry boy thought about the uniform that I left for him to clean that night.

On 31st March 1975, I was again on motorcycle patrol in Happy Valley where the traffic, as usual on a race day, was very heavy. There was nothing much that we could do about it, it was simply a case of too many vehicles for the available road space.

As I rode along Wong Nai Chung Road, beside the racecourse, I was flagged down by a traffic constable who pointed down an alleyway and said to me, 'Robbery, robbery!' I parked my bike and went down the alleyway, which led to the rear of the block of flats where I had stopped. There was a strange scene there. The rear of the building was covered in scaffolding and there was obviously major refurbishment going on. There were also wooden hoardings in place, which effectively reduced the car parking area into different sections, making it difficult to get to different parts of the area. I could see that there was a young Chinese man climbing across the scaffolding and he was being shouted at by several people who were hidden from my view by the hoardings. The man was obviously in a panic and trying to escape.

I walked around one of the wooden panels and saw another constable shouting and gesticulating to the man. Just as he did so the man jumped down and landed on the unfortunate constable who was knocked flat. Then off he went like a hare. He had an advantage over me in that from his earlier position up the scaffolding he had had a bird's eye view of the maze of hoardings and knew the way out. I chased after him but by the time I found the exit, he had a good start on me. I chased him up the alleyway. I shouted to him, in Cantonese, to stop and to my complete amazement he did! I jogged towards him and saw that he had put his right hand into his coat pocket and was fumbling with something inside. He was looking directly at me. He looked menacing. I got closer to him and then suddenly he was off again with me in pursuit.

At this time of the year, the Force was still in winter uniform and I was wearing what closely resembled a British Police-style uniform. However, as a motorcyclist, I was wearing riding breeches and knee-length boots. I was also wearing a crash helmet, and to make matters worse it was a warm day.

I continued to chase the man and once again called on him to stop. He did so again and this time I was closer to him. He was looking directly at me again, and again he fumbled in his pockets. This was quite unnerving for me, I had seen him flatten another officer and I was wondering what he had in his pockets and why had he actually stopped. The word 'robbery' was still in my mind with its implication of violence.

I was almost upon him when he turned and took to his heels again. I had had enough by now and with my brain swirling to put the information together and my heart trying to pump oxygen around my sweating body, I drew my service revolver and went after him again. With everything that was going on, I had concluded that he had some sort of weapon and was trying to decide whether to use it.

He ran out of the alley and on to the busy Wong Nai Chung Road, at the junction with Leighton Road, with me pounding after him, being driven on by grim determination, my eyes never leaving him in case he drew a weapon. It was as if I was wearing blinkers. I was aware of pushing past people and can recall a European couple with a child jumping out of my way as I ran with the revolver in hand. Nothing was going to stop me getting this man. By now my shouting had developed into: 'Stop or I will open fire'.

He ran into Leighton Road and then stopped in his tracks in the middle of that busy road and turned to face me. Again he had his hands in his pocket and looked directly at me menacingly.

Fearing the worst, I levelled my weapon at him and instinct took over. Time seemed to slow down and my concentration was focused on the man and his surroundings. I had a clear shot and there was no one in danger behind him. There was a tremendous bang as I fired.

There was a blood-curdling scream as he leapt into the air and then to my consternation he was off and running again, but this time into the waiting arms of another traffic constable.

I caught up and grabbed hold of him with my left hand, I still had my service revolver in my right. There was a terrible sound from his rear end followed by a gut wrenching stink, made all the worse by the fact that I was on my last legs and gasping for breath. I hung onto him with my left hand while he was also being held by the constable as I retched into the gutter, no doubt with a large number of onlookers. There was only one thing running through my mind now that I had my man. My brain was saying over and over to me, 'All that training and you missed him!'

In retrospect I am pleased that I had missed him. It transpired that the man had committed a burglary not a robbery, but the constable who told me didn't know the English word for burglary. No weapon was ever found and he refused to comment on his actions when interviewed. His sleeping quarters were searched and the proceeds of several other burglaries were found resulting in him getting several years in prison. This was better than the death sentence that I had tried to give him.

THE STAR, Hongkong, Tuesday, April 1, 1975. Page 3

SUSPECT ARRESTED IN SHOOTING DRAMA

A TRAFFIC police constable arrested a burglary suspect yesterday after a cops-and-robbers drama in Wongneichong Road.

The constable arrested the suspect after another policeman fired a shot at him at the junction of Leighton Road.

The suspect stopped in his tracks and gave himself up when he heard the bullet hit a wall near a bus stop and ricochetted onto the ground in front of him.

The drama started about 5 pm, when a European inspector and two constables on duty in the area directing raceday traffic were informed of an attempted burglary by a boy.

They immediately ran up to investigate and the suspect was seen escaping by a rear staircase.

The European inspector caught the suspect at the junction of Leighton Road but after a brief struggle, the suspect escaped again.

This time the inspector opened fire, missing the suspect, but another traffic policeman arrested the suspect.

The suspect is now being detained at Happy Valley police station. No charges have been laid against him as yet.

● **THE suspect**

● **THE inspector who fired the shot**

I am still unable to comprehend his actions. This was the only time that I ever fired a weapon in anger.

Tuesday evening, 29th April 1975, had been quiet. I had paraded my shift of traffic patrol officers at 3.30 pm and had sent them out to patrol Hong Kong Island. We were to finish at 11.30 pm that night. Around 11 pm I was having a last look around the places that could cause traffic problems and had just left the red-light district in the bar area of Wan Chai. I was thinking about getting home and relaxing with a cold San Miguel beer before going to bed. Sometimes after duty I went to the Bull and Bear pub where my wife worked, but she was not working that night, so it was home as soon as I had debriefed my crew at Central Police Station.

I found myself on Leighton Road at the north end of the Happy Valley racecourse. This was the exact location where I had opened fire a month earlier. I was going west on my Yamaha 650 motorcycle when I saw coming towards me three black limousines in a convoy. The problem was that, at this point, the eastbound lane was a bus-only lane and these limousines were certainly not buses.

Clicking my tongue, I turned the motorcycle round and overtook the line of vehicles and stopped them at the very end of the bus lane. I really had not made up my mind on what action I was going to take; maybe I was just intrigued as to what was going on.

As I dismounted a man got out of the rear of the first limo and approached me. He was an Asian man wearing a uniform I didn't recognise, obviously military, and he was plainly an officer. He asked me in good English what was the problem. As we spoke, another man, similarly dressed, got out of the second limo. I say similarly dressed, but he was obviously of much higher rank than the first man, who stood to attention at the second man's approach. As he got closer I could see lots of braid on his uniform and simply by his manner I had no doubt he was someone with considerable rank.

He asked me in perfect English what was the problem and I told him about the bus lane. He looked at the road and smiled. He then apologised to me for his lack of respect for the laws of the colony but explained that as it was 11 pm and there was hardly any traffic about, that he hoped that I would allow them to continue, as they were on urgent business. He was quietly spoken but he had an air of authority about him that indicated that, although he was asking me, he fully expected to get his way.

Of course, he was perfectly right in what he said about the time and the traffic. I told him to please be more careful in future and indicated that they could continue on their way. He thanked me and the little entourage then glided away, leaving me wondering who they were.

I believe that after debriefing my officers I enjoyed the beer, or maybe two, before going to bed.

The following day the whole world learned of, and saw on television, the tragic events that had occurred thereby ending the Vietnam War. Saigon, the southern capital had fallen to the communists and America had pulled out its last personnel from the embassy in absolute panic at the speed of the communist advance. It was then I realised that I did recognise the uniforms. These men were senior officers of the South Vietnamese army and were, no doubt, disappearing to some pre-arranged destination having heard that their government was about to fall. This was confirmed some weeks later when I visited the vehicle pound and saw the three limos, which had been recovered from the abandoned consulate building. I have wondered on many occasions since, what happened to those men.

The Po Sang Bank Siege

John H. T. Griffiths

Mid-afternoon on Friday, 23rd May 1974, my boss, Brian Hague, came into my office clutching a letter from the commissioner confirming that I was to be promoted to superintendent. Accordingly, we both adjourned to the Captain's Bar in the Mandarin Hotel to celebrate. At around 19.00 hrs, we were summoned back to Police Headquarters where we were briefed that a lone gunman had attempted to rob the Po Sang Bank in Mong Kok just as it was closing for the day. The alarm had been raised and the Police Emergency Unit responded in time to prevent his escape. Now there was an on-going siege of the bank with the robber holding up to a dozen bank staff as hostage. Our Close Protection Officers were the most highly trained firearms officers in the Police Force, so we were told to be ready for possible deployment. Brian Hague decided to take the first shift with one team, and I would relieve him with another team at 05.00 hrs the following morning. Once the logistics had been settled, I returned to Kowloon Tong where I was residing with my future wife, Helen Lo.

I was already in bed and asleep when Helen came home that evening and she presumed that I was getting an early night in anticipation of a heavy weekend at her riding school in the New Territories, preparing the establishment for the show-jumping season. Apparently, she was less than impressed when she awoke at dawn to find that I had already departed.

Just as I reached Police Headquarters, the heavens opened and just dashing in from my parking space in the rear yard to the main entrance resulted in my being soaked to the skin. Luckily, I had a change of shirt and underclothes in the office, but my jacket and trousers had to be hung over a chair in front of a fan in an attempt to dry them. Around 08.00 hrs, people started to arrive in the building, so I had to don my trousers which were still damp, but the jacket was still dripping water onto the floor so I left it off. I wandered down the corridor to the control room to check what was happening in Mong Kok, and met Charles Scobell, chief superintendent, who gave me a fierce dressing down for parading around with my Walther PPK, the personal-issue revolver for officers of the Close Protection Section, on display at my waist, when there were ladies present. It was pointless to offer any explanation so I promptly retired to my office to wait out my shift of duty.

Around 10.00 hrs, I was directed to take my team to Kowloon Police Headquarters and report to Paul Grace, the assistant commissioner of police, and district commander, Kowloon. On entering the office I went to approach Grace, who was seated behind his desk, but he nodded towards the figure looking out of the window and I realised that Brian Slevin, the commissioner of police, was also present. Slevin briefed me that the failed bank robber had ordered two cars, facing opposite directions, to be parked outside the bank in preparation for his departure. At this time there were huge crowds at either end of Shanghai Street, so if he tried to drive away, he would be forced to slow down. I was directed to deploy my local Chinese officers to the front ranks of the crowd at either end of the street with orders that if there was a target of opportunity, chummy was to be taken out.

We proceeded to Shanghai Street, and the team were deployed under the direction of David Chan the senior Chinese officer in the section, whilst I reported to P.J. Clancy, the deputy district commander, in his command post. Nothing seemed to be happening and I was browsing through the plans of the bank, when a shot rang out, followed about a minute later by another shot. On impulse I dashed out of the command post and ran towards the sound. After about twenty yards, I realised that I was not sure which of the shuttered buildings was the bank – first mistake! Luckily two hostages emerged from the bank building which gave me my bearings. I saw that they had come through a very narrow opening in the metal shutter, and I realised I would have to go through it sideways. I paused for a moment and cursed the impulse which had brought me to this point. It was too late and I was committed. I called out to Bob Porter, Police Tactical Unit commander, and Vince Becker, a traffic officer, who were nearby to cover me – which was a completely futile gesture but sounded good – and scrambled through the opening – second mistake! I had failed to take into account that I was moving from very bright sunlight into a darkened room, and it took three or four seconds for my eyes to adjust. I was confronted by a counter surmounted by an iron grill, and I had no idea of layout – third mistake! I should have checked the internal layout as a priority in the command post. There was a passageway to the left and assuming it would lead to an opening in the counter, I went along it with hand outstretched feeling for a gap.

There was a gap – so I ducked through it and came up behind the counter where I saw that two of the hostages were struggling with the robber, despite having their hands tied. On seeing me, they stepped away and the robber lunged in the direction of his revolver, which was lying on the floor some five feet away. Without any conscious thought, I brought the butt of my Walther PPK into contact with his forehead which stopped him in his tracks. My pistol was cocked and the impact could easily have caused it to discharge – fourth mistake! If I had paused until he had his hand on his revolver then I could have shot him, and I doubt if any jury would have blamed me in the circumstances, since for all that I knew there could have been dead or dying cashiers among the bodies lying on the floor. It later emerged that earlier in the year he had almost certainly killed a police sergeant who was shot in the head as he walked in to sign the police visiting book during another attempted bank robbery in Kowloon City.

I had my weapon thrust under his chin whilst Bob Porter relieved him of a knife that he had on his belt. During this time he kept muttering 'Only arrived in Hong Kong on 2nd April', which made no sense at the time, but did after the connection with the Kowloon City robbery emerged.

I picked up a discarded jacket and draped it over his head to mask the bloodstain on his forehead. David Chan and I then rushed him off to the command post to hand him over to the detectives.

I wandered out in the street to have a much-needed cigarette but my hand was shaking so much that I could not connect the lighter to the cigarette – someone had to do the honours for me. David Chan and I were ordered to 'disappear' from the scene quickly and be kept away from the press. We were taken to the Gazetted Officers' Mess and plied with drinks by fellow officers.

I have absolutely no idea as to how or when I got home that night but when Helen arrived home, it did not please her in the slightest to find me lying on the bed in a drunken stupor. In the morning I was still away with the fairies. When she returned that Sunday night, thoroughly exhausted from two days of toil without my help, the atmosphere was very frigid and I was banished to the spare bedroom, still nursing a kingsize hangover. The following morning, I left very early to seek refuge in the office. Shortly after 10.00 hrs, I received a phone call from Helen who had only become aware of the events of Saturday morning after receiving calls from friends and colleagues. At first she was a little contrite but soon turned the tables around on the grounds that I should have, at least, called her to put her in the picture – fifth mistake!

At least the domestic scene was settled in my favour when later in the year Helen and I were married.

Marksman Unit 1973–1978

Bill Duncanson

In the early 1970s, the Royal Hong Kong Police, like many other police forces, was faced with the possibility of air piracy or terrorist-related incidents. Generally, these took the form of an armed attack followed by hostage taking, and a demand for safe passage, usually by air out of the country. With the ready availability of Police Tactical Unit companies, the Force was initially better placed than most others in its ability to contain such incidents. As a small added capability, a number of officers who were known to be good shots had been identified who could be called upon to respond to an incident, probably in a sniping role.

Overseas incidents, such as that at the Munich Olympics, quickly made it very obvious that there was a critical demand to have a highly trained sniping capability. In early 1973 I, then a superintendent, was required to attend a meeting with the Senior Superintendent (SSP) Operations, Jim Harris, at Police Headquarters. He explained in detail the Force requirement to expand its response across the whole spectrum of possible terrorist incidents and that I had been selected to form and command a unit to provide this capability. There was urgency in getting the unit operationally competent, and a broad outline was settled upon:

- A full-time unit was not required, although some part of it had to be available for immediate callout.
- The unit was to consist of six two-man teams. Myself and my deputy, Hugh Healy-Brown were to be a fully operational seventh team. In this way we could cover leave, sickness, etc.
- Rank was not important but a proven capability and temperament were prime requirements. Other skills such as

lock picking, negotiating skills or knowledge of explosives were a bonus.
• The unit was not an assault unit and only a good general fitness was needed.

These were the general headings and Jim Harris arranged for us to take them immediately to the commissioner where further points were agreed:
• The unit was to be known as the Marksman Unit (MU).
• The MU was under PHQ command through the SSP/Ops.
• Team member selection, training and equipment were my responsibility.
• The MU could be called out by any incident commander and would normally involve one two-man team. Whilst generally I would also be present, they were to be controlled by the incident commander who must be aware of the team capabilities.

Marksman Unit Teams

The police have a long history of producing very good shots right up to Olympic competition standard. Having myself represented Hong Kong at the Commonwealth and Asian games, I was familiar as to who were the very best shots in the Force and four were invited to join. At our first meeting I had seven inspectorate officers and five sergeant/station sergeants. They were told to form up into two-man teams as they wished.

Each team had one member armed with an AR-15 rifle, fitted with a military telescopic sight and a Trilux night sight. The other was armed with a Remington bolt-action hunting rifle which was widely used at the time as a sniping rifle. It was fitted with a high-powered telescopic sight. Both rifles used the same .223 ammunition.

Our first training sessions were only to get the sights accurately calibrated and the rifles zeroed to a particular officer.

The Force Armoury made fourteen identical boxes designed to hold a team member's personal weapons. It was imperative that the weapons were securely stored so that the calibration and zeroing of each rifle would not be altered by rough handling during transportation to an incident.

It became obvious that the requirement for the MU to engage a target might be at very close or mid-range, where the use of a rifle was just not appropriate. Our training covered this possibility and the arms stored in the box reflected that.

The MU box contained either an AR-15 or Remington rifle with standard and specialist ammunition. A lightweight bipod for the rifle. A Sterling sub-machine gun, a police radio, a one-piece camouflaged military-style uniform, a webbing belt with pouches and a holster for a hand gun. A knife, torch, binoculars, boots, camouflage creams, hat or cap and other personal items such as sunglasses and notepads were also included. Every member carried a standard issue Police Colt .38 revolver and ammunition, but specialist ammunition was stored in the box.

It was arranged and practised that in the event of the unit being called upon that the Emergency Unit (999 response vehicles) on

W. Duncanson, Marksman Unit, with AR-15 rifle
fitted with Trilux night sight (Courtesy W. Duncanson)

Hong Kong Island would quickly deliver the relevant boxes from Central Police Station to wherever they were required.

The MU was amongst the first police formations to be officially issued with pagers, which had to be carried at all times. All the pagers did was to vibrate and/or give an alarm sound, on receipt of which you were required to call Colony Police/Military Command Centre. Crude by today's standards but they permitted a very quick response from the MU members.

Training

The prime requirement of the MU was to provide an incident commander with an option to resolve a dangerous situation.

We practised constantly and training shoots were never cancelled due to weather, even when typhoon signals were hoisted.

Our main training target was the standard police silhouette of a standing figure depicted from the thigh upwards. The head was about the size of a small fist and the hand about two inches square. The head had ears each about the size and shape of a little finger. An MU target was either an ear, the fist or the small gap between the body and the bent arm. The required standard was to consistently hit these spots. The teams became massively confident that because they could hit such a small target, they would undoubtedly strike a full size human target.

Shooting at a target exactly one hundred yards away from a prone position is also unrealistic compared to what might be encountered. To cater for this, an element of stress was introduced by running or jogging up and down steps, and engaging targets at different distances whilst standing or lying in a drain, street, or on a hillside.

The AR-15 had a military telescopic sight fitted, but to give a night or poor light capability, the rifle could be fitted with a Trilux night sight. We experimented endlessly with this sight and also used passive infrared and light intensifiers but were never confident with the accuracy. There is so much ambient light in Hong Kong, even in dark ranges in the hills, that we found the Remington, with its powerful telescopic sight, outperformed technologically superior sights. It was easy to see the crosshairs of its sight against any shade other than total blackness.

The range at the Police Training School had target frames that could be raised from the butts which then left gaps between them that resembled doorways or windows. Standing-man targets, described previously, were attached to poles and could be moved to various positions in the butts. I placed stickers on the targets, about one inch wide, in six or seven colours and different shapes such as triangles, squares or crescents, which gave a large number of permutations. A team would be tasked to engage a target, identified by a particular shape and colour and shoot when they were certain they could hit it. The teams in the butts would then move around six or seven silhouettes between the gaps, all bearing different identifiers, and the deployed team had to locate their specified target. Sometimes to add to their problem two teams would be tasked with different targets and the solution required both targets be hit simultaneously. Very difficult, and required a lot of time and patient cooperation between the two teams. We devised a radio system with which the teams could operate and talk to each other using very little physical movement.

Because the MU might have to engage a target at close range, we were equipped with Sterling sub-machine guns. There was little requirement for training with this gun other than instinctive shooting from the hip.

On one occasion the unit was invited to the British Army indoor range where there was a facility to run a film showing various scenarios and at which live ammunition could be fired. The one in which we took part depicted a foot patrol moving along a country lane and through a small village. The objective was to spot an ambush situation and, to keep it very simple, any person that was spotted in the trees, bushes or suddenly appearing from behind gates, doorways and windows, was to be considered hostile, and engaged. The presented targets were usually depicted as being about ten to twenty yards away. It was an unrealistic scenario for police and even more so when we were required to engage with our rifles from a prone position, when the film was really for an army foot patrol. This made it very difficult to bring the weapons to bear. We nevertheless did quite well.

We asked if the team which had not seen the scenario could use their Sterling and this was agreed. The team instinctively engaged the nearest targets from the hip and the accurate fire power brought to bear on automatic was astonishing. Whilst an unlikely scenario for us, it was a fantastic training session as there was a lot of stress – not least from performing in front of very critical and knowledgeable army observers. The army were impressed and complimentary despite the extensive damage to the film screen by the automatic fire.

We had thought of producing an appropriate film for our training purposes, but they are expensive and not easy to make. More importantly, and as this session confirmed, once seen they are quickly learnt. They are therefore of very limited value.

Over the span of the MU's existence we were sometimes required to perform close-escort duties, for which the standard Police .38 Colt revolver or a 9 mm pistol was thought adequate. Training with handguns was generally conducted at the PHQ indoor range where the lighting controls provided quite dark conditions. To create a requirement to quickly recognise a target before engaging, I again used various stickers as identifiers. On these occasions however, they were on slides which were projected on to a blank target at a range of between five and ten yards. There could be between six or eight identifiers projected on each slide. To simulate a personal protection deployment, the teams were required to be wearing a jacket and the handgun holstered. On recognising their target, they had to draw and engage. From the target being presented to shots being accurately fired was just less than three seconds.

To enhance handgun training we began practising in disused buildings. We also trained underground in the abandoned and sealed World War II military complex on Mount Davis. There appeared to be bomb damage in one area and we managed to enter. The complex provided us with a totally dark environment where we could train using our passive infrared goggles. This is an amazing experience because, if you could control your breathing, you could be standing next to someone and they would have no idea that you were there. I once took the commissioner underground and when we switched on a torch, his reaction to being within inches of eight armed officers was a good illustration of what could be achieved in total darkness.

To further advance handgun training, the Force Ballistics Office removed the bullet from standard police revolver rounds and the bullet cases were then pushed into a tray of candle wax which had been melted and allowed to harden to about an eighth of an inch thick. This allowed us to engage in live firing at each other. The wax bullet would not penetrate clothing but being hit was quite painful and left a mark that made it impossible to deny that you had been careless enough to be hit. I was struck on the ankle in one training shoot and as much as I was tempted to try and hide it, my limp generated the usual amount of good-humoured mockery.

I supplemented training with very regular shooting competitions against teams from visiting American warships and the United States Marines at the US Consulate in Hong Kong. Most ships had a US Marine pistol team who were only too pleased to take part in competitions.

Training scenarios were generally for one team to be holding a hostage and one or two teams tasked to rescue him, if possible. The 'if possible' was critical because the setting was so realistic that to achieve the required positive result was not always effected, and that fact had to be recognised as a result. I often, in a scenario like this, called the exercise off, sometimes after 90 minutes, without a shot being fired. All exercises were afterwards subject to critical analysis as to what alternatives could have been tried or what could have been done better.

This is a general account of MU training which, by today's standards with computer-assisted facilities, is somewhat rudimentary but it was effective.

Deployment

It was not at all uncommon for an MU team to be required by an incident commander to attend as a back-up in case an incident escalated. However, to my certain knowledge, the MU was never required to actively engage a human target, although it came close to doing so on a number of occasions.

One incident which MU teams attended, did however cause a profound change to our training.

The teams were at Kai Tak Airport in response to the hijacking of an aircraft from the Philippines which had landed in Hong Kong. The passengers and cabin crew had been allowed to disembark in Manila and the aircraft was then flown to Hong Kong. Negotiations quickly established that the hijackers were farmers and that their grievance related to issues with their farmland. The aircrew did not consider themselves to be under any immediate threat, although the hijackers were armed with .45 pistols and possibly hand grenades.

The MU were ordered to not allow the aircraft to depart Hong Kong and if necessary, shoot out the front tyres of the aircraft if it attempted to do so. This was not the appropriate time for me to question the order but I later went to the Command Centre in the airport and raised my concerns. Fortunately, the hijackers, once they had handed over their arms in Hong Kong, were apparently satisfied that their grievances would be dealt with appropriately in Manila and the aircraft was permitted to depart.

It was clear at the debrief that shooting aircraft tyres had not been properly thought through. The possible problems were:

- Would the tyre(s) actually deflate and how many rounds would it take to make it do so?
- Would the pilot be aware that the tyre was deflating?
- If it was deflating, would he be able to convince the hijackers that a take-off was now not possible, without them believing it was an excuse and possibly then becoming violent?
- The chance of there being an accident with deflating tyres during take-off was high and probably certain during landing.
- It was very difficult to ensure from our firing positions that only the tyre would be hit and once the aircraft was moving almost impossible. It was therefore likely that damage could be caused to the landing gear structure and function, and possibly to the braking system.

I realised this was a type of scenario that the MU would be called upon to deal with, and I should have researched answers to my own questions. Whilst retaining our core training requirements, I therefore began to research what would be the expected result if we were to engage a target under other predictable situations.

Engaging a target behind a glass window, for example. I began a shooting programme of firing at targets placed behind glass. This appears simple until one considers the specialist types of glass used in modern buildings, including shop and bank windows. There is also the question of the angle at which the bullet strikes the glass and which type of bullet would give the required result. For example, would the initial bullet actually continue on its trajectory and strike the target and having hit the target, would it penetrate further and possibly hit hostages? Would it be necessary for accuracy to fire one shot to smash the glass and create a clear path a split second before the other rounds arrived to strike the target?

Another likely task was dealing with a terrorist in a moving vehicle. Could the engine be disabled to bring it to a stop, and if so, which ammunition should be used to achieve this? Some old cars and other vehicle types due for destruction in the Police Vehicle Pound were taken to a remote range to answer that question.

A more difficult question to resolve was: Could a terrorist in a vehicle with a hostage be shot at with a high probability of success? What were the possible effects of different types of windscreens? Many windscreens, again at a range of angles, were destroyed until we understood what the result would be.

Another problem was how to deal with a terrorist who might be seated in any one of the positions inside the car, together with a hostage(s). Various permutations were tried with regard to seating. To answer the question with regard to the likely result of glass fragmentation, we used pigs' heads at various distances behind the windscreens. Whilst it would be much easier to engage with the vehicle coming head on, it was necessary to also evaluate shots having to be taken from the side, and also with a range of vehicles, e.g., a small bus.

With this detailed pre-examination and understanding of the different forms which terrorist incidents could take, I felt very confident that we knew the answers to many questions and I would have been able to give very detailed advice to an incident commander.

With this knowledge, it was nevertheless more likely the operation would be successful if it took place at a location of our choosing. With the likelihood of the terrorist demanding to be taken to Kai Tak Airport, a small team from the unit began a programme of identifying locations suitable for an ambush. Locations were selected and we became very familiar with their individual characteristics. For example, To Kwa Wan Road, a heavily used approach road to the airport, ran directly up to the airport perimeter fence to the junction with Sung Wong Toi Road before turning sharp left to run alongside the fence. Just on the other side of the perimeter fence was a drainage ditch, easily large enough to conceal an MU team(s) with excellent firing positions to engage a vehicle coming straight towards them. There was always some rubbish such as old cardboard boxes and litter caught up in the fencing on this windy corner, which created very natural cover. On one side of the last hundred yards or so of To Kwa Wan Road was a high factory wall and on the other, an equally high wall of a Public Works Department storage area. These would reduce the possibility of ricocheting rounds leaving the area. We knew the exact range of markers, such as street lights, from the firing positions.

The intention would be to have the teams in position and to keep them informed of the vehicle's movements and the terrorists' seating positions in it. This would have been updated as necessary along the route. If there had been a demand for a police vehicle to lead, and the order given to engage, the police vehicle could have turned along Sung Wong Toi Road and be safely out of the way. If after engaging, the terrorists' vehicle kept moving forward, it would run into the perimeter fence and the occupants dealt with by the teams in position there. If it came to a stop, the team(s) concealed behind the PWD wall would deal with it. If a decision was made, for whatever reason not to trigger the ambush, then one of the most important requirements of selecting the position would come into play – the teams could remain concealed and there would be no indication that an attack had been considered.

Incidents of MU Deployment

The MU was involved in dealing with a number of serious incidents.

I have mentioned the incoming hijacking from Manila, which became quite tense when the hijackers came to handing over the .45 automatic pistols and a hand grenade. One hijacker had the grenade rolled up in a bandage taken from the plane's first aid box. When they first took over the aircraft he thought that he might be jumped by the passengers and so removed the safety pin from the grenade, only to subsequently lose it. To avoid having to continuously hold the firing lever down, he wrapped it in the bandage. We provided him with a box full of different types of pins, hair grips, paper clips and nails and sent him a distance away from us behind a sea wall for him to find one that fitted. I must say that he took the very dangerous act of unwrapping the grenade and replacing the pin very casually and with humour.

There was also the very strange incident when the flight engineer on a Korean Airlines flight attacked the two pilots with an axe while the aircraft was on its final approach into Kai Tak. The aircraft came to a stop on the main runway and remained there for a long time until what had occurred was understood and the aircraft boarded by police.

On another occasion, three or four British soldiers, drunk and armed with handguns and military rifles, stole an army Land Rover. The police were not informed of the incident until they appeared at Kai Tak Airport, where they demanded a flight to take them to the United Kingdom. They took a police sergeant hostage and then became trapped in an office after which negotiations began. What they did not know was that the sergeant had switched his beat radio to continuous transmit and the Kowloon Command Centre could therefore monitor all that was being said. The incident was eventually resolved and the soldiers handed over to the Military Police.

Some other deployments appeared unnecessary but actually contained a considerable threat level. A good example was the 1976 Miss Universe contest. There was no initial requirement for police involvement other than local crowd control. However, given that there were a number of political situations in the world at that time, intelligence sources identified a direct threat to five contestants because of their nationality. The MU was deployed to provide close personal protection to these five contestants. Three days later, Miss Israel won the contest and I was informed that the threat level against her had risen considerably. The team guarding her was immediately strengthened and a woman police officer joined the team. By winning the contest, she was moved to a hotel suite, which for reasons of security, was changed to a different one every day. The MU team occupied the outer rooms of the suite and CID provided a discreet presence in the foyer. We were visited by security personnel from Israel who confirmed the level of threat and which remained high until her departure.

There were quite a number of incidents involving animals.

The Lai Chi Kok Zoo contained one tiger and the animal was apparently given a sedative in its food in order to allow cage cleaning. Unfortunately on this occasion, the tiger recovered rather quicker than expected and walked out of its cage into the public area. The crowd fled the zoo, the gates were closed and the police notified. The MU were deployed and Mark Godfrey responded. There was no designated handler for the animal, nor anyone from the zoo who was prepared to go near it, so with very little chance of it being enticed back into its cage, the order was for it to be shot before it could enter the city.

When Mark arrived, the tiger had jumped over the low fence of the porcupine enclosure and was attempting to catch them. A Hong Kong government vet arrived with a brand-new tranquilliser gun in a box. He had no idea of how the gun functioned and wasn't prepared to find out. He gave the box to Mark and left. The mechanism was quite straightforward and Mark climbed onto the low flat roof of an adjacent building where he could look down on the tiger which was by now lying on its side in the porcupine enclosure. He loaded and fired a dart which struck the tiger on its thigh but because the brightly coloured marker fell out, he believed that the dart had not penetrated. He fired the two other darts with the same result. The tiger remained motionless for a long time before anyone dared to approach, but it was later found to be dead.

An examination revealed that cause of death was tranquilliser overdose. The dart hadn't actually fallen out but the marker was a built-in indicator that the shot had been successful. This detail was 'in the small print' which Mark hadn't seen in his haste to take possibly the only opportunity to have a good safe shot. Apparently, the poor creature could have survived being hit with the three darts but it was never revealed just how much tranquilliser it had been given in its food.

Another deployment involving animals came when the MU was required to provide escort to twelve elephants. The elephants had been brought to Hong Kong from Thailand to play exhibition football matches with a ball the size of a small car. After possibly two games, it was obviously a financial failure and the organisers disappeared, leaving the elephants in the care of three or four handlers. The elephants were moved to Lai Chi Kok Zoo where their presence became a major logistical and financial problem. With no one accepting responsibility for them, consideration was being given to their destruction when the C.Y. Tung Shipping Company offered to return them to Thailand so long as they could be boarded on one of their ships in the harbour. Plans were made and the MU were deployed to escort them from the zoo to the nearest barge loading point, at Mei Foo Sun Chuen. The Force Ballistics Officer, Al Camino, gave advice on which ammunition to use to kill these animals should it become necessary.

The move commenced at about two o'clock in the morning with the animals walking in a chain holding the tail of the animal in front. They were very calm and the lead animals were being guided by two or three handlers. The MU were deployed to walk alongside the animals. When we reached Mei Foo Sun Chuen waterfront, the lead elephant was led onto a very large cargo net to be lifted onto the barge. The very second its feet left the ground, it trumpeted and instantly the other eleven elephants took off in eleven different directions. It was astonishing! One moment they were standing very quietly and the next they were gone. They spread throughout Mei Foo Sun Chuen, a densely populated residential estate, and then just stood there. Our concern was whether and how to shoot them if they began wildly running about. However, they were all very calm, easily approached, and were soon led back to the loading point. The handlers thought that the lead elephant felt insecure once its feet had left the ground. Fortunately, there were a number of wooden pallets available and one was placed onto the cargo net and the elephant guided to stand on that. The net was then lifted and the elephant, and eventually all the others, were safely hoisted aboard without further incident.

Many urban legends grew out of that night in Mei Foo Sun Chuen.

On another occasion, a large buffalo fell or jumped from a barge in the harbour whilst being taken at night to the abattoir. It swam to the shore and entered a large, underground drainage nullah and kept walking in the network of large pipes until it reached somewhere near Boundary Street and Prince Edward Road. I was never able to clarify why there was urgency to shoot the animal before morning but that is what some government department required of the police. The Fire Services were also in attendance because they understood where all the manholes were. Together we got this very large buffalo into a position underground where it was shot. A very heavy rainstorm later in the morning conveniently washed the body into the harbour.

By late 1978, the Special Duties Unit (SDU) had reached a level in numbers and efficiency to deal with terrorist and major incidents, which meant that they could take over the commitments of the MU. The MU was only ever planned to be temporary, but lasted five years.

I am extremely proud to have commanded the unit and to have worked with very skilled, conscientious and capable officers who took the unit to a level of competence that very few in the Police Force ever knew. And here I would like to record that this could not have been achieved without the very close support, advice and provision of equipment the unit always received from the Force Ballistics Office and Armoury.

Vietnamese Refugees Arrive

Ian Lacy-Smith

The sixth day of May, 1975, was to be like no other day during my long service with the Royal Hong Kong Police Force.

During the previous fortnight I had been following the final chaotic days in South Vietnam. When the Viet Cong decided on an outright attack on Saigon, I thought: 'What a catastrophic turn of events, how did it ever come to this?' Their recent atrocities and massacres in the surrounding provinces seemed to spell disaster for Saigon. It didn't help either that the American Ambassador, Graham Martin, was reluctant to order an evacuation of his embassy until the situation was hopeless, 'for fear of spreading panic'. Perhaps he had also been hoping that further negotiations might halt the Viet Cong advance. No such luck, and panic to escape their clutches did spread across Saigon, especially when it became known that President Thieu of South Vietnam had himself fled on 27th April, leaving the vice-president in charge. Ambassador Martin was one of the last Americans to be airlifted from the embassy, just hours before the surrender of the nation by General Minh on 30th April, 1975.

Another to flee before the surrender was Tran Dinh Truong, the owner of Vishipco Lines, the largest shipping company in South Vietnam. At least he left several freighters behind for his employees to help evacuate refugees if they could. His company had made him a fortune by supplying the American forces with all kinds of war materiel and so resettlement in the USA must have been a formality for him and his wife and four children. He was to make another fortune there in real estate, much of it in New York.

One of the freighters he left behind was the MS *Truong Xuan* and on 29th April, despite being grossly overloaded, it managed to sail from Saigon with 3,628 refugees on board. However, on reaching international waters of the South China Sea, after sporadic engine failures and once running aground, it ran into really serious trouble. Water was rising in the engine-room because the pumps had stopped working and no amount of manual effort could prevent the vessel from slowly sinking. As it did so, its captain, Pham Ngoc Luy, put out a distress signal and the Danish container ship MS *Clara Maersk*, en route to Hong Kong, came to its rescue on 2nd May. On humanitarian grounds, its captain, Anton Olsen, agreed that everyone including the crew could board his vessel and despite the increase in his own ship's load, he was able to steer it unhindered all the way to Hong Kong, arriving there on 4th May.

Vietnamese refugees aboard MS Truong Xuan

Once the Hong Kong government had agreed that this first massive number of Vietnamese refugees could stay in Hong Kong until resettlement, they disembarked and were taken to two camps hastily prepared for them in the New Territories and one temporary camp in Harcourt Road on Hong Kong Island. Breaking down the numbers, just over 2,000 refugees went to the recently vacated British Army camp at Dodwell's Ridge; 1,055 to another Army camp in Sai Kung; and 513 single men were moved from Harcourt Road to a third Army camp in Sek Kong when spare barrack accommodation was ready for them. The total from the MS *Clara Maersk* being duly recorded as 3,743, including the crew of the MS *Truong Xuan* and three babies born at sea.

The MS Clara Maersk *about to receive
Vietnamese refugees from MS* Truong Xuan

Her Majesty the Queen, and the Duke of Edinburgh, would have been given all this news by a hard-pressed Hong Kong Governor, Sir Murray MacLehose, as they too had arrived in Hong Kong on 4th May, at the start of their first state visit to the territory!

One of the three new babies was named Chieu Anh and her touching life story can be found on the internet site titled 'MS *Truong Xuan* – Voyage to Freedom'. Her hero is Captain Pham who went on in 1994 to be the founder of the Vietnam Human Rights Network in the USA. His action in evacuating so many people had already been recognised by the United Nations High Commissioner for Refugees (UNHCR). His own hero is Captain Olsen, who was later knighted by the Queen of Denmark for his humane deed. In 2009, Captain Pham honoured Captain Olsen's grave in the Faroe Islands; and he himself is still working in Virginia despite being in his nineties. What a remarkable life for an outstanding man.

Late on 6th May, the number of refugees at Dodwell's Ridge Camp was boosted by another seventy arriving by road from Shau Kei Wan Police Station, and this is where I enter the story. At that time I happened to be the officer-in-charge of this sub-divisional station in the northeast of Hong Kong Island where there is a small harbour. At about 08.00 am that morning, my duty sergeant came to my office to report that he had just received a message from a local resident that a large number of Vietnamese refugees were gathered in his garden after a journey in two fishing boats from Saigon. 'Port of First Asylum, what an achievement, a day to remember, get it right'; all these thoughts crossed my mind.

'Tell the gentleman,' I said to the sergeant, 'that they will have to come here for processing and also tell the barrack sergeant he is to arrange to have them transported to the station. He is also to set up benches, tables, chairs and a few desks in the shady part of the compound and warn the kitchen that we will need extra food and water, how much I don't yet know. I'm on my way to see them and the boats.' Before leaving the station, I broke the news to my Divisional Superintendent, John Macdonald. He then set the wheels in motion to basically treat our police station as a mini port of entry for the day, or for as long as it took the Security Branch to arrange for the refugees' next abode.

In the garden of a house near the Shau Kei Wan harbour were seventy outwardly calm but tired Vietnamese and the basics of their journey were described to me. The two fishing boats were shrimp trawlers owned by a joint South Vietnamese/Hong Kong consortium which would explain how the skippers knew their way around the far reaches of Hong Kong harbour. I learnt more on the way to the boats. The owners and crews had been preparing for their escape by sea while the Viet Cong were closing in on Saigon and most of those who managed to join them were their families or friends. But on the way down the Saigon River they had been boarded by a group of about a dozen South Vietnamese military officers who were taking flight in speedboats but which obviously could not go far before running out of fuel. These officers were relieved to hear that the trawlers' skippers hoped to reach the safety of Hong Kong and settled down on board for the journey. This was uneventful until the engine of one of the boats failed and the two had to be strapped together. Fuel was transferred from the ailing boat to the other one as needed, and in relatively calm seas, they were able to reach Hong Kong by the early hours of 6th May.

I asked if any of the military officers were still with the main group. 'Oh no,' I was told, 'they said they would take public transport into the centre of Hong Kong and seek asylum at the American Consulate.' I later heard that they had indeed jumped on a public light bus in the centre of Shau Kei Wan but I could not confirm anything about their subsequent movements.

John Macdonald and I then examined the two boats. All appeared as expected with fishing boats except for several small arms and some loose ammunition scattered around one of them. I was told that they had been jettisoned by the military officers before catching their bus, and wisely so. I later passed them on to the Force Armourer for disposal, apart from nine flare cartridges which I handed over to the Force Bomb Disposal Officer, Ron Bagrie, who then happened to be living in a quarter at Shau Kei Wan Police Station. As regards the actual boats, Hong Kong members of the consortium took responsibility for them and I assume that after repairs and servicing, they carried on trawling in the peaceful areas of the South China Sea. It would also have made sense for the fishing families amongst the seventy to have applied for resettlement in Hong Kong. Some of these first thousands of refugees certainly did apply for Hong Kong residency and were accepted.

Returning to the police station, I found the processing under way exactly as if the group of seventy had arrived at a normal port of entry. This activity was to carry on for most of the day. The government's secretary for security had been advised of the situation and officials from the Immigration, Customs and Excise, and Port Health Departments, quickly arrived to perform their statutory duties. During the afternoon I learnt that all of the seventy refugees would join those who had been sent to Dodwell's Ridge from the MS *Clara Maersk* the previous day.

With the aid of an English-speaking refugee, I was able to chat with some of the heads of the families. They were understandably very strained after their stressful experiences, but relieved and grateful to be in safe British hands. I clearly remember one family consisting of two parents, nine lovely daughters aged from about ten to twenty years and two of their grandparents. Putting myself in the father's shoes, how much more traumatic could it have been for him to be firstly uprooted from his native country and then to undertake a potentially perilous journey with such a large family and an uncertain future ahead of them? I wished him and his family an early resettlement and every good fortune, as I did with all of the others, as they left Shau Kei Wan for Dodwell's Ridge that evening. The next day, I contacted the camp manager and former police colleague David Weeks and was told that they were glad to be there and were settling in well with all the others.

In 1976, the Hong Kong government applied to the UNHCR for more material aid and faster processing of the hundreds or even thousands still being cared for in the three camps. By the end of 1977, all had been resettled in the USA, France, Germany, Australia or Hong Kong. As at 31st May 2000, when the last Hong Kong refugee camp closed at Pillar Point near Tuen Mun in the New Territories, a total of 143,700 from both South and North Vietnam had been resettled in the free world, and over 67,000 repatriated back to Vietnam, the last of them forcibly by the Special Administrative Region government following the return of sovereignty of Hong Kong to China in 1997. This does not tell the whole story but what a tremendous job the UNHCR, the Security Branch and disciplined services of Hong Kong had done, often in the most trying of circumstances.

Thanks to the Internet, many records of this twenty-five-year period can be studied, including the experiences of numerous passengers of the ill-fated MS *Truong Xuan* and their subsequent wait for resettlement. One of the passengers was nine-year-old Debbie Nguyen Xuan Diep, whose story of her family's eventful journey starting fifty miles outside Saigon was to appear in the 628-page book *Truong Xuan – Journey to Freedom,* published in 2010. Her whole family was blessed with enormous slices of good luck along the way, not least that while at Sai Kung Camp they were accepted by Australia, a country they now love. By 2016, her family group of ten escapees, including two grandparents, had grown to thirty five, all thriving in and around Sydney. They, and everyone else, arriving in Hong Kong on the MS *Clara Maersk* on 4th May, 1975, will never forget that they almost certainly owe their lives to the skill and humanitarian action of two outstanding ships' captains, Pham Ngoc Luy and Anton Olsen. Debbie Nguyen is now an accountant with a family of her own and is still gathering stories provided by her fellow refugee passengers.

I will always remember the gratitude shown to the staff of Shau Kei Wan Police Station by the group of seventy Vietnamese refugees who, in common with those from the MS *Clara Maersk*, would have suffered many an anxious moment in their search for freedom. It was a privilege to briefly look after them on 6th May, 1975, and I hope that they went on to prosper in the countries that accepted them.

The *Huey Fong* and *Skyluck* Refugees

John Turner

The Vietnam War ended in 1975, two years after the withdrawal of American forces, and the country was unified under communist control. Over the course of the next ten years, tens of thousands of refugees, including many ethnic Chinese, left the country by sea. They initially departed in small boats, to escape the communist regime and seek resettlement, either in other Southeast Asian countries or preferably in the United States. When Malaysia, Singapore and the Philippines turned them away, they headed further north across the South China Sea, and very soon, a tide of refugees began reaching Hong Kong.

Initially, the refugees attempted the hazardous journey in fishing boats and other small craft. There is no record of the thousands who died en route. The majority paid traffickers in Vietnam who were only able to guide them to exit points out of sight of the Vietnamese authorities. The long voyage, often in small unseaworthy small craft, was even attempted during the typhoon season in the South China Sea, frequently with tragic results.

From the mid-seventies, the Marine Police in Hong Kong were kept busy intercepting the hundreds of small, overloaded craft carrying the 'boat people', as they became known, as they entered Hong Kong waters. Late in 1978, the refugee traffickers decided that it would be more profitable to use larger ships to transport the human cargo. To this end they began to purchase old cargo ships, of which there was a plentiful number available for sale in Southeast Asia. The first of these was a Taiwan-owned freighter, the *Huey Fong*, which was chartered to convey 2,700 refugees from Vietnam to Kaohsiung, Taiwan. The ship was denied entry to Taiwan and so the vessel headed for Hong Kong. In late December it arrived south of Hong Kong where the master requested permission to enter the harbour. He described conditions on board as 'crowded, unsanitary, with babies crying and all suffering from the cold'. This proved an understatement of the actual situation on board.

The Hong Kong Marine Department refused the master's request and ordered him to proceed to the ship's designated port, i.e. Kaohsiung. Police Headquarters (POLMIL – Police/Military Combined Command and Control Centre) were informed by the Marine Department. Marine Police District Headquarters was instructed to dispatch a police launch to intercept the *Huey Fong* and report conditions on board. I decided to go out with the launch to see the situation for myself. Not knowing what to expect, I kitted myself out in riot gear together with a similarly equipped section of Marine Police officers. On embarking from Kowloon Public Pier late in the afternoon on board *Police Launch 58*, we were informed by Marine Department that the *Huey Fong* was believed to have anchored near Waglan Island, a point south of Hong Kong Island and just inside Hong Kong waters.

The journey over to Waglan took approximately one hour. The weather was overcast, with a moderate sea once we had left Hong Kong harbour. En route I briefed the 'boarding party' on the action to be taken. Envisaging a situation where the crew and/or some of the refugees became hostile, my plan was to secure the bridge, apprehend the ship's master, and establish some form of communication with those on board. Unfortunately my Police Tactical Unit training had not prepared me for this type of operation! In the event we boarded the vessel and reached the bridge where we were welcomed with open arms by the captain, and a Vietnamese male who claimed to be the refugees' representative. This man performed miracles some weeks later when the 2,700 refugees were disembarked and processed by the Immigration Department. The operation went extremely smoothly thanks to this one man's assistance.

I then carried out an inspection of the vessel. On opening the hatch covers on deck and looking down into the hold, I was met with hundreds of human faces gazing up into the light. Men, women, children and even babies, (four had been born since leaving

Vietnam), surrounded by the small amount of personal possessions they had been allowed to bring with them. Many appeared sick and were obviously in need of urgent medical treatment, especially the elderly and very young. The stench coming from the hold was indescribable, and the condition of the refugees shocked all of us. The contrast between their situation and the seasonal festivities we had all been enjoying in Hong Kong so recently was difficult to comprehend!

I returned to the police launch and reported my findings to Marine Police District Control and POLMIL. I requested food and water for those on board plus medical staff and supplies. This was promised provided the vessel made no attempt to enter further into Hong Kong waters and remained at anchor. I conveyed these instructions to the ship's master who appeared satisfied. Additional police launches later arrived at the scene and I was able to return to Marine District HQ in Kowloon. Food and water were later delivered to the ship and the seriously ill among the refugees airlifted to hospital in Kowloon. This gave me some satisfaction having observed the awful conditions on board at first hand. A few days later the government allowed the ship to move into a more sheltered anchorage off Lamma Island where regular supplies of food and water were delivered to those on board.

A few weeks later, on 28th February, 1979, a second large freighter, named *Skyluck*, carrying over 2,400 refugees, attempted to enter the western harbour area after darkness by way of Green Island. The ship's master had ignored requests by the Marine Department not to enter the harbour, and Marine Police were instructed to intercept the vessel and prevent any further movement into the central harbour area. I arrived at the scene on a police launch with Geoff Cox, the sector commander, and boarded the ship at about midnight. The master, Shu Wen-shin, was of Taiwanese nationality, and was able to speak a little English. I asked him to produce the ship's log books in an effort to establish the vessel's port of departure. Mr Shu replied that these had been lost, and the refugees on board had been picked up from small boats off the coast of Vietnam. We knew this to be untrue, and that the ship had in fact been purchased in Singapore for the specific purpose of transporting refugees from Vietnam to either Hong Kong or, failing that, Taiwan.

The refugees were also held in the ship's enormous holds and were in a pitiful condition, albeit slightly better than those I had seen on the *Huey Fong* in December. Many of the elderly and the babies, (no less than five had been born during the voyage), were suffering from the cold and exposure and were in urgent need of medical treatment. Having completed a preliminary inspection, I informed the master that he did not have permission to enter Hong Kong harbour. I told him the ship was causing an obstruction, and he must move to a more suitable anchorage outside the harbour. I also informed him that no decision regarding the refugees and the crew would be made until the ship had moved to a designated anchorage. The information was debated at length by the master and some of his officers, with several refugees joining in. Voices were raised at times, but at no time did we feel threatened.

The master finally agreed to move the vessel and was directed to an anchorage off Lamma Island. I then left the ship and returned to HQ to write a report on the whole incident, which I managed to complete just as dawn was breaking. Looking out onto the harbour I was very relieved to see no sign of the *Skyluck*. Later that morning fifteen doctors and auxiliary medical staff boarded the ship to attend to the sick, and supplies of food and water commenced on a regular basis. The *Skyluck* and its passengers remained at this location for several weeks, during which time relations with the Hong Kong authorities became increasingly hostile. Many of the younger refugees grew tired of waiting and jumped from the ship in attempts to swim ashore. Others organised hunger strikes and, on one occasion, cut the anchor chains. They also threw missiles and Molotov cocktails at the police and government launches surrounding the ship. Fortunately, by this time I had been trans-ferred out of Marine Police District so the *Skyluck* was no longer my problem.

In the meantime the government had decided to permit the 2,700 refugees on the *Huey Fong* to be given temporary shelter in Hong Kong pending permanent resettlement elsewhere – UK and the USA were possibilities. The vessel was brought into Hong Kong harbour and moored at the Kowloon Wharf, opposite the Ocean Terminal and below Marine Police District HQ. The task for the team consisting of Marine Police, CID/HQ, Immigration Department, and Customs and Excise, was to disembark the crew and passengers, process them, i.e. fingerprinting and documentation, search the vessel and any cargo, and finally remove them to a detention camp in Kowloon. I found myself in charge of the team, possibly because I had already met the refugee representative in December when we first boarded the ship, and he seemed pleased to meet up with me again, promising his full support.

The whole operation proceeded smoothly and without incident over the course of the next four days, thanks largely to the cooperation of the refugees themselves and their hardworking representative who seemed to know them all by name! At the end of the fourth day the ship had been cleared of refugees and the master and his crew had been taken away for further questioning – they were later charged with various immigration, marine and human trafficking offences. One task remained – where was the gold? We had reliable intelligence that payment in gold intended for the traffickers was to be delivered in Hong Kong or Taiwan. Already gold to the value of HK$1.5m had been recovered from crew members and refugees, and after several hours searching the ship's engine room by a CID team led by Detective Superintendent John Clemence and Detective Chief Inspector Lionel Lam, the extraordinary sight of a gold-encased propeller shaft was revealed! The gold was valued at $5m. Total value of gold recovered, $6.5m. Case closed! Time to celebrate!

My time spent in the Marine Police during those hectic weeks in the late seventies was truly memorable. Marine Police District up until then, had always been considered the 'poor relation of the Force'. It was not a popular posting, unless you happened to be a former seafarer, and the junior police officers disliked their 'sailor' uniforms intensely. The Vietnamese refugee crisis changed this view and the Marine Police were praised by the governor, the commissioner of police and the media for the efficient manner in which they had responded to the crisis, spending long hours on duty at sea, often in difficult and stressful conditions, and always showing compassion to the plight of the refugees.

In fact, the Hong Kong government was so impressed with the performance of the Marine Police that it immediately ordered the purchase of thirty modern patrol boats, a welcome addition to the ageing fleet, and a most welcome reward for very hard work!

Marine Police and the Huey Fong *refugees (Courtesy J. Turner)*

The Police Negotiation Cadre

Tom Delbridge

One of the most memorable items of TV news coverage in Hong Kong was of a robbery and hostage taking at a branch of the Po Sang Bank in 1974. A lone gunman had entered the bank intent on a swift robbery and fast exit. But police officers reached the scene so quickly that he found himself trapped in the bank and so instead took all the customers and staff hostage, tying them hand and foot.

The footage was just starting to become boring, with nothing happening, when suddenly the bank door opened, and several men bounced – literally – out onto the street. Somehow the hostages, despite still being bound hand and foot, had managed to overpower the gunman. When the 'bouncers' appeared, there was a brief pause and then, seemingly out of nowhere, a police officer appeared on the screen, gun in hand, ran into the bank and emerged moments later with the suspect. John Griffiths earned plaudits all round, together with the endearing nickname *Gee Foo See* ('nearly died'). (Griffiths tells his story in the chapter 'The Po Sang Bank Siege'.)

The Force was by no means caught unprepared by the Po Sang Bank incident. Police forces worldwide had carefully studied the incident at the Munich Olympics in 1972 in which Palestinian terrorists had seized a group of Israeli athletes and demanded a helicopter. The German police promised them one, intending that marksmen should kill the terrorists just prior to their boarding it. Instead all the hostages died, a tragedy which most experts put down to bad luck and perhaps poor marksmanship. So, the Force, in common with most others around the globe, set up a Marksman Unit and drew up contingency plans.

The lesson from the Po Sang Bank incident was that, while some incidents might indeed be resolvable only by good police marksmanship, the Force also needed the capability to storm a hostage-taker stronghold and neutralise the terrorists or criminals in close-quarter combat. So, the Special Duties Unit (SDU) was set up in the Police Tactical Unit (PTU), Fan Ling, and quickly became highly competent in the role.

Such competence clearly needed to be tested regularly and so it was decided that Force-wide exercises with SDU playing the central role would be conducted roughly once a year. The first was planned to take place at Kai Tak Airport, with Civil Aviation Department (CAD) fully involved. To add to the realism and put SDU under pressure in preparing their assault, it was decided that the 'terrorists' should be on board an actual aircraft and should issue demands and a deadline. Ah yes, and that someone should 'negotiate' with them.

Operations Wing in Police Headquarters therefore decided to establish a Police Negotiation Cadre with one or more members which would be called out to live hostage incidents. Major formation commanders were invited to nominate officers (most of them expatriates), and a staff officer, David Holdroyd prepared and conducted a training course at the PTU. On the day of the exercise, a lone negotiator sat in a large room filled with senior officers from the Force, Security Branch of central Hong Kong government, and CAD. The negotiations were carried out over a land line simulating the aircraft radio. The conversation between the two sides was blared out over a speaker system in the room and treated as entertainment by everyone but the poor negotiator.

A first major turning point for the cadre came in 1979, with a hostage-taking inside the Realty Building in Central District. A disgruntled contractor had entered the offices of a development company and, after an argument, had pulled out a gun and taken six female staff hostage. Operations Wing sent four negotiators to the scene: Eric Lockeyear, Gerry Frith, Lawrence Tsui and myself. Because of the nature of the company's telephone switchboard, there was no way of providing a dedicated line to the hostage-taker. Lawrence Tsui therefore spoke directly, from a corner halfway down a long corridor leading from 'the stronghold', the door of which was left open. Finally, the gunman was brought to his senses and decided to surrender to the sub-divisional inspector of Waterfront Police Station, Jock Atkinson, who had stood throughout, in uniform, at the end of the corridor.

With a lot of help from Operations Wing, the cadre spent most of the next five years improving its expertise, and a three-person 'negotiating team' (rather than a lone negotiator) became standard practice. Overseas agencies which provided training courses included the London Metropolitan Police, who recommended the purchase of a 'Negotiator's Box'; a desktop device into which a landline link to the 'stronghold' could be plugged, with dual recording so that one tape could be replayed at any time. Funds were not immediately available for this but Tony Robbins, a radio engineer with Communications Branch, cobbled one together from odds and ends that he had collected over the years and it served the cadre well for close to a decade.

Brian Tully had meanwhile been appointed as Senior Force Clinical Psychologist (SFCP) and was sharpening up the cadre's grasp of negotiating psychology. He also played a major role in the several negotiator training courses held for new members, all now volunteers and most local Chinese officers. And around this time, CAD completely revamped the incident command centre at Kai Tak Airport, complete with a 'Negotiator's Cubicle'; a massive improvement over the earlier arrangement.

Just as important as all this, a series of further live incidents occurred which gave individual negotiators and the cadre as a whole greater confidence, and increased their credibility within the Force.

One of these incidents was at Kai Tak Airport and involved a drunken British soldier who, armed with a rifle, took an Airport Police constable hostage. Cadre member, Jerry Kidner, was at the airport at the time and quickly moved in to negotiate with the soldier, who surrendered his weapon an hour or so later.

Another incident was in an educational institution in Kwun Tong, Kowloon, where, in the early evening, an elderly caretaker with a grudge took a young male teacher hostage at knifepoint. Charles Wong was the lead negotiator on this occasion and did well, but after matters dragged on until late into the night, the incident commander decided to send in a baton-wielding assault team. Fortunately, the hostage suffered only minor abrasions.

The outstanding incident during this period was in 1983 in Wan Chai, where a gunman hijacked a public light bus and its passengers. The lead negotiator was again Charles Wong, with Beta Tam as debriefer and Peter Morgan as strategist. Wong had no option but to go face-to-face and finally persuaded the hostage taker to surrender. His skill and bravery earned him a Commissioner of Police Commendation.

A second major turning point for the cadre came in 1984, when a threatened suicide in Wong Tai Sin, Kowloon, was attended by the Fire Services Department (FSD) and, for the first time, by a police negotiator; yet again, Charles Wong. The incident ended tragically with the suicidal man falling to his death after a failed attempt to snatch him to safety. Operations Wing decided that, in future, negotiators should be called to all threatened suicides, and the cadre geared up for this, with special training sessions for its own members, and also for FSD. Brian Tully, the SFCP, again played a key role in this.

For the next few years, dealing with threatened suicides became the main operational activity of the cadre. This naturally gave many members hands-on experience and that in turn brought a flood of important new ideas; everyone was now thinking about what negotiating really meant.

Psychology became more widely understood, especially after Charles Wong and Peter Morgan started playing more active roles in the cadre. Also, ideas used in business negotiations helped the cadre finally to establish a firm theoretical basis for its negotiating – namely the 'Win-Win' principle. In any criminal hostage-taking for example, the best outcome for the Force would be the surrender of the criminal and the safe release of the hostages. A dead hostage-taker would portray police as trigger-happy; a dead or badly injured hostage would portray us as uncaring and incompetent. And surrender is also in the criminal's best interests; avoiding his own death or the possibility of a murder charge. So, the real job of the negotiators is, subtly and slowly, to bring the hijackers/ criminals/ suicidal person to realise that their own interests would be best served by releasing any hostage, and by opting for a non-violent ending.

Most of the incidents to which negotiators were called in succeeding years were resolved successfully in line with the 'Win-Win' principle. Many lives of potential suicides were saved and then improved by referral to the Social Welfare Department and other relevant agencies. There were inevitably a few exceptions however, of which two incidents were particularly vexing to the cadre.

The first incident led to a Force-level investigation. A man fatally stabbed his wife and then barricaded himself inside the family home. When police arrived, they could see the woman's motionless and bloodstained body through one of the windows in the flat. Believing her to be dead and suspecting that the man may have a hostage – a child – the incident commander and the negotiators decided to talk to the man rather than immediately storm the premises. The man surrendered in due course but it turned out that there was no hostage, prompting criticism in the press which asked whether officers involved 'had medical backgrounds qualifying them to judge whether the woman was dead or alive when they arrived'.

In the other incident, a man set fire to himself, suffering very severe burns, and then threatened to jump from a rooftop. The negotiators eventually persuaded him to surrender, but no one could pretend that the outcome was a 'Win-Win'. Edmund Lee, who had by now had taken over as SFCP, eased a lot of concern here by explaining the important principle of 'problem ownership' when dealing with some of the more traumatic suicide incidents.

As the years went by, other major developments came along and the role of the cadre gradually expanded. In 2014, the cadre negotiators played a valuable role during the 'Occupy Central' period. This was a major incident when up to 100,000 demonstrators, mostly students and young people, protesting in support of greater democracy, occupied the area around the Central Government Complex in Admiralty for ten weeks, blocking roads and causing serious traffic problems. Tension between demonstrators and police, and between the demonstrators and some members of the public who did not hold the same views, were eased on the ground by the employment of negotiators.

In 2015, the Police Negotiation Cadre celebrated its fortieth anniversary.

Leading Her Majesty Astray

Barry Griffin

It was a wet night in May 1975 when I was sitting on my police motorcycle with the engine running outside the front door of Government House. As part of the Force Escort Group I was Red Team Leader and was awaiting Her Majesty the Queen to escort her across the harbour to Whitfield Barracks in Austin Road for a special performance. Our departure was delayed and all traffic had already been stopped on the escort route through Hong Kong Island. I was being yelled at by the Traffic Police commander to get moving and eventually we did, with some concern about traffic conditions and the slippery deck of the Hongkong and Yaumati Ferry Company's vehicular ferry on which we were to embark the royal motorcade for transit to Kowloon. Fortunately, we arrived in Kowloon without incident.

The planned route in Kowloon was via Argyle Street to Nathan Road and then down the wrong side of Nathan Road to Austin Road. This would facilitate viewing of Her Majesty by members of the public, as she always sits on the right-hand side of vehicles. As we approached the junction of Nathan Road there was some chatter on the radio channel concerning a traffic accident on the escort route. We only had one dedicated radio channel that was immediately usurped by the Kowloon Traffic Police Commander who was in a helicopter overhead. He unfortunately had taken on the role of a media commentator, reporting on what a wonderful night it was with all the Kowloon lights shining brightly and the royal motorcade moving slowly along the route.

It was at this time to my horror, that I observed the lead member of my escort team, followed by the 'protocol vehicle', turn into the left-hand carriageway of Nathan Road, instead of the agreed route down the right side. I tried to use the traffic radio channel to seek clarification but it was still occupied by the Traffic commander. As I was under strict orders not to stop when escorting the motorcade, I made the decision to follow the lead vehicles down the left-hand carriageway of Nathan Road and the rest of the motorcade followed suit behind me. We were immediately confronted by a 130-member Police Tactical Unit company on foot who were scrambling to get out of our way. I realised that something was terribly wrong. I had to get the motorcade back on the other carriageway, and the next few minutes were the longest of my life as we passed various junctions and I was rapidly running out of options.

I was aware that police vehicles were parked on Nathan Road just south of Gascoigne Road and therefore, blocking the route ahead. I decided to move the motorcade across the junction at Public Square Street, which was probably the narrowest junction along Nathan Road. Needless to say, throughout this time, the radio net had remained ominously silent until I signalled a right turn and transmitted 'Red Leader! Red Leader to all! Turn right! Turn right! Follow me!'

I made the turn and was relieved to note that the close protection security vehicle and the royal vehicle followed me across the junction, together with the rest of the motorcade. Just as my stress levels were reducing somewhat, my escort sergeant, riding immediately in front of me, skidded on a manhole cover and dropped his bike. As I slowed down the motorcade he feverishly righted his machine and got out of my way, just before we had to stop! Less than one minute later we arrived at the venue in Whitfield Barracks and Her Majesty the Queen and party were safely delivered.

I had only just alighted from my motorcycle when the senior assistant commissioner, Kowloon Police Commander, descended on me demanding to know why I deviated from the agreed route. I replied that I had understood that there had been a traffic accident on the planned route and that we had to divert. He proceeded to thank me for doing a good job.

I was then immediately accosted by the close protection commander and reprimanded for going down the wrong side of Nathan

Road. I pointed out that he had the traffic net radio in his vehicle and I had received no instructions to correct the error.

Some months later, when all the excitement had died down, I was surprised to receive a Commissioner of Police's Commendation for 'excellent duty performance during the Royal Visit'. During the next few years I carried out numerous escort duties and managed to lead at least one other member of the royal family astray – but that is another story!

Building an International Drug Case

Paul Dalton

In 1979, about halfway through my first three-year tour of duty in the Royal Hong Kong Police, I was posted to the Narcotics Bureau. I had previously served in the Leicestershire Police drug squad for nearly three years so I was pleased to trade uniform at Wong Tai Sin Division for a far more interesting role in C Section of the Narcotics Bureau.

My primary role was liaison with overseas drug enforcement offices. The American Drug Enforcement Agency and the Royal Canadian Mounted Police both maintained liaison offices in Hong Kong, as did the Dutch who seemed to be at the centre of things. I was also required to be available as a case officer for drug seizures identified by the Intelligence Section. This led to my involvement with a fascinating case that even today demonstrates the breadth and capability of the bureau.

By way of background, the bureau had been responsible in the early 1970s for the dismantling of a well-developed amphetamine factory, and the subsequent imprisonment of the organiser, Peter Wong. As his time for release from detention was approaching and because of his previous prolific drug activities, he was placed on low-level monitoring. Thus, we were not surprised to learn that he was well advanced in a plan to import opium into Hong Kong through China, although by this time opium was a drug that had almost lost its popularity due to the availability of heroin.

I became involved in the case during the summer of 1980, when I was tasked to meet a surveillance team who had arrested a man named Andrew Chan. It transpired that a Canadian female named Mary Holmwood had crossed from China earlier that day and after booking into a Mong Kok hotel, she had handed over a suitcase to

Andrew Chan. Chan, in turn, was followed to his flat in Mei Foo Sun Chuen where he had opened the false bottom of the case to remove a sample of opium before going out to find a buyer.

Chan and Holmwood were arrested and interviewed. I carried out a routine check with the Royal Canadian Mounted Police with regard to Holmwood, and in doing so, I noticed that it was her birthday next day. Being keen to build a relationship with a person who could be a key witness and knowing I was in for a long interview, I arrived at Mong Kok Police Station armed with statement forms and a dozen red roses. In hindsight, I shudder. Yet, I was rewarded with tears and a full confession of her involvement, and an agreement to be a crown witness.

Thus, we were able to develop a case against Peter Wong, although despite extensive enquiries he was nowhere to be found.

Paul Dalton with the false-bottomed suitcase (Courtesy Paul Dalton)

What we did have was a willing and credible witness in Mary Holmwood who had received the opium from Wong in Bombay, and had also met the supplier, a man named Rushi Mistry. While waiting to appear before the Kowloon magistrates on drug charges, Holmwood was found to have a quantity of heroin hidden internally. Her prospects looked rather dim. Chief Inspector John Thompson, my senior officer, directed we should present a case to use Mary Holmwood as a crown witness. She duly obliged and was eventually imprisoned for one year with the agreement to give evidence against Wong and Chan. The clock was ticking to find Peter Wong.

It was thought wise to corroborate as far as possible Holmwood's evidence. Accordingly, John Thompson and I were delighted when we were given permission to continue the investigation in Bombay. On arrival, at first we were passed like a hot potato between various Customs and Police Departments until we arrived at Crawford Market, the headquarters of Bombay CID. After a short meeting with an assistant commissioner of police, we were introduced to the splendidly named Inspector Bernard George Shaw, an Anglo-Indian who was accompanied everywhere by two detectives who could have moonlighted as Bollywood dacoits!

Bernard quickly got a grasp of the case, although we were surprised when at 7 pm a postman arrived flanked by his two detectives. We were told the best way to find Rushi Mistry in the slums of Bombay was by a postman at three in the morning! When John and I arrived the following morning, there sitting under the swirling fans sat Mr Mistry accompanied by his family, who provided his food for the next three days while he remained handcuffed to a bench.

We were able to obtain a full statement from Mistry, who took us to where the suitcase with the false bottom was manufactured. He also agreed to accompany us back to Hong Kong as a witness, which was not quite as easy as it sounds. This was due to Mistry having previously been deported from Hong Kong, so the signature of Governor MacLehose was needed on a rarely used form. Mistry subsequently left Bombay and resided in a Wan Chai safe house for six months. Thus we had two good witnesses and a large amount of evidence that provided corroboration, yet we still needed to find Peter Wong.

As part of the search for Wong we learnt that his wife was friendly with a mid-level manager at a local bank, and it was decided to approach him. I met him in a tea house and after a short discussion, he was very eager to tell us that Peter Wong was in Australia and that the following week his wife was flying out to join him.

We set in motion a surveillance operation by the Australian Federal Police who arrested Wong in the airport car park as he greeted his wife. He was later extradited to Hong Kong where he stood trial, was convicted and sentenced to another five years at Stanley Prison.

As a postscript, my face was rather red when the Canadians revealed, following the routine check and before her court hearing, that the real Mary Holmwood had died some three years previously, and the passport with date of birth had been fraudulently obtained. When I re-interviewed her, she admitted this and gave her real name, and the address of her parents. I did notice that the dried roses were still in her cell.

During this investigation John Thompson and I were assisted by a large number of police officers and legal teams whose names I regret have faded with time, but who made significant contributions to a very successful international drug law enforcement case.

A Junior Inspector in Sha Tin and Tai Po

Simon Roberts

In the summer of 1980, after scraping through training, I was posted to Sha Tin Division in the New Territories. This was my first posting after somehow managing to attain an unimpressive 52 per cent in all my final exams. Sha Tin Police Station had just been built in 1978, and was in the centre of the development of the 'new town' of Sha Tin. The Sha Tin racecourse had also been built in 1978, and there were two public housing estates. Apart from some pig farms and paddy fields and some empty six-lane highways, there was not much else there. My first boss was Chief Inspector Dick Lee. Dick was six feet four inches tall and very charismatic. It was no surprise to me that he eventually became the police commissioner. Because of the construction all around us, the town was full of engineers, and many were given visiting membership of the officers' mess. Every Friday was curry-lunch day. Dick would often shout: 'Come on young Simon, let's go up for a curry lunch.'

The curry was usually mutton or chicken. It was served with a ladle out of huge stainless steel pots by one of the Shantung cooks. Another pot contained steamed rice. There would be side dishes of sliced banana, mango chutney, diced tomatoes and diced onions. This would be washed down with copious amounts of beer, usually San Miguel or Carlsberg. Many of the engineers were British and Australian, and they were usually very thirsty. The banter was good but as the youngest I was often the butt of the teasing. Often I would stagger out at about 6 pm to get changed and make my way home for a shower and then crash into bed in order to make an early start the next morning. My conditioned hours then were 56 hours over six days per week.

Like most junior inspectors, I was reliant on my NCOs to guide me each day. At the start of each shift I would be required to inspect the sub-unit to ensure their turnout was smart and they were properly equipped. I, and they, carried a revolver with six rounds of ammunition, but at that time, female officers were not armed. As I did not know much about anything, I quickly learned the most important three words for a sub-unit inspector: 'Carry on sergeant'. I think everyone knew I was pretty clueless but they were all polite and the sergeant would salute and continue with his briefing in Cantonese. I would then walk the beat with one of the local officers and check that visiting books had been signed. I would listen to the chatter on the heavy beat radios, and try to understand what was happening. Sha Tin at the time was quiet, as many families were reluctant to relocate there. So the sparkling new housing blocks took a while to fill up.

Perhaps the government might have tried harder to promote the place. The 1979 *Hong Kong Yearbook* describes how Sha Tin would be revitalised. It states that 'as Sha Tin is surrounded by steep hills it is vulnerable to smoke pollution', and adds 'the Shing Mun river is heavily polluted and the plan is to clean the septic mud from the river bed'. In order to entice new residents further, it goes on to explain that 'disposal of sewage is a problem and that water inlets can be subject to cyclonic surge and flooding'. It's not surprising that it took time to encourage people to move out of their Kowloon squatter villages.

I found that getting around such a large geographical area was not easy so I applied to take a police motorcycle course. Once I had passed, it meant I could take out a small 175cc Kawasaki police patrol bike. This I really enjoyed because it gave me the freedom to patrol a much wider area and explore the edges of the district. It was odd riding along the empty highways. One evening, when I was out on the motorbike, I came across a small herd of buffalo that had escaped from a farmer's field. They had rings through their noses and a couple were still attached to a wooden stake that had been pulled from the earth. The buffalo were trotting down the middle of a wide motorway and I was keen to get them back to the safety of the fields. I called for back-up on the large black Motorola radio in my motorcycle pannier. All I got was static. I had to sort it myself. The bike was not a properly equipped patrol vehicle so I had no siren. I decided to put my headlamp on full beam, and constantly press the bike horn whilst shouting at the top of my voice. At the same time I was wheeling the bike round in 180-degree turns to try to startle the beasts. I must have looked a complete idiot but it seemed to work. Gradually they started to move back and eventually I got them off the highway and back into the fields. When I returned to the station and told my colleagues what had happened, everyone laughed.

One of the odd things about Sha Tin at the time was that the cells were often full of people who were not prisoners. As part of my routine duties, I had to check the cells and the prisoners regularly. Our cells in 1980 were frequently full of women, children and families. They always seemed to be in good humour but could speak no Cantonese or English. I asked Dick Lee who they were. I discovered they were from Mainland China but they were not illegal immigrants. They were in transit, waiting for residence visas to relocate to other countries. In most cases this meant the USA. The problem was the process sometimes took weeks. The government had nowhere to put them so they were housed in our police cells. They did not have access to outside exercise or fresh air and I always felt really sorry for them cramped up in such a place. Whenever I was on duty, I would collect local newspapers and magazines and take sweets for the children. In spite of their surroundings they always smiled when they saw me and seemed to be in high spirits. Perhaps this was because they were already dreaming of a new life overseas.

At the Police Training School, I had bought a green MG midget sports car for HK$6,000. I thought it was very cool, but in reality it was really unsuited for Hong Kong. It had a heavy clutch, no air conditioning or power steering and was always breaking down. After my shift at Sha Tin, I would drive my MG along Tai Po Road to my quarters in Tai Po Kau. The building was a detached low-rise white structure with some single quarters, a communal sitting room, and a communal kitchen. The place was up a small hill from the road and was surrounded by trees. We had an amah called Ah

Kee who always wore traditional Chinese costume, a black tunic and trousers and black flat canvas slippers. She did not speak the Cantonese dialect and was often found cooking strange stews and soups on a small gas stove on the floor. I had a decent group of colleagues although they had appropriated most of the serviceable furniture from my room before I had moved in. As in most communal areas, any food left in the refrigerator had often disappeared by the time I came home from my shift. The thing I disliked most about the place though was it was so remote. I never saw anyone, and to buy bread I had to drive into a Wellcome supermarket in Tai Po.

One of the things I did enjoy was that we were able to move around in new roles on a regular basis, which meant I was always learning something new. After a year in Sha Tin I was moved to the Tai Po subdivision. This was the old station up the hill from the market. It was a lovely place surrounded by tall acacia trees. I liked the older colonial feel of Tai Po station. The place was wonderfully self-contained with a laundry and a canteen. We even created an area with a small refrigerator for the inspectors to relax. There were very few Europeans in Tai Po in 1981 and so, whenever I was on patrol, people would stare and children often cried when they saw me. I was still trying to get used to the culture and habits of local people and was always trying to improve my Cantonese skills. The latter I found very helpful when attempting to chat up local girls.

When I was sitting in my small office in Tai Po station one day, catching up on paperwork, I heard a terrible commotion coming from the report room. I got up and walked along the corridor to see what was happening. I saw two constables trying to restrain two elderly men who were screaming obscenities and trying to punch each other. Their faces were bright red and from the abrasions I could see that they'd landed a few blows already. It was an odd scene so I asked the sergeant on duty what was going on. 'Well sir,' he explained, 'they are very old friends.' I interrupted him, 'It doesn't look like it!' but he continued to patiently relate the story. It was all about a loss of face. It seemed that the two old men had not seen each other in almost a year but they had known each other for a long time. They had agreed to meet for a *dim sum* lunch that day.

Everything had been very cordial until they finished. Each had then insisted that he should pay the bill, and neither would back down. Gradually they lost their tempers and first shouts, then punches were exchanged. The restaurant had then called police.

I decided to separate them and ordered them to be placed in separate cells. I left them there to cool off for about forty minutes and then went into each cell with Sergeant Chan. I laid down the law to the first chap and told him what an idiot he was, then that he should let his friend pay today and they could agree he would pay the next time. I went into the next cell and told the other chap to pay this time and let his friend pay next time. After ten more minutes I took them both out, and gave them a final warning. They walked out together with their tails between their legs, but we watched them chatting together as they walked back down the hill towards the market. We never saw them again.

In Tai Po, there were not many Western restaurants, and because I was the only expatriate in the station there was not much access to the food I was used to. I could tolerate the breakfasts of white bread, fried eggs and luncheon meat washed down with tea and condensed milk. I did find the lunches in the canteen to be hard going though. There was always rice, with small fried fish and some meat, both of which seemed to be mostly bones. The dishes were accompanied by various vegetables, none of which I recognised. It was probably very healthy, and in spite of all the beer I drank, I never put on weight in those years. I was very glad when a small European restaurant opened near the market which served black pepper steak with crinkle-cut chips.

I was in this restaurant a few months later and enjoying a meal at the end of my shift. Having just taken a couple of bites of my food, the waiter ran up to my table looking very agitated. He grabbed my arm and said: 'Bam!' I looked at him without a clue what he wanted. 'Barm ... bem ... bom,' he kept insisting. He indicated we should go outside.

I followed him into the street and then I saw the road full of smoke and heard people screaming. I ran up the road and saw the local Jockey Club off-course betting centre was in flames. Some people inside had their clothes on fire and there was a lot of damage to the interior. I realised that the waiter had been trying to tell me there was a 'bomb'. I ran inside and grabbed a large red fire extinguisher off the wall. I was able to activate it and aimed the water jet at the people with burning clothes and then at the burning betting slips around the floor. Within a short time, the fires were extinguished. I requested that someone call 999 and summon the police, ambulance, and fire brigade. I waited at the scene and tried to ensure any evidence was preserved and that witnesses did not leave. Fortunately it seemed no-one had been killed or seriously injured. We decided to request the Force Bomb Disposal Officer, Ron Bagley, to attend the scene. As it was late on a Wednesday evening, it took him almost two hours to make his way from Hong Kong Island. When he arrived, the first thing he said was: 'Have you searched the area for further devices?' I hadn't, and the thought that I could have been standing next to another bomb did not improve my mood. The story was on all the front pages of the newspapers next day. It seemed that someone had placed a home-made pipe bomb in a wastepaper basket. The motive was unknown and I don't think anyone was arrested for it.

Towards the end of 1981, I took over the vice squad, known as the Special Duty Squad (SDS). This was a plain-clothes job and meant working various hours on an ad-hoc basis depending on what was required. I had a small team and our role was to counter the trade in drugs, gambling and prostitution. There wasn't much of the latter in the New Territories in 1981, so most of our efforts were investigating drugs and gambling. We were not well equipped and were expected to use our own private cars. Fortunately Sergeant Wong had a nondescript four-door Mazda saloon which we used to get around. Beat radios were too large to carry unless we hid them in small rucksacks. We mainly used pagers to communicate. As a European I stood out like a sore thumb, so covert policing was very difficult for me. Much of the time we followed very poor information from some low-level paid informers. On one occasion we spotted a small-time drug trafficker we wanted to stop and search. He spotted me first and in spite of me giving chase on foot, he managed to escape by jumping on an old bicycle and pedalling furiously down the street.

One evening when we came on duty in Tai Po, Sergeant Wong said he had some information about drug activity in one of the village houses. We decided to check it out. We arrived after dark and parked up some distance from the house. When we walked along a narrow footpath and peered in from behind some trees, we did not see any lights. We crept closer and found the front door open. We decided to go inside, and finding no-one there, we thought we would wait for the house owner to return. About two hours later, the house owner came back up the path and through the door with his girlfriend. As he switched the lights on, we jumped up and shouted '*Chai-yan!*' (police). Sergeant Wong grabbed the suspect who did not put up any resistance. We showed our police warrant cards, and he was cautioned. Sergeant Wong said he was going to search him. In his jeans pocket, a few straws of number three heroin were found but nothing else. We also did not find any more drugs in the house. Being a bit disappointed Sergeant Wong decided to search the suspect properly. After the girlfriend was led to another room, a thorough body search was conducted. The suspect was told to drop his jeans and underpants, and before I knew what was happening the suspect was bent forwards with his bottom being examined with a flashlight for concealed contraband. Unfortunately this was done whilst I was in clear line of sight. We took the suspect to the station and charged him, and whilst I praised my sergeant for his thoroughness, I made sure to stand back next time he conducted a body search.

Probably the highlight of my time in Sha Tin SDS was when we uncovered an opium divan. By the 1980s, these were quite rare as most drug addicts inhaled heroin by 'chasing the dragon' and opium had fallen out of fashion. The information we received said the location was in a smallholding next to a village just outside Tai Po. When we turned up at the scene we found an orchard, a vegetable plot and some old pigsties and not much else. There was an old man called Ah Keung who owned the land. I decided to look a bit closer at the land. On approaching one of the pigsties, I noticed that the entrance looked different to the others. I had to get down on my hands and knees as the entrance was only about three feet high. I noticed an old curtain which I thought was a strange thing to have in a pigsty. I crawled inside. The interior was a revelation. The floor was tiled and clean, there were lamps, carpets, and curtains, it was really very cosy. Then I noticed a familiar musky smell of opium, a little like truffles. I examined the area closer and found a hidden cupboard under a bench, and there I saw what I was looking for: an opium pipe! There was other drug paraphernalia and a small ball of the tar-like opium wrapped up in cellophane. I was actually quite excited because I realised how unusual it was. When I went back and confronted Ah Keung with the evidence he just shrugged and pulled out an ancient laminated and stained paper which he claimed was a government licence to smoke opium. I was intrigued and felt a bit sorry for him. He looked quite healthy and didn't seem any the worse for his long addiction. We had to seize the evidence and charge him. I think the magistrate must also have had sympathy for old Ah Keung, as he let him off with a caution after ordering the destruction of the exhibits.

Towards the end of my first tour I was posted to POLMIL, the Police/Military Control Centre in Police HQ. It was the first time I had worked in Police HQ and was surrounded by senior officers the whole time. I was back in uniform, and the Falklands war was beginning. Another adventure was unfolding, but that, as they say, is another story.

A Detective Inspector in Tsim Sha Tsui, 1981–3

Gordon Elsden

I arrived at Tsim Sha Tsui (TST) Police Station in November 1981, equipped with a sum total of nine months instruction at the Police Training School, four months in Uniform Branch at Yau Ma Tei Sub-Division and a one-week crash course at the Detective Training Wing. For the next two years I was in charge of one of the TST CID teams based in the west wing of the Marine Police Headquarters.

On first impressions, the Marine Police Headquarters building was impressive, the blue wooden shutters contrasting well with the white painted façade and the green towering palms hanging over the mounted naval gun. I was fortunate to have an office with a balcony at the front of the building and at this time we could still see the harbour from the first floor. Many a time did I retreat to the quiet of the balcony to enjoy a cup of tea leaving the hustle and bustle behind me. My detectives never could see the attraction of leaving the air-conditioned interior for a bit of peace and quiet.

The hilltop location gave the station an air of aloofness, sitting at the front of the TST Division overlooking the harbour, feeling remote from the bustling activity immediately behind. After all, it was one of the original buildings on the Kowloon Peninsula, now out of step with the rapid development of modern hotels, shopping centres and cultural centres on every side.

The steep slope leading up the hill to the station was always a challenge especially for overzealous police drivers. They had not only to negotiate the sharp turn into the concrete-lined slope but also avoid the hordes of tourists massed at the bottom waiting to cross Canton Road en route to the Star Ferry. It gave the impression of being more of a fortress, which was its original intention, than a welcoming Police Station. At the height of a humid sweltering summer, the slope was also a physical challenge for the fully laden Uniform Branch officers at the end of a busy shift. Despite the steepness of the hill and the seasonal typhoons, a large banyan tree tenaciously clung to the hillside with its spread roots marking the entrance to the station. It remains there to this day.

This was in many ways the end of an era. Pagers were just being introduced to keep us in contact with the station when out investigating cases. For the majority of a shift my busy assistant was competing to use the telex machine just behind the report room to send out the crime reports to Kowloon Police HQ. On occasions, we were allowed into the mysterious darkened Marine Control Room to send our despatches.

Air conditioners rattled away incessantly, the typewriters clattering away in tune. The usage of Tipp-Ex differentiated the new inspectors from the veterans. Mistakes on case papers were a nightmare because there were up to four carbon copies, each of which had to be corrected.

We always had a good relationship with the Marine Police officers and they made us feel welcome in their mess, the 'Mariners Rest', on the first floor of the East Wing. After the hurly-burly of a shift it was an ideal sanctuary where fellow officers were only too ready to share their own grisly experiences over a bottle or two of San Miguel. I clearly remember the large chest fridge behind the bar in the Marine mess cooling the never-ending supply of brown bottles of San Miguel.

The west wing of the station where TST Police Division was based was always a hive of activity, the lights of the offices burning throughout the night. The remainder of the building, used by Marine HQ, maintained a more dignified pace in keeping with its prominence and history. The Marine officers who worked there managed a calmer demeanour and were invariably better dressed and less harassed at the end of their shift.

Occasionally we were invited to a curry and San Miguel lunch on the lawn below the mast at the front of the station. The rooftop of the Marine Headquarters also afforded a great view of the seasonal harbour firework displays.

Old Marine Police Headquarters, Tsim Sha Tsui, 1980s

Between the lawn and the venerable old building lay a sprawl of untidy huts which also housed the junior police officers' canteen. Here I occasionally experienced a full breakfast of fried egg, ham toast and *nai cha* (milk tea). It was an acquired taste with the *nai cha* sometimes being more congealed than the fried egg!

The cell blocks were ancient and designed for security rather than comfort. We speculated that they were originally made to secure notorious pirates! When housed with a drunk and disorderly mendicant in the height of summer it was not a place where you would wish to linger. They were useful for dissuading recalcitrant teenagers on their first shoplifting arrest, from following a life of crime.

The building was cramped, with the partitioned offices housing Uniform Branch on the ground floor and CID on the first floor, a 'temporary' arrangement that had already lasted many, many years. Nevertheless, it had met the demands of an operational force working twenty-four hours a day, seven days a week.

In the early 1980s we witnessed the change in nomenclature of the command structure, from sub-divisional inspectors (SDI) running stations to divisional commanders, and the top CID man changing his title from officer commanding (OC) CID to assistant divisional commander, crime (ADVC/C). For those of us relatively new to the police force this was a transition that we readily took in our stride, soon adopting the new vocabulary. After all, we had only relatively recently cracked Cantonese!

Living at the Hermitage, Government Quarters in the Mid-Levels, I travelled daily on the Star Ferry across to TST. In retrospect I was a proud holder of one of the most exotic monthly travel passes in the world.

I remember in 1982 working throughout the night shift listening to BBC World Service news bulletins giving the latest progress of the British Forces fighting for the Falkland Islands. I comment on this because only shortly before I had witnessed the remarkable spectacle of two of the ships involved in the Falklands, the *QE2* and the *Canberra*, docked on either side of Ocean Terminal.

At times the job was exhausting, working six days a week, with a staggered shift pattern that resulted in you never really knowing what time of the day it was. The never-ending case load was mentally fatiguing and it was impossible to set aside time to clear it while on the morning and afternoon shifts. Something always came up and this was a division distinguished by a cosmopolitan transient population where the expatriate CID inspectors were expected to take many witness statements themselves. We never seemed to be able to catch up and at times it proved quite intense and unforgiving.

The early eighties were marked by an explosion of violence in the newly developed TST East area. The triads were fighting over control of the extremely lucrative nightclubs, bars and restaurants. Not only did this make a mess of the restaurants and the pavement outside but also caused a frustrating disruption to the already steep backlog of case papers, court papers and other paperwork that we sought to reduce on the night C shift.

This was also when the 'Big Circle' criminal gangs from Mainland China, equipped with automatic rifles and hand grenades, were beginning to make increasingly bold and vicious forays in TST, targeting the gold and jewellery shops on Nathan Road.

The 'Hole in the Wall' gang was a bane for the CID teams on night shift. This team of very professional and determined burglars targeted jewellery and other high-value goods shops, working through the night literally opening a hole in an outside wall of the shop. It was always better to be investigating one of these cases at the beginning of the morning shift than at the end of the night shift! But it all depended on exactly the time when the crime was reported.

Over the years, we met a motley crew of local and international criminals. An assortment of local triad celebrities, or so they thought! An all-star cast of B-grade *kung fu* actors continuing to act out their screen roles in the nightclubs of TST. On more than one occasion, some of these actors fuelled by alcohol and the sycophantic praise of their followers had arrived at the Report Room following their arrest for 'disorderly conduct', very brave, and vocally very abusive. They were a little less confident after taking the long walk up the wide staircase from the report room to the CID *Daai Fong* ('Big Room') on the first floor.

One lunchtime in midsummer, a middle-aged Pakistani male working as a security guard in an international bank in Middle Road, armed with a loaded shotgun, suddenly recalled a long-term village dispute between his family and that of a fellow security guard. The apparent affront was so real that it resulted in him discharging three rounds of pellets across the bank at his colleague. The pellets miraculously missed the guard and, despite shattering the window behind him, also spared the multitude of people outside the bank. Oh, the paperwork! First information reports, court papers, committal proceedings, then a Supreme Court trial for 'attempted murder' and 'shooting with intent'.

A dame from Australia leading her clutch of precious and beautiful models on a fashion tour of the region gave testimony to the diversity of the crime experience in TST. An elderly pickpocket had managed to sneak into their converted dressing room in a local hotel and hid under one of the tables supporting their garments. Not only had he managed to gain a memorable preview but also helped himself to their valuables. Taking statements from these beautiful girls was one of my less onerous tasks. . . .

For a period, a Filipino gang successfully targeted the jewellery shops, one member of the gang creating a diversion while another reached over the counter to steal high-valued items. We finally caught up with them in one of the local apartment houses. The accumulation of all the individual cases created a monster of a file but at least the subsequent District Court trial removed the culprits from the streets of Hong Kong.

We met tourists from every corner of the globe who had unfortunately encountered the local pickpocket gangs or had been deceived in one of the many dishonest camera shops. We thwarted the ambitions of the latter, who had planned on their victims having to leave Hong Kong before a court case could be arranged, by removing every member of staff of the shop to be independently interviewed and by so doing effectively closing the shop.

The occasional visits of the US Seventh Fleet brought with them a large number of rest & recreation sailors. An evening's drinking combined with provocation from the resident British squaddies proved an explosive mixture. Nevertheless the situation was easily resolved. Calls to the immaculate US Shore Patrol and the Royal Military Police resulted in the incident being dealt with in a very efficient military manner!

The Orient also spun its charm on a multitude of middle-aged international businessmen. Alcohol, hubris and an attractive young lady offering a trip to the moon and back, made so many of this distinguished group so easily take leave of their senses and their wallets. What was even more surprising was how a fit of indignation brought them to the police station in the early hours of the morning to give a detailed statement on the details of the promised liaison and what bit had been reneged on. Late the following morning we invariably received a sheepish call from the victim wishing to withdraw his allegation.

Crime reports crossing our desks included transgressions in all the notable drinking establishments, Bottoms Up, Red Lips, Waltzing Matilda's, Ned Kelly's, Rick's Café, Someplace Else. . . .

Chungking Mansions, a virtual 'United Nations' refuge, invariably filled investigating officers with a sense of apprehension, not so much from the nature of the case but rather the embarrassment of getting lost in the maze of apartments, corridors and staircases within the building. Nevertheless, it was a great place for a good curry provided that you followed the string trail in and out.

Detective Inspector Elsden with members of his CID/TST team in the CID Daai Fong of the Old Marine Police Headquarters, 1983 (Courtesy G. Elsden)

We had to be mindful of the political sensitivity of the cases that we were handling. The arrest of certain nationalities provoked an immediate visit by staff of the local consulate, more concerned with the potential embarrassment to their country than their citizens' welfare. Invariably the offenders were swiftly removed from the colony, ostensibly never to return.

Because we spent so much time together it was important that the team got on well. We would relax on occasions by driving to Clearwater Bay after the late shift and then enjoy a barbecue through the night, returning as dawn was breaking. To this day, some four decades later, I have retained contact with some of these detectives.

This period of my life provided a catalogue of memorable and fulfilling experiences. I feel privileged to have spent two energetic years not only as a CID inspector in TST, but with an office in a grand old building overlooking Hong Kong's Victoria Harbour.

Light-Hearted Leadership

Peter Webb

When I was still under training at the Police Training School (PTS), a bunch of us probationary officers met a group of expatriate girls on Deep Water Bay Beach, one of whom was the daughter of Peter Law, then a senior superintendent of police in Special Branch. I took her out several times and one day her father asked if I would like to join the family, and the Ostromovs (manager of the Repulse Bay Hotel), on an outing on their respective boats. I, of course, jumped at the chance. On Peter Law's boat was another youngish couple, who were introduced as Chris and Elaine Dawson. I spent a wonderful afternoon off Lamma Island, swimming, drinking, eating and conversing, during which I casually called this couple Chris or Elaine as occasion arose. The day ended well.

Later, when I was duty 'dog' at the PTS, to pass the time I was looking down the government telephone directory for Police Headquarters when, to my horror, I noticed the name 'C.J.R. Dawson, Senior Superintendent, Establishment'. Calling a colonel by his first name when I was a young subaltern would probably have resulted in banishment! Well, I thought, he will probably not remember me.

A couple of years later when I had been working in Sham Shui Po Division for a while, an inquiry into the attitudes of young inspectors, 'the new breed', towards corruption was instituted. Each inspector was called up in turn to Kowloon Police HQ. On my turn, lo and behold, who should be sitting at the desk of a very long office as I marched in, was none other than Chris Dawson. I marched up, saluted, and wondered what was going to happen next. 'Sit down Peter. This time you will have to call me 'sir'. Let us get on with it'.

Some years later, I was a newly promoted senior inspector. I was working in Anti-Corruption Branch as the secretary of the Target Committee, and as senior inspector, administration. The chief superintendent in charge was Peter Law. One day his secretary came into my office with a leave chit in her hand and said: 'Mr Law says you are to take a week's leave to study for the Senior Professional Examination.' I went to see him and explained that I was newly promoted and the system was that one had to work for three years as a senior inspector before being eligible for the next promotion step to assistant superintendent. He looked at me from behind his two-volume *Oxford English Dictionary* and said: 'Peter, I have already signed it, now you sign it and go and study.' I duly took my week's leave, studied hard and passed the examination only to find that in the interim the powers that be had changed the qualification period and I was promoted soon after.

Later, as a superintendent, I was secretary of the Gazetted Officers' Mess, when the president of the Mess Committee obtained a spectator box at the Jockey Club for our use. There were only about twenty places available, and after discussion, he decided that I was to put out a circular announcing this and asking for applications to attend, the selection to be by a draw from a hat. 'Of course,' he said, 'the commissioner and I must attend. Please arrange.' After the circular went out, the commissioner's indomitable secretary rang me saying that the commissioner wishes to go and for me to make sure this happens. I suppose I was feeling a little suicidal that day as I cheekily said: 'Well of course, his name will go in the hat.' She harrumphed a bit and put the phone down. I soon had a call from Jimmy Morrin, the committee president, who wanted to know what had taken place with the commissioner's secretary. I explained that I was merely implying that in fairness all names would go in the hat, but of course he and the commissioner would be successful. All went well, the box became a regular feature of mess life and I thought nothing more of it.

I should have known better. On my pre-annual leave interview, I went to see Chris Dawson, by then deputy commissioner, administration, and was surprised to see him sitting there with a statement form, and pen in hand. 'I hear you tried to usurp the commissioner's authority when he applied to attend the races in the mess box.' I could not believe my ears, and I must admit I laughed, saying: 'I am a lowly, newly promoted superintendent and I was only pulling the secretary's leg.' His reply was: 'Do not laugh Peter. Can you not see I am trying to help you?' He duly took a statement and I heard no more.

Many years later, I was the parade commander for the farewell parade for His Excellency (HE) the Governor, Sir David Wilson, as he was in those days. This took place at the Police Training School where, of course, Superintendent Bill Fullerton was the major-domo in charge of drill. I knew Bill well, having conducted his recruitment interview with David Deptford some years earlier, when Bill shook us all by arriving on the parade ground in the Commander, British Forces helicopter. Bill was then serving in the Scots Guards with the British Army and it was typical of his personality to arrive in such dramatic fashion and only a Guard's regimental sergeant major could have carried it off successfully. We all practised hard, with Bill at his best, able to coach the most willing response out of all on parade with his personality and under-standing. We had a week to rehearse during which various requests came down from Government House. These included building a room in the drill shed to which Sir David could retire to comb his hair before greeting guests. Bill's contribution to this room was to install a dummy WC with a label 'For HE use only'. Once Sir David went into the room after the parade, he immediately came out again and called with mirth to his wife 'Natasha, you have got to come and see this!'.

But back to rehearsals. I must admit I was becoming a little fed up with all the requests, enquiries and additions. Just before the rehearsal for the dress rehearsal, I commented casually to Bill that I expected the next request from Government House to be that HE wished to have the whole parade ground covered in grass. The rehearsal duly took place and all was going smoothly. We marched past the saluting dais, me with sword drawn at the head of the column, only to find that when I reached my spot in the front of the halting squads, I had been given six square feet of grass turf to stand on. Later I discovered from the photographic record PTS had made that the Physical Training Instructors had sprinted on while my back was turned and placed the turf on my spot. Such was the character of a man who, with no Cantonese knowledge, had young constables literally 'eating out of his hand' within two weeks of arriving at the Police Training School as the chief drill and musketry instructor.

Special Duties Unit – Water Team

Sandy Macalister

By the early 1980s, the Special Duties Unit (SDU) had become a very capable counter-terrorism response unit in the Royal Hong Kong Police Force. Regularly trained by the British Special Air Service, the two operational teams were primarily focused on land-based scenarios, such as aircraft hijacking, high rise, key point and building options.

Following a threat assessment by the United Kingdom government in 1981, it was recommended that the SDU's capability be expanded to counter the growing threat of maritime terrorism. Hong Kong was thought to be particularly vulnerable to this aspect at that time.

A team of specialists from the UK's Special Boat Squadron (SBS) visited the SDU to assess its capabilities and confirmed that they would conduct training of a team, provided the team was first diver-trained and qualified to Royal Navy ships diver standard.

To achieve this, Station Sergeant Tsang Kan Ping, an experienced civilian diver, and Chief Inspector Sandy Macalister, a qualified New Zealand police and navy diver, both from the SDU's Alpha Team, were sent to the Royal Navy's Diving School at HMS Vernon in Portsmouth, to first qualify as Royal Navy ships divers and then as diver supervisors.

After they returned to Hong Kong from a very cold English winter of diving, Tsang and Macalister sought volunteers from the existing SDU land teams to undergo a water-team selection course. The selection, designed to eliminate those susceptible to panicking in a water environment, led to a group of ten. This group then embarked on a demanding course with an emphasis on performing in zero visibility to develop sensory skills, night diving and under-water endurance.

All the participants completed the course. The photograph below shows the team on an anchor chain during that first course, and was taken off Lantau Island, where Chek Lap Kok Airport is today. Having been delayed by the Falklands War, a full SBS training team finally returned in early 1983 and the SDU team was trained in tactical diving and specialised maritime operational skills.

Around this time, there was an international rush to form maritime anti-terrorist teams, and to perfect and practise the various techniques, in particular ship boarding. Hong Kong had exceptional training resources in the form of a variety of laid-up vessels awaiting scrapping, and in addition, had excellent relationships with shipping companies which would allow their ships to be used for boarding training as the vessels entered or left harbour. This attracted other teams to visit Hong Kong and cross train with the SDU. Several of the specialised methods, techniques and equipment were jointly developed and honed through these interchanges.

The Water Team became very skilled both above and below the water, and their diving skills outside of the counter-terrorism role were regularly called upon and used in a variety of cases, including security operations, homicide investigations, and drug and vehicle smuggling.

First Tactical Diving Course (Courtesy S. Macalister)

The Phantom Wire Cutter

John Macdonald

Once upon a time in the early 1980s, while employed as regional commander of Hong Kong Island, my morning reports from Wan Chai Division began to report some alarming crime numbers. The alarm was not so much at the nature of the (minor) crimes being committed as the potential pain they were likely to inflict on a certain gentleman, a very senior officer who disliked large numbers disturbing crime trends. Fortunately, when they first surfaced, the said officer was on leave and I was confident of an early resolution of the problem.

The Hong Kong Telephone Company's (HKTC) service to pre-war tenements was underground until it reached the customer premises, where it was ducted up the street wall before being split into lines attached to the stair wall going to individual flats. So a stairway averaged six exposed telephone lines which could be interfered with – or simply severed.

My early confidence was soon shattered, the number of cases reached thousands, the trend was upwards and said gentleman returned from leave. Before the inevitable phone call, a review (one of many) had established that all offences were being committed only in Wan Chai Sub-division; there was no other discernible location pattern; there was no identifiable time pattern; and HKTC personnel had been looked at for possible grudge action (failed promotion, transfers, etc.). Zilch! Absolutely nothing to go on!

The expected call came and a conference was convened with the gentleman, myself and a wizard of electronics from CID Head-quarters who had connections to HKTC. I will spare you the details but bells, whistles and alarms allied to ambushes were mooted. The electronics wizard was not inclined to dig into his spell book and

normal service was resumed including that by the 'phantom telephone wire cutter'. But now I got lucky – the racing season ended
and Alpha Company of the Police Tactical Unit (PTU) commanded
by the redoubtable Spencer Foo Tsun Kong, ceased crowd-control
duties and became available for other tasks.

Single-man ambushes on previously attacked premises were
established and 'Eureka!' One was attacked when manned. There
was no arrest but the constable on duty claimed that it must have
been one or more of three schoolboys who had entered and who
he checked out as living in the top-floor flat. They were identified
and placed under discreet surveillance although ambush activity
continued. Then, while the boys were being watched, another
address was attacked. So our constable was immediately 'inter-
rogated'. It turned out he had felt hungry on his way to his post,
so had stopped off for breakfast and was late arriving at the location.
He was playing a game on a hand-held computer console when a
'huge monster of a figure pushed past him, went up the stairway
and shortly after left'.

As we needed more details about the large man, we decided to
use 'remembering hypnosis' which was supposed to help victims
(normally rape cases) recall recent events. The constable was persuaded to undergo the treatment and under hypnosis, he provided
a physical description, including clothing, to be developed into a
photofit. All ambush points were provided with the likeness and
within days the culprit was arrested. He proved to be as big as
described and had to be quite vigorously subdued on arrest, but
well done Alpha!

The suspect lived in Cross Street and was one of four brothers.
He worked at an electronics store in North Point but was not the
brightest of the work force. The other workers used to make fun of
him. So he left that employ. Unfortunately, his former colleagues
kept ringing his home telephone and mocking him, so he arranged
to change the number. All went well for a while then the nuisance
calls resumed. The suspect found out that some of his tormenters
had left to join the HKTC, so an indirect revenge was planned.

His family proved very supportive of our investigation, so he was
charged with a specimen number of the offences and the above

story was put to the court. Happily, he was fined only $500, bound over and to my knowledge has never re-offended. Our crime statistics also recovered. Interestingly, the information divulged under hypnosis was spot on, the physical description and the clothes worn were all absolutely right. Hypnosis as an investigative tool had convinced this previous sceptic.

Having identified Spencer Foo and Alpha Company in this narrative, it would be remiss not to acknowledge the achievements of Senior Inspector Li Ho Yin, Officer Commanding CID Wan Chai and his team who, of course, bore the investigative burden and Senior Inspector Patrick Yeung Chee To who conducted the hypnosis under medical supervision.

Snakes and Lawyers

Rose Johnston

I arrived in Hong Kong in May 1982, not an auspicious time to move to a far-flung corner of the Empire. I had been appointed legal aid counsel in the Legal Aid Department, which was then in Sincere Building in Western, to work as a litigation lawyer.

As soon as I had my air tickets from the Hong Kong government, I arranged to leave a week early and stopover in Sri Lanka on the way. My new arrival time did not percolate through to the director of Legal Aid and I arrived at Kai Tak on a Sunday afternoon with no-one to meet me. I made my way to the Lee Gardens Hotel, where there was no room booked.

So, when a few weeks later I was allocated a flat at the Hermitage on Kennedy Road, I decided not to check out of the hotel until I had made my first cup of tea on the Baby Belling. I was right. When I went to collect the key from Mrs Choi, the manager, someone else had already moved in. It was not entirely a wasted journey however as I met a tall, dark, handsome police inspector in the lift. Reader, I married him.

My first post was in the family law section to replace a lawyer on maternity leave. Mrs Tam had a beautiful daughter and I had an on-the-job crash course in HK matrimonial law.

The first step to a divorce is marriage. Proof of marriage is usually a certificate, but up to October 1971, when registration became a legal requirement in HK, you could marry by traditional ceremony. This was a collection of rituals which varied according to where you came from and your social standing. Many of our clients had done this. To prove they were married, we had to take a detailed account as to how they had celebrated the marriage and send it to a specialist barrister, who would return a truly impressive advice on thick parchment, triple spaced and sometimes even tied up in pink ribbon. The client would then be sent to the Registry Office to post-register the marriage. Sometimes they forgot to take the paperwork with them and ended up married again instead, which took a bit of disentangling.

Some, of course, were disappointed. One woman had had a wedding feast in a restaurant and poured tea to her in-laws, but the couple had not worshipped the ancestral tablets as they were too poor to have any. Nor had she been brought to her new home in a sedan chair by her husband. Fatally, although they correctly kept the restaurant door open during the feast, they had no banner outside to announce the wedding. In the bingo of traditional matrimony, she was not even sweating on a line, let alone a full house. More tactfully than this, I explained to her that she had not been properly married.

'I thought so,' she said ruefully. 'That's why I want a proper divorce'.

(I imagine that the sedan chair was a communal asset, a bit like the laying-out board in Britain in the old days. 'Now who had it last?')

We also did a good trade in Filipina divorces as many worked in Hong Kong and there was no divorce in the Philippines. I was often drawn to one side at social events by European men asking for advice 'for a friend'.

From the fur-flying wrangles of divorce, I escaped into the criminal law department, making weekly visits to clients in Lai Chi Kok Prison. This was in a garment-making area of Kowloon and outside the prison, the nullah carried discharge from the dyeing works. I enjoyed bets with the law clerks, who came with me to interpret, on what colour the nullah would be when we emerged hours later. Gory red could turn to acid blue in minutes. No money changed hands as gambling was illegal and I had to buy lunch in any case, as even to allow a junior officer to pay their half was an offence of corruption, or so I was told.

Legal aid was not available for the Magistrates' Court so most of our cases were serious offences. Much was triad-led organised crime and you could tell from the allegation how far up the pecking order the prisoner was, especially with drug dealing. I knew which men would decline the offer of legal aid: 'My family is getting me a lawyer' was their code for 'Don't bother, the Boss is paying'.

The death penalty for murder still existed then, though it was never carried out. One of my lighter duties was drafting petitions for clemency to convert a death sentence to life imprisonment. I would see the condemned on 'death row' in Stanley Prison, most of them quite pleased to see me, to collect their account of events and expressions of remorse. Moved to tears by my prose, the Governor, Sir Edward Youde, would commute their sentence.

Although this may have seemed an academic exercise, it was necessary as there was genuine concern over what would happen to the prisoners in 1997, as China had, and still has, the death penalty.

'It'll be great when it's finished,' was my brother's assessment of Hong Kong when he visited in 1983. The city was a giant building site. Cranes littered the skyline and the ructions from the pile driving on the plot next to Sincere Building prompted my New Zealand colleagues to reminisce about earthquakes. Site accidents were rife, to add to the casualties of manufacturing, shipping and road traffic. Most accident compensation claims found their way to the Legal Aid Department. Personal injury litigation was a legal and emotional war-zone. Many stories do not bear re-telling but even wars have their brighter moments.

One construction-site labourer had fallen down an unguarded lift shaft on the thirtieth floor. Luckily, someone had left planks across the shaft on the fifteenth floor, breaking his fall and several bones. When I saw him, he was mended and back at work. Not on building sites, as he had lost his head for heights. He had a job in a restaurant.

'What kind of restaurant?' I asked.

'A snake restaurant,' he mumbled.

'What do you do?

'I kill the poisonous snakes.'

For once, we were fighting laughter not tears. And yes, he had heard of James Bond.

I asked an old lady her age. She gazed through the office window, over to Kowloon and the Lion Rock as if searching for China in the distance. 'I don't know. But I was born on the fifth day of the third moon in the Year of the Ox and that year there were floods in Yunnan province.' How was it that she came to be at the foot of the stairs in a *dim sum* restaurant, pinned down by an overturned crockery cupboard? It was going to be a long afternoon.

A welder was working on a goods chute on the outside wall of a factory. To do this, he was standing on a seventh-floor window ledge. He overbalanced and fell feet first into the chute in a manoeuvre that ended on the ground floor, where his sparks had preceded him. Piles of anoraks were in flames. He wrenched open the locked door and escaped with broken ribs and singed hair. I caught a whiff of contributory negligence.

'Didn't you think it might be dangerous not using a safety line?'

'I'd been working there three days and I hadn't fallen off before!'

Luckily his employer shared his confidence and hadn't supplied any safety equipment, so his claim was successful.

Many clients had little formal education and most of the older ones were illiterate. Even with excellent interpreters, communication could be difficult, and sometimes we had to stage re-enactments of accidents in the office, taking care not to add to the injury toll. I had a stock of toy vehicles for action replays of road accidents. One by one, these slipped away in the hands of small children who had sat, patient and bewildered, while their mothers wept into my Kleenex tissues. I kept the tram for myself and it sits on my bookshelf in Yorkshire, advertising Cathay Pacific and the Rugby Sevens.

Sitting on the upper deck of the number 15 bus in a traffic jam on the way home, I would pass the time by scanning the name boards on construction sites for companies I had not sued. Occasionally I found one.

Democracy arrived in Hong Kong about the same time as me and the government appealed for staff with experience of running elections to act as presiding officers. I had, so I found myself after only a few weeks in Hong Kong, in a nursery schoolroom in

Causeway Bay with a team of Chinese staff and an electoral roll of over 6,000, about 4,000 of whom turned up enthusiastically to vote. The election was planned like a military operation with written instructions to cover every eventuality, which my deputy had apparently memorised. Apart from occasionally having to gently separate families who tried to huddle together in polling booths, everything went smoothly.

Next time, I was at a housing estate in Kwun Tong. At 6.00 am the streets were already busy with smartly dressed workers heading for the bus and Mass Transit Railway; students in school uniform and old people shepherding kindergarten children, and of course groups practising *tai chi* in the sitting out areas. There was a sense of energy and purpose I have never experienced anywhere else. In those boom years of the 1980s, Hong Kong was something special.

My next election posting was across the sea to Lantau Island. A group of us were taken on board the governor's launch, the *Lady Maurine,* a slow and stately vessel. With its thickly varnished wood it seemed to be carved out of toffee, and its brass rails and lamps gleamed. We were put up in a government bungalow overnight, then taxied next morning to the polling stations. Mine was a community centre in a small coastal village. Our most colourful voters were a group of Buddhist monks who arrived together by sea. One voter, an old lady who lived on a boat, was dressed completely in black in the Mainland style. She dug deep into layers of clothing to produce a wallet with her identity card. The wad of notes which flashed would have bought a small yacht.

At the close, two of us carried the wooden ballot box along the rocky trail to the pier in the dark for over a mile, escorted by a police constable, who apologised for not being able to help us with it, for fear of exposing his gun to theft.

The caretaker's two small grandsons had kept us entertained during lulls in voting. As we left, their shorts and T-shirts hung on the washing line as a postscript to a long day.

Pictures such as this are clearer in my memory, even after thirty years, than the photos I took which were often dulled by the humidity and pollution of Hong Kong.

Another vivid image is the flock of sulphur-crested cockatoos which lived in Victoria Barracks around my quarters on the top floor of Alexander Block. Their morning screeches woke me up and when I came back from work they would sit in the trees eating fruit and pelting me with the stones. The barracks dated from the mid-nineteenth century and lay between Kennedy Road and Admiralty, where Hong Kong Park now is. They attracted an eccentric collection of expatriates, some of them more flaky than the buildings.

The British Army was still stationed in Hong Kong and one of their roles was to patrol the China border. On a visit to Mai Po marshes, a restricted area, I saw them riding round on BMX bikes checking for illegal immigrants. Behind a bush crouched a Gurkha in camouflage, a red transistor clamped to his ear. He was listening to *The Archers* on British Forces (BF) radio.

In that pre-digital age, English language television in Hong Kong was dismal. BF radio was a welcome addition to Radio Television Hong Kong services.

My most dramatic image is from 1989. The No. 3 typhoon signal went up on Friday, 9th June. As usual, we dragged potted plants from the balcony and battened down for the storm. By Sunday, after the signal went down, desperate to escape the flat and the TV reports of the terrible events in Tiananmen Square, I got the minibus from Mansfield Road to Happy Valley and walked through quiet streets to Causeway Bay. I came out on to an overhead walkway, clutching a new teapot in a Daimaru carrier and looked down to see the traffic at a standstill. I feared a bad accident but going down to the street could see nothing.

Walking towards Central, I found myself facing a marching mass of protesters. Some were carrying banners, some chanting. They filled the road and pavement. Normally a handful of pedestrians could block a pavement but that day thousands of them flowed round me like a stream. I could see no end to the human trail. I turned into a narrow side street where a woman was buying oranges. Both she and the stallholder seemed oblivious to the history marching by only twenty yards away. In Central were buses with banners. Able to get by in spoken Cantonese but not read

Chinese, I asked a passerby what they said. 'Li Peng stand down,' he replied. We all waved and cheered.

And what of those 1980s photos, now as pale as antique water-colours? At random, I grab an album from the box which one day I will sort.

Here I have one of a group from Legal Aid gathered around a table laden with food. I can make out roast meats, prawns and a salmon. It could be one of many outings but someone is holding a ticket and grinning. It is the Governor's Box at Happy Valley Racecourse. Sir Edward Youde was a non-gambling Methodist and did not attend the races, lending the box instead to a rota of government departments. Sir Edward was a scholarly diplomat, whose quiet demeanour at first troubled then endeared the people of Hong Kong. I recall coming out of court in Tsim Sha Tsui on a chilly day in December 1986 to find men and women crying in the street. Sir Edward had died on a visit to Beijing.

Next is one of a passing-out parade at the Police Training School in Aberdeen, where Frank (of the Hermitage lift) trained inspectors. Uniformed officers line up on the parade ground where a dignitary is waiting to take the salute. With their inspector's pips safely attached to their shoulders, many trainees would then marry. For weeks afterwards, the unmistakable red and gold envelopes of wedding invitations would shower into our mailbox.

And here is a photo of a friend's wedding with City Hall in the background. The registrars would get through the queue of waiting brides and grooms faster than the checkout staff at Park'n'Shop.

Now one of countryside. Three lawyers, a librarian and a fisheries officer all in shorts and carrying water bottles, are walking to Po Lin. After a ferry ride, it was more than two hours' trek across the Lantau hills to the hidden tranquility of the monastery, where in the refectory for ten dollars, we chased slippery mushrooms and cabbage round a plate with chopsticks. Whatever your religion, this was a pilgrimage to restore equilibrium, away from the frantic city life.

Finally, we have Macau, the only place we could go to outside Hong Kong without flying, as at that time RHKP officers weren't allowed to go into China. Here we are on the veranda of the Bela

Vista Hotel, a crumbling colonial cousin of Victoria Barracks; in front of us, glasses of white port and plates of Portuguese sausage.

I was fortunate to see more of Hong Kong than most. I drank tea in a squatter hut and wine in the Mandarin Hotel; photographed machinery at a pig farm and ate fatty pork at a police station Bai Kwan Dai ceremony; heard international concert pianists at City Hall and the clash of cymbals at the Cheung Chau Bun Festival.

I will never regret going to work in Hong Kong. Nor will I regret coming home nine years later. After all, there's only so much excitement you can take in one lifetime.

The 1984 Taxi Riots

Jim Prisk

I joined the Royal Hong Kong Police Force as a probationary inspector on 13th August 1981. Following instruction at the Police Training School (PTS) in Aberdeen, I was posted to a busy Kowloon Division, Wong Tai Sin, in April 1982.

I learnt a lot about practical leadership and management during eight months as a patrol sub-unit commander, supervising constables and NCOs on beat duties, and also about police station management. I then spent six months as the officer-in-charge of the plain-clothes Wong Tai Sin District Special Duties Squad which combatted narcotics activities, illegal gambling and vice.

Young inspectors in their first three-year tour of duty were often given further intensive training in riot drill and internal security tactics, and to this end I was sent to the Police Tactical Unit (PTU), based at a former British Army camp at Volunteer Slopes in Fanling in the New Territories. I arrived there on 30th May 1983 as an officer in 'Foxtrot' Company where I spent two weeks in a cadre course, along with other officers and NCOs receiving training which we subsequently imparted to our constables over a twelve-week period. After this, we were a fully trained company of around 160 policemen, structured into four platoons. Over the next few months the company was available as the Commissioner's Reserve for internal security, and for other duties which needed a large body of officers, usually crowd control.

Tuesday, January 10th 1984, was like most other days. I supervised my lads in 'Foxtrot' Company on the streets of Kowloon for what I thought would be the last time. The twenty weeks had rocketed by since our passing-out parade in Fanling on a blisteringly hot summer's day in August 1983. Following this, I and my 'oppo', Inspector Galer To, had commanded a platoon engaged in constabulary duties in Kowloon, and here we were on the verge of company disbandment and a return to normal police duties. I recall thinking that the day's news concerning the announcement in the Legislative Council by Alan Scott, secretary for transport, that there would be an increase of 80 per cent for a taxi licence renewal fee, plus a 17 per cent increase in fare charges, could be unpopular, but I had no inkling of what was to come!

Our company commander, Superintendent Ed Hillier, had agreed that once platoon administration had been tied up, we could drop the men at their new station postings and then relax for the last few days. Galer and I had completed these tasks by lunchtime on the Wednesday and returned to our base at Mong Kok Police Station. On arrival back at the office, we met the boss and our company 2 i/c, Chief Inspector Alan To Kin-chung. Both Ed and Alan had been watching the TV news, and I was greeted with a terse 'Get them all back Jim, *jik haak* (quickly), we might be out on the streets soon.' TV scenes of taxi blockades in Tsim Sha Tsui, Central and the New Territories told me the reason why. . . .

My mind wandered back to some eight months earlier when I had turned up at the training school medical centre for the medical examination required due to the stringent nature of PTU training. Having just come from the aforesaid six-month stint as the Special Duty Squad officer-in-charge at Wong Tai Sin, I arrived with long

'Foxtrot' PTU Co. From left: Oscar Avila, Gurbej Singh 'Jimmy' Chima, Albert Ho, Harold Chan. Mike Groves, Company Commander Ed Hillier, 2 i/c Alan To Kin Chung, Sean Lavelle, Jim Prisk and Galer To (Courtesy J. Prisk)

hair and wearing jeans, to meet seven other guys whom I believed would be my fellow inspectors, four of whom were contemporaries at the PTS and thus I knew well. Whilst waiting, we naturally chatted about the tough training ahead of us and I spoke to one of the others about what they knew of our new company commander, Ed Hillier. This chap told me that he thought Hillier might be a bit of a problem to us, as he came from Traffic, to which I boldly replied 'Well, if he is, we'll soon sort him out!' On 30 May 1983, some two weeks after the medical, I and seven other inspectors reported in uniform to the said gentleman, who was none other than Ed Hillier himself! 'Good morning Mr Prisk,' he said, clearly enjoying the moment, whilst I sheepishly saluted him!

Ed was a tough, no-nonsense Bristolian, who did not suffer fools gladly and had an often unorthodox approach, not always to the liking of very senior officers of the 'old school'.

Ed created an 'all together' spirit during training at PTU, which carried forward into our Kowloon attachment. For example, the Force in mid-1983, was phasing out the use of Land Rovers for PTU companies and replacing them with vans. However, Ed felt that whilst less comfortable, the Land Rovers gave a tougher impression for PTU officers arriving at the scene of an incident or travelling in convoy. We inspectors, to a man, agreed with him. We were thus the only Company allowed to carry on with Land Rovers.

It was also Ed's innovation to have a company tune, which he felt would make the troops identify with it and increase morale and overall *esprit de corps*. He chose Wagner's *Ride of the Valkyries,* which had been used by the air cavalry for the same purpose in the film *Apocalypse Now*. Prior to the taxi riots, we performed crowd-control duties in Tsim Sha Tsui on New Year's Eve going into 1984. I have a wonderful memory of amazed looks on the faces of the public when our company travelled down Nathan Road on the early evening of 31 December 1983, with the tune blaring loudly out from the on board tannoy systems!

Whilst under training at PTU during the cadre course, Ed kept me and the other seven *bom baans* (inspectors) on our toes, with the weekly presentation of a rather rude award for the officer/ platoon who made the biggest blunder. The prize was designed by

Ed and took the form of an RHKP wooden plinth with a letter 'W' and an anchor carved into it. Whoever qualified for this award during the week was presented with it during the expected after-work drinks in the mess each Friday evening. At our passing-out parade, the plinth was presented to the commandant as a gift to the mess. Quite naturally, we all worked very hard to avoid winning this 'prestigious' award! It really became a sort of rallying point for the guys and also used by our platoon NCOs to urge their constables on during the various aspects of training. A simple idea, with brilliant results.

Ed also had a bet with Superintendent Benny Lau Wai-ming, the commander of the other Kowloon District company under training, 'Bravo Company'. The bet was that Foxtrot would beat them hands down during the famous and gruelling PTU cross-country course. Having loudly proclaimed that his company were by far the fitter lot, Benny declared that he was so confident of victory that the losers would not only pay for all the beers in the mess afterwards, but that he would also pay for the entire victorious company NCOs and PCs to have a massive barbecue.

The event was thus held on a Friday. As captain of our team, I kept the selected runners busy during the week, with lots of extra training. Ed deliberately kept goading Benny during the week about our inevitable victory, with the latter of course declaring otherwise, until he upped the ante to such an extent that the winning team would also receive several crates of cold Carlsberg and San Miguel beer.

On the day of the event, this had been built up to such an extent that all company staff, including the commandant of the Police Tactical Unit, Bob Steele, and many of the resident Special Duties Unit Officers gathered to watch. The SDU were the anti-terrorist formation whose members included one K.S. Tang – a future commissioner of police, who on a visit to the UK in March 2009 recalled this event with me at a Royal Hong Kong Police Association lunch in London.

In the end, I won the race myself and then watched my team finish in the main, much ahead. Benny's dejection and Ed's whooping with delight when the former forlornly presented us with all the beer and food afterwards, led to a very late night indeed.

The aforementioned 'idiots award' really kept us tight as a group of officers (Galer To, Sean Lavelle, Gurbej 'Jimmy' Chima, Mike Groves, Albert Hui, Harold Chan, Oscar Avila). Ed also designed our company T-shirts, which bore a picture of Wile E. Coyote wearing a beret and holding the Road Runner by the neck, with the slogan, 'Disperse or I use Greater Force'; a special edition shirt for the officers, on the back of which were Ed's name, that of company 2 i/c Alan To and the eight of ours, each with some suitable epithet by which we had become known during training – mine was 'Jim *"Yat for the Lo"* Prisk'. 'Yat for the Lo' is Chinglish 'one for the road', due to my well-known enjoyment of a beer – or two.

My reverie stopped. I was in the PTU offices at our Mong Kok Police Station base and I realised the task ahead. I got together with the other inspectors to get our troops back to the base.

The required clarion call was made and the full complement of 160 men were all back at base within two hours, a fine testimony to Ed's leadership.

Over the next couple of days, we kept the men busy at our Mong Kok base, whilst keeping abreast of events on the streets via the TV and radio news.

We watched the build-up of problems on the streets, exacerbated by the arrival of rabble-rousers and various criminal elements in large numbers. Friday the 13th of January 1984 arrived, a portent of doom for the superstitious among us! The taxi blockades eventually dispersed peacefully, to be replaced by the aforesaid insurgents whose numbers had by now grown considerably. Looting of department stores, hijacking of vehicles and double-decker buses, and arson had replaced what had been essentially a peaceful protest.

The telephone call came. Ed rose from his desk and told me and the other platoon inspectors, 'We're going downtown lads!' Briefings in the station compound followed. It had been decided that my platoon and No. 2 Platoon, led by Sean Lavelle and Gurbej Chima, would lead the foray into Nathan Road, with the other two platoons taking kit, equipment and men as back-up to our 'holding' station at Yau Ma Tei. Whilst I was sure that there would be quite a crowd awaiting us, nothing could really prepare me or the troops for the spectacle as we deployed on foot in platoon formation at 21.00 hours.

As we turned into Nathan Road itself I was absolutely stunned by the size of the crowd confronting us. What seemed to be thousands of jeering *laan jais* (bad characters), bent and buckled sections of central road divide fencing, some abandoned or over-turned cars, even the odd burning bus, with hordes of onlookers in various buildings shouting and bawling. I remember thinking, at first, 'How the hell are we going to get through this lot!' particularly as we had come out in initial 'soft order', which meant berets as head gear, and sidearms only.

As we started our platoon advances on both sides of Nathan Road, heading in a sweep towards Tsim Sha Tsui, the bottles, plant pots, general debris, and other heavy objects rained down from a height, with even the odd Molotov cocktail. It was pretty clear after less than an hour that a re-think was needed. We thus needed to get into our holding compound at Yau Ma Tei Police Station to re-equip with anti-riot gear, and this we achieved although under attack. My feelings throughout were full of confidence – such was the brilliance of our PTU training – that at the head of my platoon I was never once in the slightest doubt as to who was going to win!

I briefed the boys again prior to redeploying out. The spirit and morale was high.

We returned to the streets at around 22.15 hours in 'hard order', with helmets, shields and the men with their full complement of weapons.

The vision of the full-scale confrontation that the police must have faced every day for months during the 1967 Disturbances momentarily amazed me, as I stood at the head of my platoon in Nathan Road. No. 2 Platoon was on the other side of the central fencing, and we were facing the mob.

Led from the front by Ed, closely followed by Alan, my men and I performed the ritualistic and disciplined baton charges that we had been taught at PTU, but never expected to have to perform in anger. My memories of the next few hours of that night will never leave me: Ed with his massive long baton, standing in the centre of Nathan Road directing the individual charges, engaging at close quarters those who refused to flee, dodging the objects thrown from the adjacent buildings and rooftops, and the sheer spirit of the men. I had the marvellous feeling, amidst all the chaos, that I was really doing something for the greater good. The arrests of five young men for looting a goldsmith shop caused a brief sojourn while we took them back to Yau Ma Tei Police Station, where I deposited them with CID and returned to the fray.

We continued our baton charges and occasional arrests, with the odd canister of tear gas used to persuade the crowd that this event was really not that good an idea. Radio transmissions from Kowloon HQ in Argyle Street relaying the Scottish tones of the Deputy Regional Commander, Bill Ross, giving encouragement to Ed Hillier to 'Get the job done, laddie', filled me with a certain confidence. The wonderful spirit and camaraderie displayed by my men and officers from other units throughout the night made me proud to be a member of 'Asia's Finest'. We reached Salisbury Road at about 06.00 hours, tired, filthy, but exuberant.

Finally, after a few 'clear ups', moving on some remaining stragglers, the whole operation was over. It was now about 07.30 hrs. We had been repeatedly baton charging, amidst breaks whilst taking prisoners back to Yau Ma Tei station. We had just reached the junction with Salisbury Road and the adjoining Tsim Sha Tsui streets had been cleared. The mob was gone.

In disciplined fashion, we boarded our Land Rovers and lorries and returned to Mong Kok Compound. I had many good moments throughout the rest of my police career, but none were as vivid as during this period. I recall hugging several of my men and all the troops were fired up. The overall sense of camaraderie was encapsulated by numerous Mong Kok Police Station staff, both Uniform Branch and CID, together with a number of Traffic Kowloon officers, standing there applauding us! Our platoons were all there, all the guys chanting 'Foxtrot, Foxtrot, Super Foxtrot!' Then we, the officers, conducted another early-morning deployment, this time up to the officers' mess, Mong Kok Police Station's renowned

'Bugs Retreat'. Cold beer, Carlsberg and San Miguel, led to the singing of that old football favourite *We are the Champions!*

What an eventful night. I have met up with my men on many social occasions over the years up to 1997 and on my subsequent return trips to Hong Kong, when they sought me out for dinner and a 'few' beers, at which we relived that unforgettable time together in PTU.

As a postscript, Alan Scott in due course left the Hong Kong administration and went on to be appointed governor of the Cayman Islands.

Gun Battle In Causeway Bay

R.A. (Bob) Steele

There are good postings and there are bad postings. Commandant, Police Tactical Unit (PTU) is a good posting and I was fortunate enough to hold that post in the early 1980s. At that time the unit was still housed at an ex-army base at Volunteer Slopes by Luen Wo Hui, Fanling in post-war Nissen huts – the same huts that I had first seen on posting there as an inspector platoon commander in 1966 and again as a superintendent company commander in 1975. I swear that each time I returned I was welcomed back by the same spiders and mosquitos.

PTU's main task was to train the Force from constable through to superintendent to deal with public order incidents and provide a Commissioner's Reserve in case of emergency, be it a public order incident or a natural disaster. Most officers in the Force went through PTU – many more than once, as I did, in different ranks. In addition to this, the commandant PTU was also responsible for the administration of the Special Duties Unit (SDU), though its operational use had to be sanctioned by the deputy director, operations, at Police Headquarters. The SDU, under the command of a superintendent, was housed close to PTU and was Hong Kong's counter-terrorist unit. They were highly trained in this work and the structure was modelled on that of the UK's 22nd Regiment Special Air Service. Only in very rare circumstances were the SDU permitted to be used to deal with 'civilian' criminal incidents. As I was about to finish my time at PTU, one such occasion arose.

On 31st January 1984, five men, each armed with a handgun, robbed the Po Sang Bank in Des Voeux Road, Central of 138.4 million Japanese yen (approximately HK$10 million) as the cash was being transferred from a security van to the bank. During the course of the robbery a Remington shotgun was seized from one of the cash-in-transit security guards.

The robbers made off on foot but soon commandeered a private car, forcing the driver out at gunpoint, and then drove off towards Eastern District. Beat patrol officers attempted to follow but lost the vehicle in traffic. A general alert was put out and, shortly thereafter, an officer on patrol reported seeing the vehicle near Lai Tak Tsuen in Causeway Bay.

Another officer reported seeing the vehicle enter the multi-storey car park in Fortress Hill Road and a number of Emergency Unit cars and patrol officers converged on the carpark. Sergeant 11811 Fu Siu-wing of EU alighted from his EU car and followed two beat patrol police officers into the car park. As the patrol officers entered the car park, four of the robbers opened fire – all were armed and one had a firearm in each hand! The officers took cover and returned fire. The robbers then ran out in the direction of Sergeant Fu who engaged them in fire, taking cover as he could. In his attempts to apprehend the robbers, he exposed himself to a fusillade of shots and considerable danger. By some miracle he was not hit though his uniform was subsequently found to be holed by at least one bullet and a car park employee was injured. In spite of this, Sergeant Fu showed great presence of mind and only fired four rounds from his service weapon.

The robbers ran off along King's Road with Sergeant Fu and others in pursuit. More shots were fired at the pursuing officers and another EU car arrived on the scene which also came under fire. Police Constable (PC) 1862 Yu Chau-pui and the other officers alighted from the vehicle and, with the others, chased the robbers into Fuk Yuen Street when they were again fired upon. Taking cover behind a fire hydrant, Yu fired two more shots and hit one of the robbers in the leg. The injured robber helped by one of his accomplices fired again at Yu but hit and killed a female pedestrian.

The robbers hijacked another vehicle and made off along Electric Road against the traffic flow and firing at a press vehicle which had stopped behind the robber's vehicle. Blocked by traffic at Hing Fat Street, the robbers were confronted by PC 17377 Cheng Chi-ming of Eastern District, Traffic Team. Having seen the robbers' vehicle driving the wrong way along Electric Road, Cheng had taken his motorcycle to the junction of Hing Fat Street to intercept them. He immediately came under fire and took shelter in a doorway, calling for pedestrians to take cover. He then fired once at the robbers who were still in their car. Cheng fired again hitting the vehicle. Still shooting and hitting a male pedestrian in the thigh, the robbers abandoned the vehicle and fled on foot into Victoria Park Road. They commandeered yet another vehicle and though Sergeant Fu, who had followed on foot from the start arrived, they drove off and evaded capture.

The ¥138.4 million and a Remington shotgun were recovered from the vehicle which had been abandoned in the multi-storey car park.

In the early hours of 5th February, a male surrendered to Kowloon City Police Station in need of treatment for a gunshot wound to the leg. This was the robber who had been shot by Yu in Fuk Yuen Street. Questioning of this suspect by Chief Inspector R.J. Pierce of CID Hong Kong Island elicited the information that the other robbers might have been hiding in Flat 2303, Wun Sha Tower, Causeway Bay. Pierce, having assessed the danger posed by these robbers, requested that the Special Duties Unit be utilised to effect the arrest. This was approved. While waiting for the SDU officers to arrive, Pierce prepared as detailed a plan of the interior of the premises as he could, from the information provided by the injured suspect.

Acting Chief Inspector C.M. Davey, SDU's operations officer, undertook the detailed planning and operational briefing for the elements of BRAVO Team SDU, under the command of Inspector M.J. Lovatt, who were to conduct the assault.

At 08.00 hours on 5th February, Inspector Lovatt and another member of BRAVO Team made a close reconnaissance of the flat. Like many flats, the front door was protected by an iron grille and Lovatt, undetected, managed to lay an explosive charge on the grille.

At 08.15, Lovatt detonated the charge which removed the grille cleanly from its hinges and also demolished the wooden front door to the flat. Upon entering, Lovatt met a hail of gunfire and returned five shots, hitting one robber in the chest. The robbers continued to fire from the end room of the flat at Lovatt who was in an exposed position. Lovatt's second-in-command, Sergeant Ng Kwan-wai, followed him into the flat and though now himself exposed to the fire from the end room, opened fire with his H&K MP5 sub-machine gun to provide cover for Lovatt. Ng's weapon then jammed but he drew his sidearm and continued to cover Lovatt.

One member of BRAVO team providing backup was shot in the leg. Two stun grenades were thrown by other members of BRAVO team. The robbers then retreated, locking themselves in the end room. Sergeant Ng called on them to surrender, which they eventually did without further gunfire. Four men emerged from the end room and after some initial resistance they were subdued and arrested. Lovatt then secured the premises, seizing seven firearms including semi-automatic heavy-calibre pistols and loaded magazines. Given the number of rounds fired in that small flat it is something of a miracle that casualties were relatively light.

Subsequent investigations led to a factory block in Kwai Chung where, on 8th February, five police revolvers that had been stolen between 1975 and 1980, five other pistols, two shotguns, spare parts, silencers, over 1,000 rounds of ammunition, as well as a number of knives were seized; then four days later a further 9mm pistol, one .45 pistol and three magazines and two .38 pistols. All in all, 23 firearms were seized as a result of this case.

As I left PTU, all five suspects were awaiting trial on charges of murder, shooting with intent and robbery. For their parts in bringing this dangerous gang of criminals to justice, a number of officers received honours and awards ranging from a Queen's Gallantry Medal for Inspector Lovatt and Queen's Commendations for Brave Conduct to Sergeants Fu and Ng, to Commissioner's Commendations.

Special Duties Unit Selection

Gordon Elsden

The Special Duties Unit (SDU) was the anti-terrorist formation of the Royal Hong Kong Police, and as such required a very high standard of fitness and motivation. Selection of suitable personnel was rigorous.

Thursday 5th September 1985
Our fourth day on selection and dawn broke with the news that Typhoon Tess had changed direction and was moving fast towards Hong Kong. The raising of Typhoon Signal Number 3 was marked by a noticeable increase in the intensity of wind and heavy rain rattling off the streets and buildings. What a dramatic change to the hot and humid climate that we had experienced at the beginning of the week! Yet the reduction in temperature was to prove a temporary relief to our torment.

We were meant to be taken by helicopter from the Police Tactical Unit (PTU) at Volunteer Slopes to Tai Lam Chung Marine Base. The increasing winds of the typhoon put paid to that and so we were driven across the New Territories through furious unrelenting rain and savage gusts of wind. The staff had planned to drop us out of the helicopters at an interesting height above the ocean, a kilometre from the shore to see if we could take a joke. Plan B now came into effect: a warm-up run, lasting an hour, with a variety of press-ups, sit-ups and shuttle runs in the pouring rain and strengthening wind. We found ourselves quickly soaked. Then, in groups of four, we fitted crude, cork-lined life jackets and boarded rigid inflatable speed boats to be dropped unceremoniously in the ocean at a respectable distance from the shore. The sea was running fast with a sizeable drop between the crest and trough of the waves; so much so that for periods we lost sight of the land and were deluged with sheets of water descending on us from the heavens as we rode the huge swell.

Our support boat directed us to a ship anchored in mid-channel with a scaling ladder dropped at the rear of the vessel. This proved an interesting exercise in timing, to catch a wave and grab and securely hold the ladder before being slammed into the unyielding steel hull. Not that there was going to be any relief once we had managed to climb to the top of the ladder. A slow jog along the sloping deck to the bow of the ship where one of the staff was grimly waiting for us. He had been hanging about for longer than expected and was now beginning to get wet and uncomfortable. Here we go! A phobia test in unnerving conditions with the wind whipping round the bow of the ship and the waves rearing up to meet us. One by one we had to climb over the rail at the bow and on the count of three, with no hesitation, immediately drop into the ocean from a height of above thirty feet.

As the count reached three I let go, not because I was especially brave but simply because my fear of failing the course overwhelmed my fear of dropping into the ocean. But as I dropped, the full force of the wind turned me in mid-air, resulting in me hitting the surface of the water on my side. The cork lining of the life jacket smashed into my rib cage. Ouch, that really, really hurt! But now, despite the shock of that, I had to get back to the surface, negotiate the rolling mass of waves to get to the stern of the ship, then climb the scaling ladder again, with ribs that were protesting their utmost discomfort. Amidst the violence of the wind and the hammering rain, I slowly ascended to the deck, swaying on the tenuous ladder, only to repeat the exercise on two more occasions. Thankfully, the staff had realised the danger of the wind at the bow and so we were now dropping from a lesser height into the turbulent cauldron below.

After the third jump, we remained in the ocean and formed up as a team of four, being tossed around on the surface. Riding the surging waves and going nowhere in particular for about forty-five minutes, with the rain slashing down on us in torrential bursts, we simply focused on remaining together and keeping as much of the salt water out of our mouths and noses as we could. Despite the noise of the storm, which made it difficult to hear each other, we endeavoured to maintain banter and see the humorous side to our predicament. After all, it is not every day on Her Majesty's Service that you get to go on a swim in the ocean in the midst of a typhoon!

We were dumped like drowned rats back on the pier of the Marine Police base. Now on terra firma, on our knees, we had the opportunity to throw up some of the excess water that we had taken on board. In the background, one of the staff strolled up and down lamenting our pitiable state and bragging how when he had done selection he had jumped from above forty feet. Fortunately, the noise of the storm and the rattle of spinnakers on boats moored nearby served as a convenient mute button.

Our ocean ordeal was not yet concluded as the staff had another interesting experience planned for us. It went like this: put a hood over the victim's head, tie their hands together behind the back, tie their feet together, and as a precaution fix a rope around the waist, though you have to remember to keep hold of the other end. Then get your tethered subject to lie down on the edge of the pier before rolling him into the ocean, some five feet below: stand back to watch his reaction. Will he immediately freak out or will he relax, hold his breath and come to the surface to calmly take a breath, hopefully not as a wave is breaking over the top? It doesn't take long to get a reaction if there is going to be one.

Our final test of the morning was to don oxygen rebreather apparatus and descend into the ocean to see if we had any adverse reaction during a short descent. After what had preceded, this was mundane, especially as many of us had experienced diving in open water.

Bedraggled and sodden we were given lunch as the approaching typhoon increased in intensity. In the afternoon there was little respite with a planned exercise in canoes to ostensibly go and make a reconnaissance of one of the nearest moored ships. The surging waves and fierce wind were not sympathetic to such a venture and we didn't even get close. The exercise soon became a rescue mission for numerous capsized canoes and our waterlogged and now increasingly cynical group.

Three of the inspectors and numerous constables on the selection course dropped out during this ocean stage, some on the verge of extreme panic. The inspectors had been reduced to a group of five, a group that would join together and remain as a close unit for the remainder of the selection. In a way it now became a case of us against them, which was a great motivator.

Staff and surviving inspectors of September 1985 SDU selection.
Back & upper row: Martin Lovatt (staff), Lance Brown (staff), Bob McAuley,
K.S. Tang (staff – went on to become commissioner in 2007)
Front: Alan Crowther, ? Anderson, Steve Wordsworth, Gordon Elsden,
Paul Pettit (staff) (Courtesy of G. Elsden)

A New Territories Kidnapping

Peter Halliday

The 1970s and '80s saw a steady stream of kidnappings involving victims of all ages and socio-economic status. It seems likely that quite a lot of these went unreported with the victim's family or friends simply paying the ransom demanded, which may have encouraged kidnap gangs to commit more such crimes.

Kidnappings were amongst the more stressful of investigations for the simple reason that our objectives were to some extent incompatible. The main objective was to locate and recover the victim unharmed, but also not to pay any ransom and to arrest the perpetrators.

In common with others, I investigated my fair share of forcible abductions, with varying degrees of success. Some were completely successful, others a disaster. In one case I dealt with, the ransom was scooped up under our noses but the victim – a well-to-do businessman – was never seen or heard of again.

One of my successful investigations was something of a trail-blazer. We conducted what I will characterise as an audio identification parade. We had the suspect repeat sentences that had been used on the telephone calls to the victim's family, which had been recorded. We then had seven other persons record the same thing. The victim's family were asked to listen to all the recordings and identify – if they could – the suspect. They were able to do so. The *modus operandi* of the 'parade' was examined at great length in the ensuing court proceedings and the evidence was ultimately ruled admissible. In addition, at the end of the trial, the judge remarked that he thought the maximum penalty for kidnapping (at that time fourteen years imprisonment) was too low. Not long after, it was raised to life imprisonment and the number of such cases dropped dramatically.

I was involved in an interesting, partially successful, investigation in or around 1985. A three-year-old boy was taken from his flat in the Sheung Shui area of the New Territories. His mother had stepped out for a moment and returned to find him gone.

A report was made to the local station and the case was referred to the New Territories Headquarters Criminal Investigation Department, in accordance with established procedures.

Arrangements were made to monitor the victim's family telephone from the local telephone exchange and it was not long before the assumed kidnappers made contact. Their initial demand – believe it or not – was for HK$10 million, accompanied by the direst threats if the family did not comply. This led the investigators to suppose that the kidnappers had abducted the little boy by mistake as the family were of very modest means. Coincidentally, the father was a cleaning worker at the Police Tactical Unit Headquarters, also in Sheung Shui.

The next ten days or so proved exhausting for both family and investigators. A police officer moved in with the family to provide support and encouragement. The kidnappers kept up a steady barrage of menacing telephone calls, all from public telephone boxes and from all over Hong Kong. As the days passed, the family was able to convince the perpetrators that they had very little money, whereupon telephone call after telephone call became a callous, one-sided exchange as to how much they could afford. 'Playing with' the victim's family would be an apt way of describing it.

The investigating team had established its command post at the Yuen Long Police Station in the northwestern New Territories. This is a largish station with long corridors (seventy yards or more) running the length of the building. The team was housed on the first floor with the CID.

Late one afternoon, the kidnappers called again and demanded $10,000, or the victim would suffer dire consequences. The victim's family could no more afford this sum than they could afford $10 million, but it was adjudged that the kidnappers were entirely serious. As such, a command decision was made to supply the money. The kidnappers gave precise instructions as to where the money was to be left, and clearly knew their business. Ordinarily, the drop point would have been covered by undercover officers but such tactics were extremely difficult in the more rural New Territories. Nevertheless, it was decided to try and cover the drop point – which was on the outskirts of Yuen Long town – using just a few officers.

A member of the victim's family left the money at the agreed location. Despite the best efforts of the few officers on the stake out, the kidnappers managed to retrieve the money unobserved. Indeed, this did not become apparent until the kidnappers telephoned the victim's family late that evening. Despite, they said, the family having 'double-crossed' them by reporting to the police, they had decided to release the victim.

The victim could be found, they said 'at an abandoned pig farm in Pat Heung'. Pat Heung is a sizable village east of Yuen Long.

Some enquiries with the local police quickly established that there were dozens of abandoned pig farms in the area, most of their erstwhile owners having emigrated overseas. The morale of the investigating team was at a very low ebb. Nevertheless, as big a search party as possible was assembled and set off.

Without exaggeration, the next ten hours or so were a nightmare as the search parties quartered the countryside looking for the little boy. Had the kidnappers told the truth? It was the height of summer so the weather was trying – hot and wet. Back at the command post, I am told that I spent a lot of the time walking around the perimeter of the (large) station carpark, and have some recollection of staring at the stars – and probably hoping for luck.

It must have been around four in the morning when one of the investigators came running over to me and said that the little boy had been found. Joy! I ran back to the command post on the first floor.

There are staircases at each end of the building. I was with other members of the team, congregated at one end of the long corridor. Suddenly, a group of people appeared at the other end. It was difficult to see them clearly. Suffice to say that both groups started walking towards one another, and this quickly developed into a run, and we converged in the middle. In later years, I was reminded of the scene in *Gone With the Wind* when Ashley returns from the Civil War, 'from the dead', and sees Melanie, his sweetheart on the other side of the cornfield. They run towards each other and embrace.

I embraced the little boy as if my life depended on it. Strangely enough, he was not crying but his clothes were torn, he was filthy, and he was covered with mosquito bites. Otherwise, it seemed that he was none the worse for his horrifying experience.

I doubt very much if Yuen Long Station had seen such an emotional event before, or since.

The 'wash-up' the following morning (or, rather, later the same morning) with the Regional Commander, Michael Illingworth and his deputy, Gordon Jack, was a positive affair in the best traditions of the Force, and I remember it well.

Jack emphasised the difficulties of the operation and the overarching fact that we had recovered the little boy.

The discussion then moved to more delicate terrain. How, asked Illingworth, had the family managed to raise the $10,000? I had anticipated this question and had decided to face the music. I had taken it, I told him, from the Rewards and Special Services Fund, (R&SS) in my safe.

(The Rewards and Special Services Fund, as its name implies, is a fund for paying public rewards, for paying informers and for other confidential or sensitive operational expenses. It is subject to 'surprise inspections' by appropriate officers to ensure that there are no discrepancies and that the fund is being administered in accordance with the rules.)

There was a silence whilst the three of us contemplated both each other and the ceiling above. The suspense was ultimately broken by Illingworth who said: 'I imagine that for an operation of this length and complexity your operational expenses have been significant. Presumably also, you tasked informers to try and develop lines of enquiry?' I earnestly agreed that this was so. Illingworth: 'Looking at my diary, I see that you are due for a surprise inspection of your R&SS. Would around midday be convenient?'

Illingworth duly 'surprised' me later in the day and conducted a detailed inspection of the fund. It was in order and he raised no queries. He made an entry in the inspections register to that effect.

The kidnappers were never caught.

I know not what became of the little boy who would now be in his thirties. One hopes that he is carving out a successful career. He may well also by now have a family of his own.

My undying thanks go to all the officers on the investigating team, who strove night and day for two weeks trying to engineer a scenario which would both liberate the victim and net the perpetrators; to the search parties who laboured that night under atrocious conditions and did not even contemplate giving up; and to Messrs Illingworth and Jack, who behaved with dignity and honour, and provided very welcome encouragement and support. It is no exaggeration to say that these combined efforts saved a little boy from serious harm, or worse.

A Tragic Career Development

Peter Halliday

In 1986, having served most of my career in the Criminal Investigation Department (CID), I was told that it was high time that my horizons were broadened. The modern term for this is 'career development.' So I was taken out of the CID and posted to Personnel Wing.

This was a shock, not only for me but also for many around the Force. 'Halliday in Personnel?!' Heaven help us!' was the popular sentiment. They may well have been right.

It turned out that 'Personnel' needed a section to deal with all the personnel matters that did not seem to fit into the charters of other sections, for example those sections devoted to recruitment, and postings (and career development!). My charter rapidly expanded to cover a vast and inventive range of 'people issues.'

In late November, a file landed on my desk one morning which, it is fair to say, stopped me in my tracks – such was the unspeakable sadness of it.

It concerned a young constable – just twenty-seven years of age as I recall – who had been pursuing, until illness struck him down, a very successful career. He had been an operative with the Force Surveillance Unit, and such officers are not picked out with a pin. He was married with a baby son.

Tragically, he had contracted cancer of the spine. This had been diagnosed as terminal and he had been transferred to the Haven of Hope Hospice in Tseung Kwan O.

Reviewing the file, the concern was clearly what might be done to 'look after' the wife and baby after the officer's death, and I thought about this for several days.

In the event – with the agreement of my direct superior – I sought an audience with Deputy Commissioner Eric Blackburn, who in fact had posted me to Personnel Wing. I went over to his office with considerable foreboding as he had a reputation for being hard-boiled. His secretary's attempts to encourage me with platitudes including: 'He's not as rough as people think' did nothing of the sort and I was ushered, nervously, into his office.

Somehow, I managed to lay out the circumstances with reasonable coherency. Blackburn then asked me what I wanted and I replied that I was seeking advice as to how to handle the officer's impending death. 'What would you do?' asked Blackburn, impaling me. 'Lesson No 1 in getting on; don't announce a problem for someone else to solve. At least identify some options first.' I ventured that the only option that I had identified thus far was for some sort of ex-gratia payment to be made to the wife, but that I had little or no idea of whether or how this was possible.

'Alright, let's look at the issues,' said Blackburn. 'What's his record like?' I said that it was a good one. 'Any blemishes?' 'No.' 'How many years of service?' 'Seven.'

Then: 'Has he passed the sergeant promotion examination?' 'Yes.' 'Has he appeared before a board yet?' 'No'. 'He's been recommended before, but not shortlisted.' 'Hm.'

'Have you talked to his commanding officer?' 'Yes.' 'To what conclusion?' 'He's reported to have been a very good officer with potential.'

Blackburn raised his eyes slowly and looked at me (I was reminded of Paul Morphy, the great chess player, delivering the coup de grâce). 'If you were writing his promotion report this year, would you recommend him?' 'Yes.' 'If you were the chairman of the promotion board, would you promote him?'

The penny dropped. 'Most certainly!'

'So, what it amounts to is this. We have a fine officer with an equally fine record. There's no doubting his potential. Had it not been for *force majeure,* there is every likelihood that he would have been promoted this year. Does this, in your view, represent an objective assessment of the situation?'

'Very much so.'

'Alright, Peter,' said Blackburn. 'Write the whole thing up, recommending that I make a field promotion to sergeant.' We agreed that Blackburn would present the chevrons at some suitable time.

Tragically, things then moved very quickly.

On the afternoon of 4 December 1986, the hospice telephoned to advise that the officer had fallen into a coma and was fading. I called Blackburn who, dispensing with the niceties, ordered me, peremptorily, to be in uniform, standing by with a staff car, in thirty minutes. 'And do a nice letter for my signature, and don't forget the chevrons!'

At the appointed hour, Blackburn appeared in full dress uniform with sword, and with his many decorations. Not sparing the horses, we were at the hospice in half an hour or so and went immediately to the ward.

The officer was indeed in a deep coma. A large group of grieving relatives and friends was present but there was no hysteria. I have seldom seen such quiet dignity in a group of people. Tears, yes and aplenty, but everyone in firm control of his or her emotions.

Blackburn performed the promotion ceremony right down to the pinning of the chevrons on the officer's sleeve with flair and panache, and made a short suitable speech about the officer's capabilities and that his promotion was thoroughly deserved. Frankly, I was overwhelmed by the occasion and am not ashamed to say that I was very misty indeed – near to tears if the truth were known.

Blackburn had a few words with the family, whereupon we took our leave.

Later that evening, I received a telephone call from the hospice saying that the officer had died.

And why do I remember this so vividly? Why can I pinpoint the exact date?

In the early hours of 5 December 1986, Sir Edward Youde, then governor of Hong Kong, died in his sleep at the British Embassy in Beijing.

We hear a lot about leadership and what works, and what does not. In my book, it boils down to two or three very simple things: looking and acting the part; dignity; and boundless compassion.

A Murder in the Vietnamese Refugee Camp

Simon Roberts

In the late 1970s, after the victory of the communist Viet Cong in Vietnam, some of the wealthier people began to try to escape.

Over the years as more Vietnamese 'boat people' sought refuge in Hong Kong, the government's policy on handling them changed. By 1987, there was a large Vietnamese camp at Kai Tak near the international airport. Many of the accommodation blocks were similar to those used by the Royal Air Force some thirty years earlier. I was a senior inspector in the Criminal Investigation Department in Sau Mau Ping Police Station and this camp was in my district. I had attended the Detective Training School in 1986 and was transferred to the District Crime Squad a year later. The Kai Tak camp was an open camp which meant that residents had special identity cards and could travel outside the camp to work. Unfortunately, some of them decided to also steal and the crime rate outside the camp increased.

We sometimes conducted patrols in the camp where I met Mr Wong, who was in charge of managing the camp. The accommodation was very basic, consisting of bunk beds laid out on either side of a single corridor running down the middle of a large corrugated iron Nissen hut. Latrines and showers were in a separate external block. One day Mr Wong showed me a different room with its own entrance. When we walked in I couldn't believe my eyes. It was wallpapered, there was air-conditioning, a four-poster bed, carpet on the floor, a music system. I thought to myself, this is better than my government quarters! I turned to Mr Wong. 'Who lives here?' I asked.

'Oh, this is Pham's room.'

'Who is Pham?'

'Pham is the boss of Kai Tak camp,' he replied gravely.

The following February in 1988, around 9 pm, I was at home when my telephone rang. It was Chinese New Year's Eve, a time when families reunite and enjoy a festive dinner together. There are celebrations, presents of lucky money, and lion dances. It is always a very happy time. It was common for the expatriates to remain either on duty or on call during this time to allow local Chinese officers to enjoy their traditional family time. It was Detective Sergeant Chan on the line. He told me a homicide had occurred at the Kai Tak camp. In a short time I was in my car. On arriving at the scene I saw a group of officers already there ahead of me. Our District Commander Lai had also attended and looked very unhappy that his family dinner had been disturbed. Once I'd been briefed he ordered me to take the case over. I felt sorry for Sergeant Chan and my team. They had no choice but to stay behind and begin the painstaking investigations required for any homicide.

The victim's body had already been removed, so we spent time trying to ascertain the chronology of events and locate any witnesses. Photos were taken and after a couple of hours we made our way back to the station. By this time it was after 11 pm and my team were hungry. I gave detective Lau a HK$100 note and asked him to buy *siu yeh* for the team. *Siu yeh* is a late-night snack, often fried rice or noodles, served in polystyrene cartons. It was essential in order to maintain morale, and hopefully get everyone working their best. We compared notes and discussed our initial thoughts on the case. It seemed that a Vietnamese male had been murdered following a dispute during an illegal gambling session. We didn't know how the murder had taken place. The victim was in the morgue and we had no murder weapon. An urgent post-mortem had been arranged in the morning and as it was already 1 am, I decided to use a sleeping bag in my office and go directly to the mortuary from there. I let my team make their weary way home. We would meet again after the post-mortem.

At 9 am, I was in the mortuary and I introduced myself to Dr Lee, the pathologist. A post-mortem is gruesome. The smell of decomposing human flesh and the sound of a saw cutting through a skull will stay with me forever. I was led over to our victim who was already laid out on a slab. He was a strongly built, dark-skinned Vietnamese male, with tattoos on his body. His flesh was still warm to the touch. He had almost no discernible injuries and looked as if he was sleeping. I was intrigued. Dr Lee made the first incision through the victim's belly. As he did so several pints of frothy liquid burst out and splashed over the sides of the slab onto the floor and over my shoes. It was clear that our man had enjoyed many glasses of San Miguel before his demise. Once I'd dried my shoes with tissues and regained my composure, I asked Dr Lee what he thought about the lack of obvious injury. He pointed out some small puncture wounds. When he examined the body internally, he discovered massive trauma to various organs. He concluded that death had occurred as a result of multiple stabbings with a long narrow, needle-like weapon.

By noon, I was back in the station and my team started to report on duty. They were still unhappy with having to deal with this during what should be their New Year celebrations. I began to brief them about the post-mortem and the supposed murder weapon. We agreed to go back to the scene now that it was daylight and look for anything similar to a narrow lance. Once in the camp, we scoured the ground around the murder scene. We also continued to question residents and look for witnesses. It was apparent that people were very reluctant to come forward, but someone had whispered a familiar name in Sergeant Chan's ear: 'Pham'. Suddenly I heard a shout from one of my team: 'Sir, come over here.' I ran over and saw one of my detectives pointing on the ground. Two aluminium pipes about three feet long and a half-inch in diameter lay on the ground. One end had been sharpened to a razor-like point and there were blood stains near the tip. It looked like we'd found our murder weapons.

The tubes were water pipes commonly used in the camp. The Vietnamese, resourceful as ever, had realised they were easily cut and sharpened and made excellent weapons. It seemed there must be others because water was always leaking over the camp grounds. We learned our victim was named Tran and that he was an unpopular person and a bit of a bully. We understood that after consuming several beers he had tried to muscle in on a card game being run by Pham and his cronies. Being a bit drunk, he began to get loud and argumentative and before long a fight broke out. Pham and his gang decided to teach him a lesson and things became so heated that he had been murdered. This was to be the story we were hearing from confidential informants, and to us it seemed very plausible. We began to work our case around this scenario.

I learnt that Pham had been implicated in two earlier homicides, and had been arrested previously in connection with one. He was hated and feared by the camp residents. The blood group on the lances we seized matched Tran's and we were able to lift a partial fingerprint off one of the handles. We gradually built a case. Eventually, it was time to bring Pham in for questioning. When I faced him for the first time it was unnerving. His eyes were black, he showed no emotion. He refused to answer any questions. In spite of this and with the excellent work from the team, we built a case with significant circumstantial evidence that pointed the finger firmly at Pham.

It was time for me to send the case file to the Legal Department and have it examined by a crown counsel. This was a nervous time for me because the case file had to be perfect; otherwise I could expect barbed comments in reply!

A favourable decision came back and it was agreed that Pham should be arrested and charged. This was a very exciting time for the team because it meant their hard work was being rewarded. I requested Pham be held in custody until the first plea date. A murder charge had a special legal arrangement which meant an initial legal review took place in court before the case was transferred to the High Court. Therefore, it was some time before the actual trial commenced.

When eventually the first day of the High Court trial arrived, a jury had to be agreed. The whole process was very drawn out. I was of course present throughout and in my best dark suit looking as smart as possible. I sat near to the prosecuting crown counsel named Stevens, so I could assist him with witnesses, exhibits, questions of evidence and so on. Pham's defence was simple; that he wasn't at the scene and therefore could not have committed the murder. By calling a number of witnesses, we aimed to convince the jury that

Pham had been at the scene even though we had no-one directly implicating him. All the while, Pham's gang sat up in the viewing gallery glaring down at proceedings.

Eventually the case was concluded, the judge summed up the case, and the jury was sent to consider a verdict. It was late in the evening and I thought that perhaps we might need to come back the next day. At about 11 pm there was some excitement and a flurry of activity – the jury was returning. Once everyone had returned to their places, the jury foreman was asked for the verdict. It was unanimous. Pham was found guilty of murder! I felt elated. I turned to Stevens and smiled, he seemed as pleased as I was. The judge leant down, and pulled something from under his bench. He gravely placed a small black cap on his head. He turned to Pham and said: 'Pham, you have been found guilty of murder, therefore I sentence you to death.' I had completely forgotten that the death penalty remained on the statute in Hong Kong and was the normal punishment for murder. The sentence was later commuted to life imprisonment by Her Majesty. It still made for a dramatic end to the case.

Stevens was very happy with the case and the verdict, and was very complimentary in the case file. But though Stevens had said the case was watertight, Pham appealed. We were still confident that nothing would change. Having been held in custody for a few months, Pham's appeal was heard. The sentence was overturned and Pham was released. We were all in shock but we were not as upset as the poor boat people in the camp. Three murders and he was still walking around. This time his power was greater than ever, he appeared invincible.

There was a final twist to the tale. As Pham became more notorious, he became careless. Everyone feared him. He started leaving the camp late at night and returning drunk on the cognac he'd consumed in Kowloon's nightclubs. One person in the camp noticed this. He began to track Pham's movements. One night at around 1 am, Pham was returning, as usual, in an inebriated state. As Pham made his way towards the entrance gate, a dark figure leapt out. He held a razor-sharp meat cleaver, and swung it hard at the back of

Pham's neck. The heavy blade struck again and again until Pham was left in a widening pool of blood. There were numerous suspects for the murder of Pham; almost everyone in the camp had a motive. The main suspect was Tran's younger brother, Duc. As far as I know, no-one was ever charged in the case, but the camp became a more peaceful place as a result.

Baguio Villas Landslide, 1992

Keith Braithwaite

In May 1992, as officer in charge of the Narcotics Bureau of the Criminal Investigation Department, Headquarters, RHKP, I found myself in Peshawar, North Pakistan – literally 'Up the Khyber'! I was on an official liaison visit organised by the Foreign Anti-Narcotic Community of both South and Southeast Asia. National anti-narcotic agencies took it in turns to host these liaisons designed to meet and discuss mutual problems concerning drug enforcement, to attempt to set in motion better and more efficient enforcement co-ordination and to witness particular difficulties of enforcement on the ground. There was much to discuss!

On this occasion, the host was Pakistan and representatives from other South and Southeast Asian nations attended. Suffice to say that the North-West Frontier Province abutting Afghanistan, clearly poorly controlled by the Pakistan government officials, was quite an eye opener with guns and drugs on open display – but that is another story.

On the return flight to Hong Kong, we were informed that the plane would be diverted to Taiwan due to a 'black rain warning' in Hong Kong. We flew on eventually, having been delayed for a couple of hours in Taiwan, and upon arrival in Hong Kong, I was informed that Victoria Road had been closed due to a landslide.

Meanwhile that morning in Hong Kong, my wife, Christine, had driven my youngest daughter, Melanie, from our quarters in Baguio Villas, to school in Wong Chuk Hang. Melanie was taking her mock exams and therefore had intermittent attendances at school due to study leave. Prior to leaving, Christine had been listening to the radio because of the threatening weather but had not heard that the school had been closed. So off she went, driving

Melanie to school along Victoria Road and through Aberdeen to Nam Fung Road. The weather was atrocious but Christine managed to get to South Island without too much trouble apart from the heavy rain, only to find that the school was closed for the day. The return journey was made safely, albeit with much trepidation due to flooding through Wong Chuk Hang (there being no flyover through the factory area in those days). On returning home, Christine discovered that a black rain warning had indeed been issued.

The rear of our home, Flat 13, Block 42, overlooked Victoria Road and the dining room window afforded an excellent view of that, together with the foundations of the Upper Baguio Villa blocks.

A little after lunch, Melanie was on the phone to her friend, Katrina Tudor, who was living in Flat 5 of Block 42, situated about level with Victoria Road. They were discussing the most unusual and ominous looking light – a strange yellow-green-black colour piercing the heavy rain. Suddenly, they heard a rumbling and crashing sound and Katrina's mother, Fiona Tudor, scream – at which point Katrina dropped the phone and ran into the dining area to join her mother.

Fiona had been looking out of the fifth-floor dining area window and witnessed the avalanche of hillside crash down past the foundations of Upper Baguio, cross over Victoria Road and down onto and through the patio of Lower Baguio blocks 42–44. She had seen Mrs Morrison, who resided on the first floor and who had been out on the patio apparently trying to unblock drains, being engulfed by the deluge of liquid mud. Luckily her maid, Gillian, had seen what had happened and dived in to pull her to safety.

The avalanche of rock and mud fell with such momentum that it punched a hole in the first-floor rear patio of blocks 42–44. It engulfed a first-floor flat in Block 44, trapping and killing a young lad, whilst his father and brother managed to escape through the main front door. Sadly, a government duty engineer on an inspection in Block 44 was also engulfed and killed.

Both our families, led by Christine and Fiona, together with Trixie the Braithwaite dog, fled down the front staircase of Block 42, out on to the front patio and down to ground level. In their panic, they ran down to the reclaimed area of Telegraph Bay.

They feared the possible collapse of some of the Upper Baguio blocks onto the lower blocks, as had occurred in the Kotewall / Po Shan Road landslide in 1972. [9]

Luckily this did not happen. Eventually, after a couple of hours, they decided to make their way north on foot up through a very small fishing village, Kong Sin Wan Tsuen, to Victoria Road, thereby avoiding the affected blocks. Upon reaching the road, they fortuitously bumped into Paul Deal, the police divisional commander of Aberdeen, patrolling in his vehicle. He arranged for both families to be taken to the safety of his quarters in Happy Valley.

Upon my arrival at Kai Tak Airport, my driver had picked me up and had informed me of a serious problem in Victoria Road. He took me through Aberdeen to Victoria Road where we could go no further. I contacted Paul, the area being under his command and he put me in the picture. I was quite relieved to learn that both my family and the Tudors were safe and joined them in Paul's quarters. His wife Sian kindly took them in and there we all subsequently stayed for a couple of nights before being temporarily housed in a hotel in Wan Chai.

Residents of the lower blocks affected were evacuated into a hotel in Wan Chai and subsequently given limited access to their quarters to retrieve personal items. It was not until about three weeks later that we were allowed to move back into our quarters. During that time both Melanie and Katrina had to sit their mock exams – something neither of them will ever forget.

According to the subsequent report by the Geotechnical Engineering Office of the Civil Engineering Department dated June 1992,[10] a masonry containing wall at a Temporary Housing Area (THA) along Pok Fu Lam Road had collapsed that morning due to

9   In June 1992, following the worst deluge in 83 years when 640 mm of rain fell in 72 hours, a huge landslide occurred in Po Shan Road, Mid-Levels, Hong Kong Island. In less than ten seconds, it had cleared a path to Kotewall Road destroying several houses and retaining walls. Upon reaching Kotewall Road, the slip knocked Kotewall Court, a luxury block, completely off its foundations. 67 people were killed and 20 injured in less than one minute.
10 There are two interesting appendices, one showing the track of the mud slide and the other showing the hourly rainfall.

exceptionally heavy rain. On that day between 6 and 9 am, the Royal Observatory recorded a total of 179 mm of rain, which corresponds statistically to a one-in-30-year event. Short bursts of rain resumed at 11 am, intensifying at about 1:45 pm when over 40 mm fell in 20 minutes. It is thought likely that the collapse at the THA level began at this time, there having been a total of 300 mm of rain since 6 am.

At 3:15 pm, over 22.5 mm of rain fell in five minutes, a one-in-60-year event. This flushed the large volume of accumulated debris from the collapsed wall down the gully alongside Block 26 of Upper Baguio Villas. The debris was washed across Victoria Road and landed on the podium of Blocks 43–44, entering the rear of a flat on the podium level and killing the young boy. The weight of the debris was so great that it caused the collapse of a 5x9 metre area of the reinforced concrete slab forming the podium. This then fell onto the floor of the upper carpark area below, collapsing it and allowing mud to enter part of the basement carpark. Three thousand cubic metres of material were deposited onto Block 43 and 44 following an entire drop of 110 metres from the THA area in Pok Fu Lam Road.

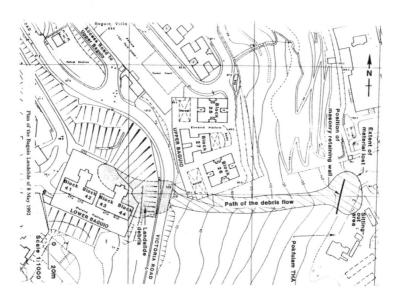

Track of the Baguio Villas mud slide

The Approach to 1997

Simon Monaghan

When I joined the Force in 1988, the Handover of the sovereignty of Hong Kong to China had already been signed and sealed, and the countdown was well underway. However, 30th June 1997 seemed a million miles away to the nine of us who departed Gatwick Airport on that August morning and it was never a concern for us during our thirty-six weeks of basic training at the Police Training School. The 1985 Joint Declaration meant that we could all continue in our positions after 1997, other than the three posts at commissioner and deputy commissioner level, so we gave it no thought.

But the events of May 1989 were a wakeup call. The ongoing student protests in Beijing were front-page news in the *South China Morning Post* for months, and after the actions of the People's Liberation Army in Tiananmen Square on June 4th there was widespread concern in Hong Kong. It didn't worry me personally, and in a sense why would it, since I could leave at any time, but it undoubtedly influenced some of those officers starting to wrestle with the decision to stay or go after 1997.

Politically, the early 1990s were dominated by the wrangling between the Chinese government and Chris Patten who had arrived as governor in Hong Kong in 1992, and spats between the two sides appeared to dampen enthusiasm in Hong Kong generally. One of my earliest recollections was whilst having drinks in Mong Kok Police Officers' Mess one evening, when an expatriate district commander and a couple of his equally senior peers were extremely negative about the future prospects for the Force and advised the junior expatriates present to consider leaving. I think they were all part of the group that went on to leave with a Her Majesty's

Overseas Civil Service (HMOCS) package after joining in the 1970s, so I can perhaps understand their feeling that things would not be the same in the future. However, it was very much an individual decision and I remember thinking that I was loving the job, and enjoying the lifestyle and the city, so why leave? But it did very much come down to personal preference, and I knew a couple of expatriates on contract terms who quite suddenly decided to call it quits, very close to the Handover. Some didn't like the thought of working for a Chinese administration, others had just had enough of Hong Kong, whereas others were concerned about future vetting issues and went off to forge careers with various departments of the United Kingdom government.

For some officers, that decision to leave was as much financial as anything, since those joining before 1985 were eligible for pensionable terms, something not open to us late joiners. Members of HMOCS were usually eligible for both compensation and deferred pensions, and so leaving was not a difficult decision for those officers in the compensation 'sweet spot', due to their age and length of service.

Discussions about pensions and terms of service were a constant part of mess life throughout my service, but I'm not one of those people who can get upset by the distinction that was created between the expats on pensionable terms or those on contract. Theoretically, I could have joined the Force in 1984 as an eighteen-year-old straight from school, but I had been in no way ready for the Force at that stage, so it's simply not relevant. There is no doubt that the officers who left with generous pensions underpinned by UK government guarantees have since done very well indeed financially. However, there was always a trade off between the security of a pension and the freedom and flexibility offered by contract terms, and the latter suited me personally. Not that I had a choice of course.

The last small group of expatriate probationary inspectors arrived in late 1994 and it seemed that their recruitment was a partly symbolic exercise since their standard three-year agreement would take them beyond the Handover date. One of that last group could be the last expatriate serving in the Force, if he stays until the normal retirement age of fifty-five, which in his case will be 2029.

Strangely, in many ways the atmosphere in the Force seemed to improve post-1997 despite the inevitable changes in policy and procedures creeping in. The declining numbers of expatriates also led to changes and some, such as the reduction in station interpreters, were unremarkable, whereas others, such as removing all expatriates from sitting on promotion boards, were more controversial.

Promotion was a big issue around 1997, as the hundreds of expatriates leaving with the HMOCS package or for other reasons, had to be replaced. For several years there was a promotion 'Big Bang' and it was a great opportunity to get ahead if you could catch the crest of the promotion wave. But the converse was also true, since not only would a board failure leave you behind your peers, the following years were expected to be extremely barren and create a promotion bottleneck. At chief inspector level this manifested itself in a promotion list of over one hundred in one year, and at that stage there were still good numbers of expatriates making the grade.

It became clear over time that a de facto quota system was operating in terms of absolute numbers of expatriates being promoted in any category. As a consequence, the expatriates were now primarily competing against each other for a limited number of promotion slots, with that number being at the whim of Personnel Wing and their manpower planners who were tasked with ensuring that enough local officers remained in the manpower pool to provide the future cadre of senior officers.

The decision gate for HMOCS officers wanting to quit the Force and take a compensation package opened several years before the Handover. The first leavers were able to depart from 1995 in order to stagger departures and ameliorate the impact. Those intending to leave commonly drifted towards less-demanding postings, but some clearly wanted to go out on a high, and at Police Tactical Unit Headquarters (PTU HQ), we ended up with a couple of expatriate inspectors who knew that they would not be there for long but wanted to regularly experience the smell of CS tear smoke nonetheless.

In January 1995, I had recently started my third tour and I was able to secure a posting on the PTU staff after five months on long leave, Intermediate Cantonese Course and yet more leave for the Christmas period. With hindsight, PTU HQ was always going to have been involved in the Handover operations, though that was not at the front of my mind when I arrived in Fanling. At that stage PTU HQ was still wrestling with the issues around the forced repatriation of tens of thousands of Vietnamese refugees. The PTU training sausage machine was operating at maximum capacity, with one new PTU company passing out every four weeks. This required four staff teams, one each for the three companies undergoing internal security training, and a fourth team preparing trainees for duties on the Hong Kong–China Border.

I started to actively plan my own career. A post in one of the Emergency Units seemed to be the obvious choice but the timing was critical. Despite always having excellent working relationships with the teams under my command, I was concerned that 1997 might have an effect on team cohesion, or to put it more bluntly, an expatriate might not be as well accepted in a post-1997 environment. For that reason, I applied to curtail my contract and in December 1996 I therefore returned all my PTU kit and headed off on leave for the Christmas period. I was pleased with my plan, it seemed like a sensible thing to do. The only problem was that the commandant PTU had decided to keep an experienced team together over the Handover period. So January 1997 saw me returning to Team 3, re-drawing my kit, and attempting to find a suitable locker and bed space upstairs in the officers' mess.

But there were far worse places to work than on the PTU staff and as time went on, PTU's role in the large-scale Handover operations became clearer. Security was paramount due to the presence of so many world leaders at the ceremonies, complicated by the number of events being held at different locations, though primarily on Hong Kong Island around the Convention and Exhibition Centre and the naval base at HMS Tamar. A large 'sterile' zone was required and the solution came in the form of hundreds of white and extremely bulky water barriers purchased specially for the occasion. Over six feet high and six feet wide, empty they were relatively light and could easily be manhandled into position by a couple of officers. However, once filled with water and linked to water barriers on either side, they became immovable objects. Unfortunately, it fell to us to fill them with water and in view of the close proximity to the harbour it was decided to use sea rather than fresh water. 'Sea water' is a somewhat euphemistic description for the liquid that went into those barriers since it was pumped straight from the harbour and at the end of that day, I was probably the hottest and smelliest of my entire career.

On the eve of the Handover, 30th June, I was tasked to man an alternate command post (CP) within the HMS Tamar site, not far from the quayside where the Royal Yacht *Britannia* was berthed. The CP was to run throughout that day and our small team were to man it from that evening until early the next morning. The whole point of an alternate was that it should have nothing to do unless serious problems emerged at the main CP, and thankfully it turned out that we had almost nothing to do throughout. Sat on the sidelines of the operations with limited views of the various goings-on, it was all rather dull. The operation went smoothly apart from the wet weather. Midnight came and went with us changing insignia of rank from 'Royal Hong Kong Police' to 'Hong Kong Police' and after that, it was just a matter of waiting for the operation to wind down and go off duty the next morning. However, the weather had other ideas and at around 4 am we discovered that our position in the Tamar site was rather too low-lying and water started to pool around our ankles. Normally that would have been just a minor inconvenience, and after all, sub-tropical Hong Kong does benefit from warm rain in the summer months. On this occasion we were based in an Air Shelta, a temporary tent-like structure which maintained its shape by air blown from an electric fan, which was in danger of being submerged. As I waded through that water to move the fan to dryer ground, I do remember thinking that my mother would really not be happy with the commissioner of police if I were to be electrocuted just a couple of hours after the Handover. Dawn arrived several hours later and I recall feeling tired and with a sense of anti-climax, if not depression, as Hong Kong started another chapter in its history.

Several days later, I was approached by one of the guard police constables at PTU HQ. I didn't know them well but their small team was always cheerful and reliable when I was acting as the duty inspector performing 'standby' on an evening or weekend. It therefore came as a lovely surprise when he took me aside and presented me with a well-used Union Flag. It wasn't clear if that was the flag flying on 30th June or just a spare, but I very much appreciated the gesture, and I've kept it as a treasured memento ever since.

In the run up to 1997, Hong Kong was quite an exciting place to be. We were temporarily the focus of world attention and innumerable visits and reports by the world's press. I had many friends and relatives visit me in Hong Kong throughout my career and it was perhaps no surprise that one of them should have arrived a matter of weeks before the Handover, and in doing so he witnessed a memorable incident.

The British military had been present throughout my service, and when I first arrived there were around 12,000 UK servicemen stationed in Hong Kong, usually comprising a UK regiment and a Gurkha regiment, in addition to Royal Navy and Royal Air Force units. The last UK regiment to serve was the Black Watch and it was to be a high-profile component of the Handover events.

One June evening found me walking along Humphreys Avenue in Tsim Sha Tsui with my wife-to-be, the UK friend and his partner, having had a couple of drinks. Out of the blue we came across three expatriates rolling around the floor in an alleyway with one of them shouting for the police. Being a hands-on type of chap I grabbed one, asked my mate from home to sit on him, then grabbed the other as the third chap exited stage left before the arrival of the cavalry in the form of the Police Emergency Unit Kowloon West. They were big lads but completely paralytic and fortunately, they weren't capable of putting up much resistance. After the short trip to Tsim Sha Tsui Police Station, it turned out that they were both squaddies from the Black Watch, and so the Royal Military Police (RMP) were called out to deal with them. Upon arrival, the RMP corporal clearly took a dim view of the two servicemen after we reported that that they had been spitting at us through the bars of the cell. Coincidentally, I met the same RMP corporal in 'Joe Bananas' bar just a few days before the Handover. After introducing myself, he told me that the two miscreants were repatriated to the UK the day after they were arrested, though not before some appropriate military 'attitude adjustment' back at the barracks.

From January 1998, I was working in Kowloon West, and my experience was that the smaller number of expatriates in the region experienced a better camaraderie than previously. We all knew each other and there were regular social events that pulled us together in one place. There were also a number of expatriates in senior positions as district commanders in the region, and it helped that a couple of them were extremely social and supportive of mess functions and curry lunches. At that stage, many stations still had an officers' mess, though that did gradually change. The relationship between the expatriates and local officers remained generally good, certainly at an individual level, and the Force seemed keen to address and allay the fears of expatriate officers.

Twenty years later I look back on the Handover with pride at a job well done by the Force, and it is satisfying to have been a small part of a significant chapter in the history of Asia's Finest.

A Postscript: The RHKP Memorial

Keith H. Lomas

The Royal Hong Kong Police ceased to exist in 1997 following the handover of sovereignty of the territory to China, although the Force continued, reverting to the name of the Hong Kong Police. At that time, there were still a few hundred expatriates, mainly British, still serving in the Force but under the terms of the Joint Declaration with China, they could continue to have a full career although they would not be appointed to the topmost ranks of the organisation. This has proved to be the case and at the time of writing, more than twenty years after the Handover, there are still about forty expatriate officers serving in Hong Kong.

During the time that Hong Kong was under British sovereignty, from 1841 until 1997, there were many deaths of officers on duty, British and Commonwealth, Chinese, Indian, and Pakistani. These numbered over 230 individuals, but did not include eleven British officers who died in World War I (1914–18), having volunteered among many others to serve in the British Army in the fighting in Europe. A further 160 officers, British, Chinese and Indian, were killed in the fighting following the invasion of Hong Kong by the Japanese in 1941 or who subsequently died by execution or from the hardships of detention.

Several years ago, the Royal Hong Kong Police Association recognised that in the United Kingdom, a monument to these sacrifices did not exist – indeed there was nothing concrete to show that the Royal Hong Kong Police had ever existed. Accordingly, the association arranged for four Chinese Juniper trees to be placed in the National Memorial Arboretum in Alrewas, Staffordshire, in honour of these officers, and later added a memorial tablet.

In 2015, the association considered that there was a need to upgrade the memorial, and with the very significant financial support from the commissioner of the present Hong Kong Police, and from association members, an impressive granite and bronze memorial was erected in the arboretum. The citation, and short description of the Force, was cast on the bronze disc, in both English and Chinese.

The execution of the project was performed by a small sub-committee consisting of Mr Keith H. Lomas, Mr Keith Braithwaite and Mr G.P.E. Guest.

The dedication ceremony was held on 27th May 2018 and was attended by some eighty members of the association and was led by Lord Wilson of Tillyorn KT GCMG FRSE, a former governor of Hong Kong (April 1987 to July 1992). Mr Kenneth Li Kin Fai, senior assistant commissioner representing the commissioner of the Hong Kong Police, and Ms Priscilla To, director general of the Hong Kong Economic and Trade Office, London, were present as honoured guests.

A warm message of congratulations from Her Royal Highness, Princess Alexandra, the former Honorary Commandant General of the Royal Hong Kong Police was read out at the ceremony.

Dedication and unveiling of the RHKP Memorial. From left: Keith H. Lomas, Ms Priscilla To, Lady and Lord Wilson, Mr and Mrs Kenneth Li Kin Fai, John Macdonald, Angus Stevenson-Hamilton

The RHKPA sub-committee tasked with the design and installation of the memorial, together with the representative of the HKP Commissioner. From left: Keith Braithwaite, Kenneth Li Kin Fai, Keith H Lomas, Paul Guest

Lady Wilson, Keith H. Lomas, Lord Wilson, Kenneth Li Kin Fai, Keith Braithwaite

References and Further Reading

Patrick J. Cummings and Hans-Georg Wolf. *A Dictionary of Hong Kong English: Words from the Fragrant Harbor.* Hong Kong University Press; 2011.

Debbie Nguyen Xuan Diep. *Truong Xuan – Journey to Freedom.* BPA Print Group: Sydney; 2010.

Chris Emmett. *Hong Kong Policeman.* Earnshaw Books: Hong Kong; 2015.

G.B. Endacott. *A History of Hong Kong.* Oxford University Press; 1958.

Norman Gunning. *Passage to Hong Kong.* Bound Biographies: Bicester; 2005.

Hong Kong Government Information Services. *Hong Kong Yearbook.* Hong Kong Government. Annual.

Hong Kong Police Force. *OffBeat.* Hong Kong Police Force. Fortnightly.

Simon Roberts. *Hong Kong Beat: True Stories From One of the Last British Police Officers in Colonial Hong Kong.* Blacksmith Books: Hong Kong; 2020.

Kevin Sinclair. *Asia's Finest: An Illustrated Account of the Royal Hong Kong Police.* Unicorn: Hong Kong; 1983.

Steve Tsang. *A Modern History of Hong Kong.* Hong Kong University Press; 2004.

Iain Ward. *Sui Geng: Hong Kong Marine Police, 1841–1950.* Hong Kong University Press; 1991.

Iain Ward. *Mariners: The Hong Kong Marine Police 1948–1997.* IEW Publications: UK; 1999.

Captain William Worrall and Kevin Sinclair. *No Cure No Pay: Memoirs of a China Sea Salvage Captain.* South China Morning Post: Hong Kong; 1981.

EXPLORE ASIA WITH BLACKSMITH BOOKS

From bookstores around the world or from *www.blacksmithbooks.com*

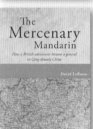

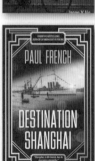